# THE
# FINAL
# CURTAIN

# THE ·F·INAL CURTAIN

## Obituaries of
## Fifty Great Actors

# MICHAEL COVENEY

UNICORN

'*Good my lord, will you see the players well bestowed?
Do you hear, let them be well used, for they are the
abstract and brief chronicles of the time.*'

Hamlet to Polonius, *Hamlet*, Act II, scene 2


'*Our revels now are ended. These our actors, as I foretold you,
were all spirits and are melted into air, into thin air.*'

Prospero in *The Tempest*, Act IV, scene 1

# Contents

# Sam Mendes

'HERE LIES ONE whose name was writ in water' reads the gravestone of John Keats. The great theatre director Tyrone Guthrie borrowed the same sentiment to describe the work of actors.

Where do we go to find the history of the arts? Who chronicles live performances – characters who lived for only months or weeks and the actors who created them? Where can we look to find the shape and meaning of a career that has all but disappeared? In a broader sense, how do you define the legacy and influence of stage actors? Not just those whose names remain familiar even now – Olivier, Gielgud, Ashcroft – but those who were perhaps equally influential, but never became household names? What will we know in years to come about Nicol Williamson, David Warner, Dilys Laye, Pete Postlethwaite, Susan Fleetwood, Alan Howard…?

This book is a beautiful collection of some of the many extraordinary obituaries written by Michael Coveney over the last twenty or thirty years. Possessed of an encyclopaedic knowledge, and an astonishing and vivid memory, Michael has made something special. I am trying to persuade him to let it be the beginning of what would be a large-scale theatre masterwork to rival David Thomson's magnificent *Biographical Dictionary of Film*. After all, the theatre needs a chronicle. It is more than a start.

For myself, this collection is a chance to reflect again on those I loved and who died far too young – Helen McCrory, Natasha Richardson; to think about and relish those whom I was lucky enough to work with and still miss – Albert Finney, Pete Postlethwaite – and perhaps to get a bit closer to those I never saw, or barely recollect: the 'yeasty' Ralph Richardson, the 'coruscating whisper' with which John Wood conjured dreams and madness, the 'rampaging farmer' that was Gerard Murphy, the 'brandy injected fruitcake' of John Hurt's voice, the mystery of Alan Howard: 'solitude was his mindset, grand spiritual debauchery his inclination'. Tellingly, Michael quotes playwright Simon Gray on his friend Alan Bates' performance in Butley: 'he thought it was the beginning, but it was, in fact, a moment of complete fulfilment that never came back'. This book is a chance to look back and see the past with clarity. The theatre art created in our lifetime, the shape of theatre history. The movement of the water.

# Introduction
# Michael Coveney

I WAS FIRST TAKEN to the London theatre, aged 11, to see the D'Oyly Carte's spick and span production of *The Gondoliers* at the Savoy Theatre in 1959 and then Paul Scofield as Sir Thomas More in Robert Bolt's *A Man for All Seasons* at the Globe (now the Gielgud) in 1960. Formative experiences, both, but I became an assiduous theatregoer with the arrival of Laurence Olivier's National Theatre at the Old Vic in 1963 and, ten years later, a practising theatre critic.

So, I make no apology in starting this collection of theatrical obituaries – 42 of the 50 were first published in the *Guardian* – with a fanfare for Olivier and the three great contemporaries of his who, it is generally acknowledged, created the possibilities leading to the glories of our contemporary theatre in new and classical work.

There was no obituaries column on my first newspaper, the *Financial Times,* but the occasional flare went up for a deceased actor, writer or producer. I managed to squeeze in short obits for Hermione Gingold, Irene Handl and Colin Blakely – all in 1987 – and had my moment of glory on the *FT*'s front page with an account of Olivier's magnificent memorial service in Westminster Abbey in 1989, shortly before I moved on to the *Observer.*

That ceremony really did mark the end of an era. Even though Olivier's memory and indeed legacy marched on, he saw himself in a line stretching from Shakespeare's leading actor, Richard Burbage, through David Garrick, Edmund Kean and Henry Irving. And yet, this protean actor, in the latter half of his career, added lustre and prestige to the ground-breaking new writing theatre, the Royal Court of George Devine and Tony Richardson, and incorporated many of the Court's actors and directors in his National Theatre.

Without Peggy Ashcroft on board, said Peter Hall, he could not possibly have launched the Royal Shakespeare Company in 1960. Ralph Richardson's historic seasons with Olivier at the New (now the Noël Coward) set the standard for the post-war repertory theatre. And Gielgud's brilliant West End seasons, directing and starring with the leading players of the day, defined the aspirations of subsequent generations in both commercial and subsidised sectors.

After the Fanfare, the actors are listed in chronological order of their passing. Acting is one way of 'performing' and a performer is certainly, in my book, an actor. Hence the inclusion of such great vaudevillians as Ken Dodd and Bruce Forsyth, and of TV stars with bona fide acting chops such as Una Stubbs, Lionel Blair and Dennis Waterman. The careers which bring down the curtain, those of Angela Lansbury and Leslie Phillips, attest to the longevity, variety and sheer bloody-minded dedication of so many of our greatest actors.

When I first wrote a book about Maggie Smith, in 1993, she accused me of being her 'premature obituarist'. When she got wind of me writing an expanded, post-*Downton Abbey* and *Harry Potter* biography, she rang up and said, 'You're digging me up again, aren't you? You've turned full-time necrologist. And if you write any more when I'm dead, I'll kill you.'

People often say, it must be depressing writing obituaries. Well, it isn't. I enjoy ransacking my cuttings and reviews, all kept in folders and scrapbooks, supplemented by the invaluable Theatre Record, now fully digitalised (but only dating from 1981), my dictionaries and reference books, hunting down interviews and film clips on-line, talking to friends and relatives of the deceased – I cannot think of a single instance, in 30 years, when someone was reluctant to help contribute towards a *Guardian* obituary.

I enjoy the excitement and, yes, the terror of the job, just as I enjoyed the same with writing reviews between February 1972 and April 2016 (8,985 in all). As with anything, deadline anxiety is the spur to my intent. Some obits are compiled in advance, when the subject is well-known, over-80 and reportedly ailing. Oddly, such people tend to hang on for ever and often – though not in my case, yet – outlive their obituarists. Out of spite, probably.

David Bowie and Alan Rickman died unexpectedly within four days of each other, both suffering from cancer known only to their nearest friends and family. (I particularly love the pairing at St Peter's Gate on Christmas Eve, and Day, 2008, of Harold Pinter and Eartha Kitt, master of the pause and mistress of the purr.) I recall hearing of Rickman's demise on entering the Finborough Theatre in Earl's Court for a new production, and of Nicol Williamson's as I arrived in Stratford-upon-Avon for a not so merry Christmas show. Panic stations! An overnight review of a play is one thing; of a life, quite another, even though both carry dread responsibilities.

✦ ✦ ✦ ✦ ✦ ✦

The *Guardian* kindly gave permission to reproduce the 42 obituaries, all of which have been edited, in some cases partly re-written, but without hindsight or updates. The *Guardian* has owned the *Observer* since 1993 and therefore rubber-stamped my *Observer* articles on Peggy Ashcroft, Alan Bates and David Warner. Permissions were also kindly advanced by the *Financial Times* (Laurence Olivier), *The Stage* (Ralph Richardson) and the *Evening Standard* (Robert Stephens and Natasha Richardson; the latter's appreciation appeared in the *Independent,* which was acquired by the *Standard* in 2010).

My John Gielgud obituary is an extract from a paper I delivered at the World Congress of the International Shakespeare Association in Valencia, Spain, on Shakespeare's birthday, 2001, 11 months after Gielgud's death. Late in life, Gielgud bemoaned the fact that he spent so much time going to other people's memorial services that it hardly seemed worthwhile to go home.

On his birthday in 1993, two recently elected MPs, Gyles Brandreth and Glenda Jackson, invited him to lunch in the House of Commons. Much to their surprise, and gratification, he accepted. Gyles asked, why exactly had he graced them with his company? 'Oh,' he said, 'It's perfectly alright. You see, all my *real* friends are dead.'

I am especially grateful to Robert Hahn and Rachel Atkinson for clearing the copyright at the *Guardian* and *Observer*. I must also thank the *Guardian* obituaries desk so graciously led by Robert White and Diana Gower and tip my cap to fellow obituarists Ryan Gilbey and Anthony Hayward who concentrate, respectively, on film and television while knowing more than enough about theatre, too.

The book was suggested by Sam Mendes, and I thank him for that, and his foreword. And it has once again been a pleasure to work with Unicorn, where chairman Ian Strathcarron enthused from the start, and where the editorial input of Lucy Duckworth and designer Felicity Price-Smith has been both sensitive and exemplary.

# Laurence Olivier

*Charismatic, heroic actor who was a Hollywood star, founder
of the National Theatre at Chichester and the Old Vic in 1963
and gave his best account of King Lear on television.*

THE SUN BLAZED, the trumpets sounded, and the bells of Westminster
Abbey rang out across London at a noonday service of thanksgiving for
the life and work of Laurence Olivier OM, Baron Olivier of Brighton,
who died in July. It was 84 years, to the very day, 20 October 1905,
since the first knight of the theatre, Sir Henry Irving, was buried in
Poets' Corner in the Abbey.

The Dean of Westminster, the Very Rev Michael Mayne, declared that
the ashes of Olivier would be laid next year alongside those of Irving
and Garrick, beneath the bust of Shakespeare 'within a stone's throw
of the graves of Henry V and The Lady Anne, Queen to Richard III'.
Thus invoking two of Olivier's greatest performances, the Dean made
way for the professionals.

A stocky Albert Finney, once touted as Olivier's natural successor, read
sonorously from Ecclesiastes, a dapper Sir John Mills spiritedly from
Corinthians. A radiant Dame Peggy Ashcroft then recited vigorously
the last 30 lines of Milton's *Lycidas* ('At last he rose, and twitched his
mantle blue / Tomorrow to fresh woods, and pastures new'). Sir John
Gielgud, looking frail after recent illness, shook his fist at death in John
Donne's *Holy Sonnet* and Hamlet's 'we defy augury' speech.

The Abbey was at its finest and most superbly organised for this
glittering occasion. The choir sang the heart-stopping arrangements
by Vaughan Williams of Bunyan's 'Death, where is thy sting?' passage
in *The Pilgrim's Progress* and of the dirge in *Cymbeline*. The composer
mostly represented was William Walton, Olivier's great friend and
collaborator on the Shakespeare films. The London Brass and Abbey
Choir, directed by Martin Neary, finally joined in a flashing, growling

and spectacular account of Walton's *Coronation Te Deum*.

Olivier spoke thrillingly for himself in a playback of the St Crispin's Day speech from *Henry V*. But his show was nearly stolen by Sir Alec Guinness, who gave the address. Musing dispassionately on Olivier's greatness, Sir Alec described the threat of danger that clung to Olivier, both onstage and off.

'There were times when it was wise to be wary of him.' He praised his pinnacle performances but dwelt on his comic side. The Abbey erupted into laughter on being told how Olivier altered punctuation on a line of Malvolio from 'My masters, are you mad, or what are you?' to 'My masters, are you mad or what? Are you?'

Sir Alec continued by invoking what Coleridge wrote of Kean: 'To see him act is like reading Shakespeare by flashes of lightning.' He paused ... 'Some of us might prefer a steadier light. Larry provided the flashes often enough but he always had an overall, workmanlike concept.

'Sometimes we read in the press of a young actor being hailed as "a second Olivier". That is nonsense of course, and unfair to the actor. If he is of outstanding talent and character then he will carve out his career in his own right and in his own name; he won't be a second anyone. In any case, there may be imitators, but there is no second Olivier. He was unique.'

The clerical procession had been followed by a thespian parade, bearing Olivieresque mementoes on blue velvet cushions. The billing had not been quite sorted out. Douglas Fairbanks Jr carried Olivier's Order of Merit, followed by Michael Caine with an Oscar.

Peter O'Toole usurped Jean Simmons to bring on the *Hamlet* film script, while Ian McKellen was obliged to trudge behind Derek Jacobi with the laurel wreath of Coriolanus. Paul Scofield carried a silver model of the National Theatre alongside Maggie Smith bearing a similar emblem representing the Chichester Festival Theatre. Frank Finlay brought up the rear with Edmund Kean's sword, a gift of Gielgud to his old sparring partner.

The stalls and pews were packed with, literally, an A to Z of theatricals: Lindsay Anderson to Franco Zeffirelli. The royal family and the government sent along support players rather than star turns: Prince Edward and Sir Geoffrey Howe. The Queen was represented by Lord Zuckerman, the Prince and Princess of Wales by Sir Richard Attenborough.

Olivier's career was often a conscious bid to stand in succession to Burbage, Garrick, Kean and Irving. He could justly claim, and often did, that he was in direct cahoots with Shakespeare, the root of our culture and his own fame.

This is what the Abbey so gloriously celebrated yesterday, and the vulgarian flipside of the great actor's demonic personality would receive many more raucous toasts as almost the entire production transferred immediately to the National Theatre at Lady Olivier's invitation.

As I mingled in the throng heading over the river to the south bank reception, images of Olivier crowded in: his slow, upstage entrance as Othello, sniffing a red rose as surely as we were sniffing danger. His epileptic fit in the same role, which I was witnessing from a two-shilling standing place at the back of the Old Vic stalls, and which sent me scurrying to the toilet where I retched up in shock and sympathy.

Passing him, unrecognisable almost, in a pin-striped suit and heavy, horn-rimmed spectacles, on the Waterloo Road. His supreme, pantherine athleticism: flashing subliminally across the stage as the bewigged fop Tattle in Congreve's *Love for Love* – was that a true illusion, or a false entrance? The defiant, stomping tarantella as the besieged Captain in Strindberg's *Dance of Death*.

In the mid-1950s, Olivier had greeted a dinner guest with the news that he had been lying on his bed upstairs thinking about his funeral: 'I could see the sun shining through the window of the Abbey,' he said, 'and I felt joyous.' He had dreamed of this day and had played his full part from beyond the grave.

---

*Laurence Kerr Olivier, actor and director, was born in Dorking, Surrey on 22 May 1907 and died in Steyning, West Sussex, on 11 July 1989.*

# Peggy Ashcroft

*Luminous and inspirational presence at both the
Royal Shakespeare Company and the National,
excelling in Ibsen, Rattigan and Beckett.*

DAME PEGGY ASHCROFT, who died on Friday aged 83, without
regaining consciousness after a stroke three weeks ago, enjoyed a
glorious Indian summer in the 1980s as Barbie Batchelor in Granada
Television's *The Jewel in the Crown* and as Mrs Moore in David Lean's
movie of *A Passage to India*. This latter performance won her an Oscar
and suddenly the world wanted to know more about Peggy Ashcroft.

If asked directly, Dame Peggy, a cricket-loving Hampstead-dweller
and indefatigable champion of left-wing causes (Binkie Beaumont,
chief West End producer of the 1940s and 1950s, called her,
affectionately, 'The Red Dame'), would firmly but politely say she
did not discuss her private life. But she was vociferous on such public
matters as the removal of VAT from the price of theatre tickets and
the preservation of the Rose Theatre in Southwark.

Her concern about the future of the subsidised theatre was never
idle. Her career, along with those of Olivier, Gielgud and Richardson,
was one of the cornerstones on which it was built. She was affiliated,
inextricably, with the most significant theatre movements of our
[20th] century: the Old Vic seasons under Lilian Baylis in the 1930s,
the West End productions of Olivier and Gielgud between the wars,
the earliest days of the English Stage Company at the Royal Court
under George Devine in the mid-1950s, and the formation of the
Royal Shakespeare Company with Sir Peter Hall in 1960.

When the National Theatre finally opened on the South Bank one
wintry March afternoon in 1976, it was Dame Peggy who spoke the
first words from its stage as Samuel Beckett's bare-shouldered Winnie in
*Happy Days*, sitting under a parasol, buried up to her waist in a mound

of grey post-nuclear detritus: 'Another heavenly day.' Her plangent, beautiful sigh was a signal of regret and a simultaneous announcement of business as usual.

Christened Edith Margaret Emily Ashcroft, her background in London was comfortable middle-class and mildly cultured: her father (who was killed in the First World War) was a land agent, and her part Danish, part German-Jewish mother an amateur actress who had studied with Elsie Fogerty, founder of the Central School of Speech and Drama. Peggy attended this school; Olivier was a contemporary.

She would be Juliet to Olivier's controversial Romeo in 1935, Beatrice to Gielgud's Benedick in 1950, and an over-age Katherina to Peter O'Toole's Petruchio in 1960 (Trevor Nunn described that performance as one of 'a ferocious scattiness that risked ridicule and lived dangerously, right out on the edge'.)

She said that, apart from Shakespeare, Chekhov and Ibsen provided the great experiences for an actress. 'Ibsen is like architecture; emotions are in the first place masked, then revealed which is what makes it so strong. Chekhov is more impressionistic, volatile, fluid.' She hungrily absorbed the writings of Stanislavsky and attended the famous Chekhov productions in Barnes, south London, of the Russian director Theodore Komisarjevsky, who became her guru and, later, her second husband.

Dame Peggy was first and foremost a company actor. Peter Hall said that he only went ahead with his RSC plans once he had enlisted her support. She always referred to the RSC as 'the Co' and remained a key member of the advisory directorate to the end of her life.

In 1963, the alliance was cemented with her blistering performance in *The Wars of the Roses* as Margaret of Anjou, sadistic she-wolf and vengeful Cassandra, daubing the face of Donald Sinden's Duke of York with the blood of his own son.

It was difficult, in the light of this performance, to understand how she had once been deemed too English for Lady Macbeth and Cleopatra. Both James Agate and Kenneth Tynan, hugely important critics, thought her too genteel for tragedy; the latter once unkindly dwelt on her blinking mannerism.

All actors have mannerisms, and any blemish – Dame Peggy no more disowned the blink than she did the pronounced mole above her upper lip – was subdued in her more notable attributes of tonal precision, bell-like clarity of diction, complete emotional identification with each role, a surface restraint concealing strong passion, and a thorough detestation of vulgarity.

In 1952, she played Hester Collyer in Terence Rattigan's *The Deep Blue Sea*, a woman pushed to the edge of suicidal despair. This was hailed by a semi-repentant Tynan as 'a scorchingly realistic portrait of a woman in love beyond her means' and the best part for an actress since Pinero's heyday. That great capacity for welling sorrow and emotional dignity found later outlets in plays of Harold Pinter, Edward Albee and Marguerite Duras, most of them with the RSC under Peter Hall. In Duras' *The Lovers of Viorne*, at the Royal Court in 1971, she mined new territories of schizophrenic despair and shuddering, stony-faced bewilderment as a French housewife inexplicably driven to chop up her deaf-and-dumb cousin. It was one of her favourite roles.

At home in Frognal, Hampstead, Dame Peggy continued to keep abreast of the cricket scores, the latest books and debates, surrounded by memories, friends and many fine paintings, notably one by Walter Sickert of her Juliet in profile against a view of Verona. She was in constant touch with her two grown-up children (who live in Canada and France) and their families, and had remained on good terms with their father, the lawyer Jeremy Hutchinson, to whom she was married for 25 years. Her first two marriages, which also ended in divorce, were to the publisher Rupert Hart-Davis and, more briefly, Komisarjevsky.

Michael Billington suggests that Dame Peggy was 'an exemplar of female constancy', and the toughness and security of her acting, what many directors and critics have identified as the Ellen Terry-like quality of her work, was surely an expression of her own character.

Her last stage appearance, before the late television and film fame, was as the Countess of Roussillon in the RSC's 1982 Edwardian *All's Well That Ends Well*. It was appropriate that she should be seated at the still centre of a bold and revelatory production by Trevor Nunn, her beauty unimpaired, her radiance undimmed, in a performance of sparkling, emotion-flecked vitality.

---

*Peggy Ashcroft was born in Croydon, south London, on 22 December 1907 and died in London on 14 June 1991. Her ashes were scattered around a mulberry tree at New Place, Shakespeare's house in Stratford-upon-Avon, which she had planted there in 1969.*

# Ralph Richardson

*As eccentric as he was ethereal, Richardson specialised in dreamers,*
*once playing a character of J.B. Priestley, Johnson Over Jordan, as a*
*man revisiting his past as though he were still half-alive.*

RALPH RICHARDSON ALWAYS looked as though he had come from somewhere else but wasn't going back. He'd dropped by, his presence was temporary, and he was on his way… but to where?

It's very hard to define what was so special about him, because of this ethereal, other-worldly, strangely subversive quality. He was four-square, earthy, on the stage, a little taller than average height, yeasty. 'As for my face,' he once said, 'I've seen better looking hot cross buns.' He seemed possessed of special knowledge which he had no intention of sharing.

He once pulled up smartly on the stage and turned to the audience: was there a doctor in the house, he asked? A doctor stood up. 'Ooh, I say, doctor, isn't this a terrible play?'

As a man, he was transparently genuine, though he invented an outer carapace of hoodwinking and false scent-laying. He liked his gin and tonics, and his lunch. And as an actor? Perhaps he wasn't really one at all, as Albert Finney thought, but a magician. Ironically, Prospero was one of his few inexplicable failures at the pre-war Old Vic, as indeed was Macbeth.

But he was usually unbeatable as any sort of beautiful dreamer, generally agreed to have been the greatest wild-eyed Peer Gynt of the last century, and the funniest, most moonstruck of Bottoms (he was utterly 'translated' in his ass's head, so they say, and you could see his button eyes staring like hot coals through the mask).

On stage, like all great actors, he had a total awareness of what was going on around him. And like all great light comedians – Gerald du Maurier, I imagine, or Cary Grant – you could not see how he did it.

His acting seemed as natural as breathing. His voice was a mellifluous squawk, studded with sighs, hoots and harrumphs. Whoever spoke like him? Nobody. His stresses were completely his own, and inexplicable.

He was born in Cheltenham in 1902, where his father was an art master at the Ladies' College. His parents separated when he was four, and he lived with his mother in genteel poverty in Shoreham-by-Sea in two railway carriages with brass handles on the doors. A lonely, imaginative boy, he said he 'bought' his way into an acting company aged 16. He served in the Fleet Air Arm in the war and was known as 'Pranger' Richardson: so many planes fell to pieces in his control.

The theatre he described as a magnetic forest where he climbed a few trees and marvelled at the new seeds blowing in to make it look different. He was summoned to run the Old Vic at the New Theatre (later the Albery, now the Noël Coward) with Laurence Olivier in 1944, sealing his reputation in a string of great performances: Peer and Falstaff, Bluntschli in Shaw's *Arms and the Man*, Cyrano, Vanya and Inspector Goole in *An Inspector Calls*.

He became a legend, and casually acknowledged this in even the smallest part, such as 'barmy' Waters, the waiter in Shaw's *You Never Can Tell,* a role he transmitted with ironic benevolence as if he were a famous philosopher down on his luck. The extent to which he let the audience 'in on the act', tipped the wink, even seemed to ride the coughing in the stalls like a surfer, was unlike anything else I've experienced in the theatre, before or since.

At Oxford at the end of the 1960s, I had arranged to interview him for the university newspaper when he was on tour in the first, disastrous production of Joe Orton's *What the Butler Saw*. I reported, as arranged, to the stage door of the New Theatre (now the Apollo) at the end of the performance. I had it in mind to go for a drink in the Randolph Hotel.

He emerged in leathers, crash helmet and a flying white scarf, looking like an early aviator. 'Oh, there you are. Thank you so much for coming. All the very best. Good-bye.' And he jumped on his 750cc BMW motorbike and roared off into the night, waving cheerily behind him as he went. It was the shortest, and the most unforgettable, interview I've ever conducted; and, of necessity, when I wrote it up, the most inventive.

His oddness was ever startling and never hardened into mere eccentricity. His performances with John Gielgud in two modern plays – David Storey's *Home* in 1970 and Harold Pinter's *No Man's Land* six years later – were struck with a sort of tragic jauntiness and ebullient despair. A slightly stomping walk was the framework for his extraordinary, rhythmic cadences, through which rushed fire, wind and rough weather. He drew the huge curtains with terrifying briskness in the Pinter play, and then astounded the first night audience with a sudden, cataleptic fall to the ground.

Although his last stage appearance was in 1983, the year of his death, when he played, as if sleepwalking, in Eduardo de Filippo's *Inner Voices* (translated by N.F. Simpson) at the National, his true valedictory had been as *John Gabriel Borkman* eight years earlier on the Old Vic stage alongside Peggy Ashcroft and Wendy Hiller. Whereas Scofield played Borkman as immoveable granite, Richardson soared to the last and returned to a former, and a higher, life. It was simply incredible. Gielgud remarked that the noise he made at the end was 'as if a bird had flown out of his heart'.

Olivier was a god, Gielgud divine, but who could play the creator of the universe Himself? Kenneth Tynan had only one candidate, should you imagine the Almighty to be 'a whimsical, enigmatic magician, capable of fearful blunders, sometimes inexplicably ferocious, at other times dazzling in his innocence and benignity'. Richardson had all these attributes while remaining –Tynan quoted C.S. Lewis on God – 'a positive, concrete and highly articulated character'. Oh, and audiences really loved him.

---

*Ralph David Richardson was born in Cheltenham, Gloucestershire, on 19 December 1902 and died in London on 10 October 1983. He was buried in Highgate Cemetery and, like Olivier and Ashcroft, had a memorial service in Westminster Abbey.*

# John Gielgud

*The mellifluous voice of Gielgud is one of the most imitated,*
*yet inimitable, in the British theatre. A definitive Hamlet*
*and Prospero, his intelligent, musical technique has been an*
*inspiration to actors of all later generations.*

NO OTHER ENGLISH ACTOR of the last century was better bred to the tradition he sought to emulate – that of the great Ellen Terry dynasty, to which he was connected on his mother's side. At the same time, Gielgud's perpetual air of aloofness, almost sanctity, placed him above the rabble both onstage and off.

Yet no actor – save, perhaps, Judi Dench – was more loved in his lifetime by his fellow professionals. He exerted an exemplary influence on British theatre from the moment he decided to take his new-won West End stardom to the down-at-heel Old Vic in 1929 and learn how to play Shakespeare.

He even rescued Olivier's then floundering career in 1935 by casting him as both Romeo and Mercutio and sharing the roles with him. Gielgud reckoned Olivier his superior – Italianate and dashing – in both roles, even though he himself had already played Romeo twice, once aged 19 in 1923. A silent film shows him spreading his arms imploringly in the balcony scene like a rather well-mannered pauper at the gates. James Agate declared: 'Mr Gielgud has the most meaningless legs imaginable.'

Gielgud's first drama teacher, Lady Benson, had started this line of disapproval by telling him that he walked exactly like a cat with rickets. Kenneth Tynan, adding injury to insult, averred, when he played Prospero at Stratford-upon-Avon in 1957, that he was 'perhaps the finest actor – from the neck up – in the world today'. Gielgud finally snapped: '[He] said I had only two gestures, left hand up, right hand up. What did he want me to do – bring out my prick?'

Still, Gielgud admired Tynan as a critic. 'It's wonderful when it isn't you,' he said. The truth is that Gielgud was always curious and adventurous throughout his career. He often worked with the director Peter Brook, playing a definitive Angelo in *Measure for Measure* in 1950 that restored that inexhaustibly modern play of sex, power and politics to the repertoire after decades of neglect. And who would have guessed that, in 1993, he would play his fifth Prospero for the controversial film director Peter Greenaway, speaking every single word of *The Tempest*, many of them while stark naked?

As an actor, his restless quest for truth and new meaning defined, for Brook, his modern quality. His sense of tradition, his passionate sense of quality, came from the past. In linking two ages, said Brook, he was unique. That suspension between past and present gave him his identity and defined his talent, especially as he grew older.

Yet he always retained a boyish sense of fun. In rehearsal for another Brook production — Seneca's *Oedipus* at the Old Vic in 1968 — he enthusiastically joined in a series of warm-up exercises, including, as this was a grim tragedy, an improvised confession of a terrifying prospect, something the actor feared most of all. His turn came, and he stepped forward: 'We open on Tuesday.'

Destiny, of course, came into it. Through his aunt, Ellen Terry, Henry Irving's leading lady, he inherited the style and poise of a true star, as well as the Terry tears, the ability to cry on stage at the drop of a hat, though his mother told him that this ability was due to weak lachrymal glands. His second cousin was Gordon Craig, the innovative stage designer and theoretician. And he knew of the legendary actor-managers through his great uncle, Fred Terry, whom he adored.

Gielgud's stockbroker father was of aristocratic Polish émigré extraction and his paternal great grandmother had been a Shakesperean actress of some reputation. So, on the Terry side, he inherited a commitment to the theatrical life, while his Slav ancestry no doubt explained his enduring enthusiasm for Russian music and ballet, and his affinity with the works of Chekhov, whom he championed in London in the 1930s.

While he was addicted to the grand, expansive manner of the Victorian and Edwardian touring theatre, he was exposed from an early age to all manner of entertainment. He enjoyed musical comedies and revues as much as Shakespeare or J.M. Barrie, and he always insisted, perhaps over-insisted, that he wanted colour and beauty and drama and magic in the theatre. He once told an interviewer that he couldn't read *Troilus and Cressida* or *Coriolanus* with any great pleasure; he much preferred to bolt down a cheap thriller, see the latest movie or do the *Times* crossword.

Olivier changed his career by playing Archie Rice in *The Entertainer* at the newly radical Royal Court in the 1950s. Gielgud was drawn to the same stage in the 1970s, giving several of his finest performances in plays by Charles Wood, David Storey, Edward Bond and Harold Pinter. He was initially nervous of entering the place which he imagined would be populated by young men in beards and sandals reading Proust.

He didn't much like Bond's mischievously titled *Bingo* in which he played Shakespeare living off the fat of the land in Stratford-upon-Avon, land he has cynically consigned to the socially evil consequences of the enclosures. His performance, nonetheless, was a perfect example of how his own personality and standing as an actor had become inextricable from the work itself.

Having recently played his fourth stage Prospero at the National, this was an even more telling valedictory. Shakespeare found himself, drunk and despairing, exiled in a landscape of harsh white snow: 'Wolves will drag me through the snow. I'll sit in their lair and smile and be rich. In the morning or when I die the sun will rise and melt it all away. The dream. The wolves. The iron teeth. The snow. The wind. My voice. A dream that leads to sleep.'

Gielgud the Shakespearean, playing Shakespeare at death's door, had discovered a text that both energised his gift for nostalgia and provided a blanket as protection against the icy winds of change. The blanket, however, was electric. It clung to him like Prospero's cloak and validated his final persona as the unchallenged spirit of Shakespearean farewell.

Because of his exalted status, the myth persisted that Gielgud was old-fashioned, out of touch, yesterday's news. In fact, the speed of his delivery, the perfection of his articulation and the ever-present glint of self-mockery signalled a complete break with the Victorian way of doing Shakespeare. The last insult you could hurl at him would be 'fuddy-duddy'.

He played Hamlet over 500 times, most famously in 1934 at the New (now the Noël Coward) Theatre. Hamlet, as much as Prospero, was 'his' role. Yet he always insisted that Hamlet presented new challenges to each successive generation, and should be re-discovered, re-created, every 10 or 15 years.

Still, even listening to his voice today, you wonder if anyone ever spoke as brilliantly as this. The individuality of his sound, unimpaired by a lifelong cigarette-smoking habit, was variously compared to a violin, or a cello, while to the actor and writer Emlyn Williams, it was 'an unbridled oboe'. Best of all, Alec Guinness, a protégé of Gielgud's, proclaimed 'a silver trumpet muffled in silk'.

In 1937, he presented and starred in a nine-month commercial season at the Queen's (now the Sondheim) Theatre of *Richard II*, *The School for Scandal*, *The Merchant of Venice* and *Three Sisters*, this latter the first Chekhov ever seen in the West End, with Gielgud as Vershinin, Peggy Ashcroft as Irina, Michael Redgrave as Tusenbach.

The nature of the creative network of theatre in Britain was never better shown than in this revolutionary 1930s decade. Traditions were meshed, collaborations forged, old lessons incorporated, new directions considered. Gielgud's career was the mainspring for the creation of the National Theatre and the RSC.

At the same time, he was always embarrassed by his propensity for making terrible, sometimes hurtful, gaffes. These merely reinforced the idea that a great figure had feet of clay, an essential requirement in Shakespearean tragedy. They became known as 'Gielgoodies'. He himself once said that he had dropped enough bricks to build a new Great Wall of China.

For instance, one old character actor, Clive Morton, was so terrified of Gielgud when touring with him in a play that he hardly dared speak to him. Eventually, he summoned up courage to knock on his dressing room door. 'Thank God it's you,' cried Gielgud, as Morton put his head nervously into the room, 'for one dreadful moment I thought it was going to be that ghastly old bore Clive Morton.'

In 1994, the illustrious Globe Theatre was renamed the Gielgud for one of its most illustrious sons. At an informal ceremony in the theatre's circle bar, on a magical sunlit morning, Gielgud re-called not the great figures he had known, nor the Shakespearean triumphs he had enjoyed, but his very first appearance on the new Gielgud Theatre's stage. In 1928, he had acted badly, he said, in a play called *Holding Out the Apple*... and he quoted a favourite, silly line: 'You've a way of holding out the apple that positively gives me the pip.'

He giggled so much that he nearly had to sit down.

More plaintively, he then revealed that, when he walked down Shaftesbury Avenue these days, he never knew any of the names on the marquees. At least now, at the Gielgud, he said, there would be one that he recognised. Not an actor, said Tynan, but *the* actor. We shall not, as they say, look upon his like again.

---

*Arthur John Gielgud, actor and director, was born in South Kensington, London, on 14 April 1904, and died in Wotton Underwood, Buckinghamshire, on 21 May 2000. He requested no 'fuss', but a memorial stone was unveiled in Westminster Abbey in April 2022, adjoining those of Irving, Olivier and Ashcroft, and a low key tribute was paid by Judi Dench and Ian McKellen.*

# Susan Fleetwood

*At her memorial service, I was surprised to find my name on the order of*
*service as giving 'an address'. Facing an audience of stony-faced actors and*
*directors, I said that if I did so, they might all come round and throw stones*
*through my windows. Not a titter. I ploughed on, improvising as much*
*as I could remember of my – I mean, her – Guardian obituary.*

SUSAN FLEETWOOD, WHO DIED yesterday aged 51 after a ten-year
battle against cancer – a struggle known to only a few people – was
one of the most important and gifted actresses of her generation. Her
name was a byword for integrity, quality and humanity in countless
productions at the Royal Shakespeare Company and the National
Theatre for the past two decades.

Lately she had reached a wide audience on television in the series
*Chandler and Co.* And she was admired for a string of impeccable,
funny and attractive performances in such TV series as *The Jewel in
the Crown*, *The Buddha of Suburbia* and *Summer's Lease*, opposite John
Gielgud and Michael Pennington. Her sparkling brown eyes and
silken voice were instantly recognisable.

Each character she played was carefully considered and projected
with panache. She was particularly impressive in the recent BBC TV
adaptation of Jane Austen's *Persuasion*. Her beauty was apparent, but it
glowed from within as well. She always conveyed a sense of intellect
and rapid thought in her acting.

One of her closest friends and associates at the RSC was the director
Terry Hands, with whom she lived for some years earlier in her career.
Hands directed her in 1991 as Beatrice in *Much Ado About Nothing*
and as Madam Arkadina in Chekhov's *The Seagull*. Both performances
were of matchless, impregnable beauty, tempered in fire and struck
with a golden wit. She demonstrated her profound versatility by
appearing, in the same season, in a revival of Sam Shepard's intense
domestic drama, *Curse of the Starving Classes*.

Born in St Andrews, Scotland, hers was a peripatetic childhood – her father was a high-ranking officer in the armed forces – and she attended no less than 16 schools, finally a convent in Kent. She trained at the Royal Academy of Dramatic Art and toured Arizona in 1964 with a RADA company playing Rosalind in *As You Like It* (a role she later played with memorable warmth and zest for the RSC) and Lady Macbeth.

The family home in Salisbury, Wiltshire, where she died yesterday morning, was a haven for actors and artists over many years. Her brother is the rock musician Mick Fleetwood of Fleetwood Mac, and her sister the artist Sally Fleetwood.

Tall, beautiful, supremely talented, her first professional engagement was in 1964 at the Liverpool Everyman, which Hands had founded that year with Peter James and Martin Jenkins. This gave her a solid rep grounding in many classics. She followed Hands to the RSC three years later, making her mark in the Stratford-upon-Avon 1968 season as Regan opposite Eric Porter's King Lear, as Audrey in *As You Like It* and as Cassandra in the famous sandpit *Troilus and Cressida* directed by John Barton.

She joined the Cambridge Touring Theatre in the early 1970s but returned to the RSC to play Portia, the Princess of France in *Love's Labour's Lost*, Katherina in *The Taming of the Shrew* and Imogen in *Cymbeline*. She played everything she should have done, apart from Viola and Cleopatra.

In 1975 she joined the National under Peter Hall (Olivier's successor) and achieved one of her most celebrated triumphs as Pegeen Mike in J.M. Synge's great classic *Playboy of the Western World* in an otherwise all-Irish cast led by Stephen Rea and directed by Bill Bryden. She formed an abiding friendship with Bryden's assistant director, Sebastian Graham-Jones, with whom she lived for some years.

'Susan was an astonishingly committed, ruthless actress, who never stopped working,' said Graham-Jones last night. 'She was slightly dyslexic, which made reading a problem for her. You could never say anything vague to her. She would come back and insist on an answer to a problem and then, if nothing was forthcoming, she would provide the solution herself.'

Other National appearances were in John Osborne's *Watch It Come Down*, Marlowe's *Tamburlaine* opposite Albert Finney (she was also Finney's Ophelia in an unsatisfactory *Hamlet*) and *A Midsummer Night's Dream*, again directed by Bryden, in which she played Titania alongside first Paul Scofield and then Robert Stephens as Oberon. A close friend in this period was the fine South African actress Yvonne Bryceland, with whom she played in Edward Bond's controversial epic, *The Women*, in the National's largest arena.

Sadness was unconfined yesterday as news of Fleetwood's death filtered through the grapevine. She will be sorely missed but also remembered as someone whose career both justified, and made valid, the ideals of subsidised theatre in this country as pioneered by Olivier, Ashcroft, Gielgud and Richardson. She was in their class.

When the National vacated the Old Vic to move to the South Bank in 1976, Peggy Ashcroft impersonated the founding mother of subsidised theatre, Lilian Baylis, in an Old Vic gala. Not inappropriately, Fleetwood spoke the speeches of Sybil Thorndike even while that great actress, Shaw's first Saint Joan, rose and flourished her stick to bid a final farewell in the stalls.

Fleetwood's films included Merchant/Ivory's *Heat and Dust*, *White Mischief* and *The Krays*. In 1985 she made *The Sacrifice* directed by Andrei Tarkovsky. As the critic David Thomson says, this movie 'has some of the most glorious extended shots in film history'. Tarkovsky himself was suffering from cancer and was in exile in Sweden. Fleetwood's role as an ideal woman in an unkind world meant a great deal to her. It shows in the performance. Tarkovsky fell in love with her. They bonded seriously but were never lovers. He would show her a page of outline and they would enlarge it into script form together.

She once wrote an article in praise of Maggie Smith, saying that, when she watched her, she felt excited about being an actor: 'She just makes me feel good about the job.' As Beatrice at Stratford in 1990, I recall her standing, stricken and aghast, by the topiary in a post-Civil War 17th-century garden, lively and alert, emotions rushing through her face while preparing the next severe edict to serve on Roger Allam's reluctantly besotted Benedick. A lass unparallel'd, indeed.

---

*Susan Maureen Fleetwood was born on 21 September 1944 in St Andrews, Fife, and died on 29 September 1995 in Salisbury, Wiltshire.*

# Robert Stephens

*Robert Stephens was adept at portraying weak and vacillating characters. He exuded charm and personality on the stage and was disappointed, despite his impetuous, temperamental unsuitability for the job, not to succeed Olivier as director of the National Theatre.*

ROBERT STEPHENS WHO HAS DIED aged 64, was a rogue with no malice, a vagabond with no material possessions, and a true born, truly great actor. This much was recognised earlier this year with his knighthood and his Variety Club award for his moving performance as King Lear with the Royal Shakespeare Company.

He played Lear as one who knew only too well what it meant to see your life flashing before you, and he caught the poignancy, humour and sheer grandeur of Shakespeare's tragic hero in a way unrivalled in recent times.

Audiences knew his value and relished his return to the front rank not just as Lear, but as a gloriously embittered, unsentimental Falstaff, also with the RSC, in 1991.

Prince Charles, the president of the RSC, became a close friend. He told Stephens that his Lear was the best argument he had yet come across against abdication, and he constantly bemoaned the fact that he never had a father figure comparable to his Falstaff when he was a young princeling; he felt he needed such a one.

This brace of Shakespearean triumphs constituted a comeback on a par with that of Lazarus. For Stephens had been racked with illness for most of the 1980s. The golden boy of the English Stage Company at the Royal Court, and of Laurence Olivier's National Theatre, had become a shambling shadow of his former self – always cheerful, but an unpredictable loose cannon, nonetheless.

His last days were spent on a dialysis machine in the Royal Free hospital, Hampstead, north London, where he had undergone a kidney and liver transplant in September last year. Years of hard drinking and physical misfortune had, at last, taken their toll. He was severely diabetic, had broken both hips in bad falls and, when suffering from anaemia in America several years ago, had been given an almost fatal infusion of infected blood.

Still, he invariably bounced back, an incorrigibly naughty boy. If you went to lunch with Robert, he would sneak a couple of lethal brandy cocktails while you were still parking the car. Since January, he has hardly been at peak condition but has written his autobiography, much of it spoken into my tape-recorder while he was living in Denville Hall, the actors' rest and recuperation centre in Norwood. He also recorded an album of Shakespearean speeches at the behest of Prince Charles and acted in John Osborne's last TV script as the poet John Dryden in a film about the composer Henry Purcell.

His spirit, ever indomitable, charged a will to live and a formidably robust constitution. He once discharged himself from hospital, exiting to the pub through a window after medical sedation, deemed sufficient to knock out not only a horse but also a pair of elephants. The nurse on his ward took a telephone call from the Prince of Wales, assuming it to be that aforesaid pub. It wasn't. It *was* the Prince of Wales.

The outline of his life was a classic tale of promise, achievement, decline and recovery. Born in the West Country, he was, as his best friend, the actor Jeremy Brett (whose own recent demise was a source of immeasurable sadness to him) once said 'a fairly nice old sweetheart from Bristol'; ordinary, unassuming but blessed with a special gift.

Stephens trained as an actor in Bradford, Yorkshire, and went into weekly, then monthly, rep. His experience at the Library Theatre in Manchester was formative, and instrumental in his recruitment by the Royal Court in the early days of George Devine and John Osborne. He made his name in Osborne and Anthony Creighton's *Epitaph for George Dillon* (1958) and originated the role of Peter the chef in Arnold Wesker's *The Kitchen* (1961).

When Olivier took various Royal Court alumni to start his National Theatre adventure in Chichester and the Old Vic in 1962/3, Stephens was among a phalanx of Sloane Square shooting stars – directors William Gaskill and John Dexter, and actors Joan Plowright, Frank Finlay and Colin Blakeley. He was at the heart of the operation and regarded by Olivier as his obvious successor.

His National roles included Atahualpa, the sun god, in Peter Shaffer's

*The Royal Hunt of the Sun* (1964), a performance which was shamelessly, glisteningly, influenced by Olivier's own Othello, but an astonishing achievement in itself; a preening Benedick opposite Maggie Smith in Franco Zeffirelli's joyously festive production of *Much Ado About Nothing*; an unexpectedly tortured Loevberg in Ingmar Bergman's *Hedda Gabler*, a production Maggie Smith, who played Hedda, said was the best she had ever appeared in; and a heart-wrenching Tom Wrench – an earlier, Victorian version of the failed writer he played in *George Dillon* – in Pinero's *Trelawny of the Wells*.

Stephens never played Macbeth, Leontes or Antony – all ideal parts for him – and his film career never really took off. He was a disappointing Othello in Regent's Park (Edward Fox was Iago, weirdly) and he desperately wanted to perform that role once more.

His big film break should have been as the great detective in Billy Wilder's *The Private Life of Sherlock Holmes* (1970). But although the film has since become a revered cult classic, his experience on it was catastrophic. He could not cope with Wilder's obsessiveness and punctiliousness and was simultaneously going through a rocky period in his marriage to Maggie Smith.

A last-ditch attempt to save the marriage back-fired in a 1972 production of Noël Coward's *Private Loves* directed by John Gielgud. The comic-tragic dilemma of two people who love each other too much to be able to live together was horribly appropriate, though Robert himself was grateful for the onset of triumphant triviality after coming back, he said, from the brink of suicide on the Wilder film.

Another deferment of the inevitable break-up came with a superb season at the Greenwich Theatre in 1974 when, with fellow actors Peter Eyre, Nicola Pagett and Irene Worth, under the direction of Jonathan Miller, he explored the comparable Freudian mother/son tapestries of Shakespeare's *Hamlet*, Ibsen's *Ghosts* and Chekhov's *The Seagull*.

A domestic by-product of the season was that he met the writer Antonia Fraser, a great friend of Peter Eyre, and embarked on a passionate, short-lived, but therapeutic affair with her before she settled into her final, long-lasting friendship with, and marriage to, the playwright Harold Pinter.

Back at the National in 1985, he joined Bill Bryden's company as

Herod and Pontius Pilate in *The Mysteries*, the wonderful adaptation of the medieval pageant plays by the poet Tony Harrison which had been fermenting for eight years.

On the Saturday morning press show of the finally completed trilogy, Robert was standing in the foyer and – not on stage for the early scenes – had somehow had the bar opened and was dispensing large gin and limes to the critics as they arrived, gulping two down for each one he passed round. Needless to say, he gave a turbo-charged performance, and we all delivered glowing, or at least flushed, notices.

For the past 20 years, he enjoyed a stable relationship with the actress Patricia Quinn, whom he finally married in January. She was his fourth wife. By his first, a fellow drama student from Londonderry called Nora Ann Simmonds, he had a son, Michael, a poet who now works in the music industry in America.

By his second, the actress Tarn Bassett, he had a daughter, Lucy, an international lawyer. And by Dame Maggie, with whom he began a tempestuous affair in those early seasons at the National, he had two sons, both actors, Chris Larkin and Toby Stephens. It was a great comfort to him that they all rallied round when he needed them, and that his children saw the very best of his talent almost at the end.

On the Sunday before he died, Pat, Lady Stephens, was at his bedside in the Royal Free hospital to read out a review of his book published in the Sunday Times that very morning, written by John Mortimer, in whose play *The Wrong Side of the Park* Robert had appeared in 1961: 'I remember work or play with him as times of great laughter and enjoyment ... a magnificent actor, a joy to watch and to be with. I only wish he had taken greater care of himself, but that, after all, is his own affair entirely.'

There was a magnificent sunset over Hampstead that evening. Robert died in his sleep, just after one o'clock on Monday morning. That very evening, critics and first-nighters gathered at the Vaudeville Theatre for the opening of *The Shakespeare Revue* devised by Malcolm McKee and Christopher Luscombe, who had played Francis the drawer in the Boar's Head scenes with Robert's RSC Falstaff.

In a song by Caryl Brahms and Ned Sherrin from their 1959 musical *No Bed for Bacon*, Dolls Common, Tearsheet and Overdone announced their departure for the funeral of their favourite rapscallion reprobate, Merry Sir John:

'We're ladies of London, and it won't be the same;
He was sprightly twice nightly, and lord he was game...
He owed for his drink and he owed for his rent,
He owed for his shirt, but we're sorry he went...'

---

*Robert Graham Stephens was born in Bristol on 14 July 1931 and died in Hampstead, London, on 13 November 1995. At his funeral, a 'live' recording of 'Vissi d'arte' from Tosca burst forth, the impassioned music enveloping the coffin for some time until we heard a loud onstage knocking at Scarpia's door. Someone muttered, 'It's Robert trying to get out; the pubs are open.'*

# Alan Bates

*The biggest West End star in new plays by Simon Gray,
Bates was a stylish, equivocating maestro of inner turmoil
sifted through a humorous, self-mocking exterior.*

IN HIS *UNTOLD STORIES*, Alan Bennett recalls a telephone message Alan Bates left for him about the 1999 RSC Stratford production of *Antony and Cleopatra* in which Bates was required, in the opening scene, to bury his chin in Frances de la Tour's lap.

This Bardic bearding was replaced in the London transfer by a walk-down in kingly garb: 'While this might seem a radical change,' said Bates, 'it is, I suppose only the difference between coming down and going down, though there's no doubt which one the audience prefers. Goodbye.'

Like Simon Gray's Butley, a stage role with which he defined himself in 1971, he loved women but enjoyed his closest relationships with men. (Bates slept with men, Butley didn't.) His marriage to the tragic Victoria — she was an English secretary he met in New York who became obsessive, anorexic and socially embarrassing; that, at least, is the 'official' line — and his secret life among devoted male companions can be seen as his artistic motor, a method of screening emotional unrest with dry, occasionally destructive, humour.

The death of one of his and Victoria's twin sons, Tristan, from a heroin overdose, and the subsequent death of Victoria herself, wasted with grief and unhappiness, served as a prompt for some bizarre, guilt-ridden exercises late in his career.

One of his other signature Simon Gray roles was the diffident publisher Simon Hench in *Otherwise Engaged*; in 1996, Gray wrote a sequel, *Simply Disconnected*, in which Hench, having now lost a wife and child who may not have been his own, is threatened at gun point by a drug addict (played by Bates's own surviving twin son, Benedick) for the crime of seducing and then abandoning his mother. Another late Gray play, *Life Support*, provided a further cathartic outlet for the actor: he played a character caring for an onstage wife stretched out in a vegetative state by anaphylactic shock after a bee sting.

Bates supported Victoria, as he supported his wider family at home in Derbyshire, all his life. But duty and inclination, in his case, were at war with each other. His personality was exactly caught in that first great success in *Butley*. 'He thought it was the beginning,' said Gray, 'but it was in fact a moment of complete fulfilment that never came back.'

Bates was the first of three sons of talented amateur musicians in Derbyshire. His mother was also keen on amateur dramatics. As luck would have it, a family friend, the father of theatre director John Dexter, was instrumental in gaining young Alan a place to study at RADA.

His charmed progress to the top of a new post-war meritocracy was symbolised in his recruitment by George Devine in the first English Stage Company at the Royal Court, where he appeared as Jimmy Porter's sidekick, Cliff, in *Look Back in Anger*. He was overlooked for the same role in the film version but soon made his mark as the randy draughtsman (who gets his girlfriend pregnant and settles into a reluctant marriage with her) in John Schlesinger's *A Kind of Loving*.

With Albert Finney, Tom Courtenay and Peter O'Toole, Bates transformed the British theatre and movie industries, liberating them from middle-class dominance and gentility. His film debut was alongside Finney in *The Entertainer* with Olivier. He then appeared in the stage premiere of Harold Pinter's *The Caretaker* in 1960 and forged a crucial working relationship with Pinter (who directed him in the early Gray successes) as well as with Gray, David Storey and, later, Alan Bennett, for whom he played the defecting traitor Guy Burgess in *An Englishman Abroad* on television, again directed by Schlesinger; Bates's Burgess was a wonderfully boozy, hollow man 'lost and loveless in his chosen promised land'.

This mystery and sense of unplumbed depths about Bates is what fuelled his acting, which never showed any signs of wheels going round, or technical strain. He made acting look as natural as breathing, which is why he was sometimes uncomfortable in Shakespeare, which demands rhetorical flourish, and perfectly at home in Chekhov; he was a magnificently sleek and pantherine Vershinin in the Olivier film of *Three Sisters* and the ideal, casually and charismatically destructive Trigorin in a production of *The Seagull* with which he loyally launched the new Derby Playhouse in 1975.

But the best of Bates is seen in those roles where his welling up of emotional confusion, banked down in ironic disclaimers and an attractive sort of helplessness underpins – and then undermines – his imposing physical presence.

His own favourite screen performance was Michael Henchard in Dennis Potter's dark and faithful television adaptation of Thomas Hardy's *The Mayor of Casterbridge*. Henchard sells off his wife and child in a drunken stupor and lives the rest of his life in cloud of remorse. Again, Bates found an outlet for a highly developed guilty streak.

A large, bulky man with a yeoman's head and hams for hands, Bates wore a quizzical smile for most of his life and delighted his friends with his steadily challenging green-eyed gaze. On stage or screen he was simply a star from the off. Only with him on the London stage could you imagine, briefly, a future for intelligent, witty comedy in the commercial sector.

Nowadays, Michael Frayn, Tom Stoppard and even Alan Bennett take their work to the National Theatre. Bates was a guarantee of a quality audience for quality work in the mainstream. Only Maggie Smith and possibly Judi Dench now have that box office pulling power.

Cancer took Bates in 2003, but he ended with a flourish: a knighthood, a Tony award on Broadway for an impeccable performance as a shabby, self-effacing Russian aristocrat in Turgenev's *Fortune's Fools*, and a lovely cameo as a shuffling, disdainful head servant in Robert Altman's movie *Gosford Park*.

Alan Bates may have found love, fitfully, wherever he turned, but he finally focused on his surviving son Benedick, whose burgeoning career and three young daughters in a happy marriage gave him a glimpse of the settled, simple, radiant existence his demonic talent always denied him.

---

*Alan Arthur Bates was born in Allestree, Derby, on 17 February 1934 and died in London on 27 December 2003.*

# Fritha Goodey

*A mythology can grow around a young actor dying*
*tragically young – Kay Kendall, Mary Ure, even*
*James Dean – but Fritha Goodey had no time to plant*
*a myth beyond her obvious, fragile beauty.*

FRITHA GOODEY, WHO HAS DIED aged 31, was conspicuously and classically beautiful, but it was clear that her talent ran deeper than outward show. She was blonde, willowy, graceful, entrancing; perfect casting, as she proved at the National Theatre in 2000, for Proust's alluring Odette de Crécy in *Remembrance of Things Past*, a stage version of Harold Pinter's un-filmed screenplay, written for director Joseph Losey in 1978.

One strand in Pinter's text reflected his own plays' obsession with the memory of sexual encounters glazed in poetic ambiguity, and Goodey's place in the central quartet – as the object of Swann's languish and adoration, alongside Marcel's pining for the bisexual Albertine – gave the performance an overall erotic charge beyond all expectation.

Di Trevis's production, and Goodey's assured yet gleamingly innocent performance, clearly benefited from the fact that Trevis herself had played Odette, very well, in a production at the Glasgow Citizens in 1980 which used a supple, more acidic text than Pinter's, by Robert David MacDonald, simply titled *A Waste of Time*.

At the time of her death, she was rehearsing for a revival of Terence Rattigan's *Man and Boy*, directed by Maria Aitken, at the Yvonne Arnaud Theatre, Guildford, opposite David Suchet.

Named after the girl in Paul Gallico's *The Snow Goose*, Goodey was born in Surrey and went to secondary school at Grey Court, Ham. After attending a local drama school, she was accepted at the London Academy of Music and Dramatic Art (LAMDA). While there, she suffered from anorexia, but after three years was well enough to finish the course.

Following some radio work, she took her first television job, after which she appeared with Joanna Lumley in *Dr Willoughby*, and in *Randall & Hopkirk Deceased* (both 1999). Her screen career - far more varied than might be assumed - included *About a Boy* (2002), in which she was one of Hugh Grant's former girlfriends. She will be seen in the forthcoming remake of *Alfie*, starring Jude Law.

She also had character roles as a low-life Londoner in *Hearts and Bones*, as an Irish terrorist in an American mini-series and as a foul-mouthed, horrid ballerina in the short film *Table Twelve*. She had a lovely voice and worked extensively on radio.

Goodey's was a successful career just waiting to burst into the big time; one special role would have done it. As it was, she made her mark over five years with Max Stafford-Clark's Out of Joint touring company, firstly in Mark Ravenhill's *Some Explicit Polaroids* (1999), the follow-up to his controversial success, *Shopping and Fucking*.

She played Nadia, a sexy nightclub dancer who sounded as though she had fallen off the self-help shelf in a pop psychology section. 'You're OK, I'm OK,' she would chant, mantra-like, a deluded victim of her own low self-esteem, who saw the sexual violence committed on her as a vague positive in a world where 'nothing means anything.'

In 2002, again with Out of Joint, she played a delightful Constance Neville in Oliver Goldsmith's comedy classic *She Stoops to Conquer*, and a very funny, gorgeous Mrs Garrick, keeping an eye on her great actor husband, in April de Angelis's *A Laughing Matter*, a new companion piece to Goldsmith's comedy, and performing an exquisite little dance in the entr'acte.

This pairing of a classic with a new play that bounced off and around it was a feature of Stafford-Clark's Out of Joint company, sprung from his days as artistic director of the Royal Court. Goodey seemed immediately at home in this creative environment. She displayed not only great poise and skill in her modern take on an historic character, pulling the strings behind her hapless great actor husband rejecting Goldsmith's play out of fear of censorship, but also the makings of an accomplished comic actor in the classic repertoire. She was disarmingly funny in both roles.

Stafford-Clark said Goodey was a joy to work with. She often wrote to him with ideas for projects. 'In the circumstances,' said Stafford-Clark, 'I'm glad I replied to her on at least one occasion. An actor's life can be miserable, always waiting for other people to define your existence for you. Her beauty was a blessing, and also the reverse, as her looks often determined her parts.'

Last Saturday, Goodey visited rehearsals of Stafford-Clark's new production of *Macbeth*. She had become close friends with Monica Dolan, who is playing Lady Macbeth, during their work together on the Goldsmith/Garrick plays. Dolan attested to Goodey's extraordinary range of knowledge in painting and literature, and her ability to read any social situation: 'She knew immediately how people were feeling and she loved watching rehearsals, even when she wasn't involved.'

In Stephen Poliakoff's *The Lost Prince* on television, a little boy crouching beside a garden gate sees a fleeting vision of a beautiful young woman. This was Fritha Goodey, and the tragedy of her death – she left a suicide note in the Notting Hill apartment where she stabbed herself through the heart – reinforces the poignancy of her too brief and more than promising career. She is survived by her parents and an elder sister, Tabitha.

---

*Fritha Jane Goodey was born in Kingston upon Thames, Surrey, on 23 October 1972, and died in Notting Hill, London, on 7 September 2004.*

# Ken Campbell

*There were no half measures with Ken Campbell in a career ranging from pub theatre cabaret to epic sci-fi on a shoestring to a series of brilliant, idiosyncratic monodramas he wrote and performed himself.*

KEN CAMPBELL, WHO HAS DIED suddenly aged 66, was one of the most original and unclassifiable talents in the British theatre of the past half-century. He was a writer, director and monologist, a genius at producing shows on a shoestring and honing the improvisational capabilities of the actors who were brave enough to work with him.

An Essex boy who trained at RADA, he never joined the establishment, though his 1976 play *Illuminatus!* (co-written with Chris Langham) – an eight-hour epic based on an American sci-fi trilogy – was the first production in the National Theatre's Cottesloe auditorium, with a recorded prologue spoken by John Gielgud. The great joke here was that the most beautiful voice of our time spoke the lines of a computer known as the First Universal Cybernetic Kinetic Ultramicro Programmer, or its acronym.

Campbell's official posts included a brief spell as artistic director of the Liverpool Everyman in 1980 and a professorship in ventriloquism at RADA. He was first renowned in the early 1970s for the *Ken Campbell Road Show*, in which a company including Bob Hoskins, Jane Wood, Andy Andrews, Dave Hill and Sylvester McCoy ('The Human Bomb') enacted bar-room tales of sexual and psychic mayhem while banging nails up their noses and stuffing ferrets down their trousers.

Even more remarkable than *Illuminatus!* was his ten-play (22-hour) hippie extravaganza, *The Warp* (1979), a sort of acid *Archers* co-written with the poet Neil Oram. The protagonist's search for his own female consciousness took him from 15th-century Bavaria to a flying-saucer conference in 1968. Bill Nighy and Jim Broadbent were among the cast of unknowns; characters included Turkish policemen, Chinese officials,

Buckminster Fuller, clowns, fire-eaters, military art enthusiasts, a raging landlord ('I don't have any friends; just different classes of enemy') and a comic postman.

*The Warp* – subsequently revived as a rave-music production near London Bridge by Ken's daughter, Daisy Campbell – was followed in 1980 with a magnificent hoax which seemed to encapsulate the challenge of 'What next?'

The theatre world was flooded with invitations from Trevor Nunn to come aboard the newly formed Royal Dickens Company in the wake of the RSC's hugely successful *Nicholas Nickleby*. Shakespeare was being dropped for Dickens, and offers were made on meticulously reproduced company notepaper, all apparently signed by Nunn ('Love, Trev').

Nunn's embarrassment was compounded by the fact that a lot of people had written back to him refusing, or even more disconcertingly, accepting his gushing offers of work on Snoo Wilson's *Little Dorrit* or Michael Bogdanov's equally specious *Sketches by Boz*. After a couple of weeks of panic and speculation in the press, Campbell owned up.

There have been few stranger people in Britain, let alone the theatre, than Campbell. Living in a Swiss chalet in Epping Forest, he trained his three black crossbreed dogs – Max, Gertie and Bear – to win prizes, made artwork from the random droppings of a parrot called Doris and entertained his visitors with the films of Jackie Chan, the martial arts film star, whom he regarded as the greatest living actor.

This irrepressibly jovial elf, with a thin streak of malicious devilry about him – he was Puck, hobgoblin – was in recent years most widely known for his own wild and wonderful one-man shows, which embodied the quality of 'friskajolly youngkerkins' that Kenneth Tynan, quoting the Tudor poet John Skelton, ascribed to Ralph Richardson's famously hedonistic, twinkling post-war Falstaff. Campbell gave up 'serious' acting when he realised he was enjoying what everyone else was doing too much, although he did appear in a takeover cast in Yasmina Reza's *Art* at Wyndham's in 2000.

On television he appeared memorably as a bent lawyer in GF Newman's *Law and Order* series (1978) and in one episode of *Fawlty Towers*. He was Warren Mitchell's neighbour, Fred Johnson, in the sitcom *In Sickness and in Health*. He popped up bizarrely in films such as *A Fish Called Wanda* (1988) and Derek Jarman's *The Tempest* (1979), very much the same persona, bursting at the confines of a role and never quite fitting another scheme of showbusiness.

With a gimlet eye and a pair of bushy eyebrows that had lately outgrown even Denis Healey's and acquired advanced canopy status, Campbell was a perennial reminder of the rough-house origins of the best of British theatre, from Shakespeare, music hall and Joan Littlewood to the fringe before it became fashionable, tame and subsidised.

When Richard Eyre presented Campbell's *Bendigo*, a raucous vaudeville about a legendary prize-fighter, at the Nottingham Playhouse in 1976, he thought it was one of the most enjoyable things he had ever seen in a theatre (so did I). 'Most of Campbell's capers,' said Eyre, 'look as if they are going to be follies and turn out to be inspired gestures of showmanship.'

He had pursued improvisation as a particular goal in recent years, and had just returned from the Edinburgh Fringe, where he supervised the fleshing out in performance of shows that had no existence whatsoever except in the columns of fictitious reviews written by compliant critics on national newspapers.

I saw an example of this style of riotous work in Cambridge in 2005, when I watched Campbell conduct an inspired improvisational contest in the English faculty between a group of undergraduates and a quartet of visiting Liverpudlian actors.

In a sort of *Whose Line Is It Anyway?* format, Campbell set the tasks, or took suggestions from the audience. We had cod Shakespeare, the Eurovision song contest, enemies seeing each other in a museum, simultaneous singing and 'German' acting.

Ken Campbell was born in Ilford, Essex, the only son of Colin Campbell, a Liverpudlian Irishman who worked for ITT, the commercial cable company, and his wife Elsie. He was educated at Gearies Primary School in Barkingside and Chigwell School. While at RADA he also appeared with the renowned Renegades, an amateur group in Ilford run by one of Campbell's earliest heroes, James Cooper, who also played the leading roles, painted the sets, manned the box office and talked a lot about Noël Coward.

He was hired by the comedian Dick Emery as his stooge on tour and had a pot of coffee tipped into his lap for daring to gain an unscripted laugh. 'I'm the comedian around here,' said an incensed Emery, as he poured it.

In 1964 he was understudying Warren Mitchell in the West End and showed him a script called *Events of an Average Bath Night*. Mitchell arranged for a performance, in which he appeared, at RADA. This started him off as playwright, and his *Old King Cole* (1967) for Peter Cheeseman - another early champion - at Stoke-on-Trent has proved a children's classic.

A chance encounter with Lindsay Anderson led to his key, reactive association with the Royal Court in 1969. He tasted failure as a junior director and decided to change tack completely. He heard that a benefactor at the Bolton Octagon was sponsoring a small 'road show' team to spread the good word of the theatre locally. He put in for the job, got it, then broke away from the Octagon. The *Road Show* brought him back to the Court (Anderson invited them into the tiny Theatre Upstairs) and established his place on the fringe at the first peak of its creativity in the early 1970s.

With another eccentric self-dramatiser, Ion Alexis Will, he wrote *The Great Caper* (1974), about a search across Europe and the Lapland tundra for the Perfect Woman. The practitioners he now most admired were not the career directors of the day but the liberated, liberating American companies like the Living Theatre, who had appeared at the Roundhouse, and the improvisational group Theatre Machine, whose work was based on the teaching of Keith Johnstone, an assistant director at the Court.

When Eyre took over the Nottingham Playhouse, Campbell wrote not only *Bendigo* but also *Walking Like Geoffrey*, an inspired piece of vaudevillian hokum based on the local legend of people disporting themselves in a lunatic fashion in order to avoid paying taxes. Eyre also cast Campbell as Knock'em the horse-courser in *Bartholomew Fair* and Subtle in *The Alchemist*; never was an actor more perfectly equipped for the wild excesses and linguistic relish in rare Ben Jonson.

By the end of the 1980s, Campbell's interests in trepanning, teleportation, synchronicity and the Jungian concept of archetypes were fuelling a new career as a solo artist, stitched into a dizzyingly seductive form of theatrical monologue that he delivered in his trademark nasal whine, rocking dangerously on the balls of his feet.

Campbell's three monodramas – *Recollections of a Furtive Nudist*, *Pigspurt* and *Jamais Vu* at the National in 1993 — were subtitled 'The Bald Trilogy' because the (David) Hare trilogy was playing next door in the larger Olivier auditorium. They contain some of the most exciting and entertaining writing for the stage in the past 30 years, on a par with many sections of *The Warp*, and they won the Evening Standard Best Comedy Award.

He was gloriously on form again in *I'm Not Mad: I've Just Read Different Books!* (2005), a multiple adventure of some time-travelling cave-dwellers near Turin, a visit to Jeremy Beadle's library, his career as a speaker at pet funerals in Ilford, and a demonstration of real gastromantic acting (this involves a lot of arse, as opposed to voice, projection; what Judi Dench does, apparently, is merely 'dramatic portrayal'). His heroes included the sci-fi writer Philip K. Dick, the Hollywood script fixer Robert McKee and Ken Dodd. His enthusiasms were legion and unshakeable. A maniacal telephone call in the small hours was both a dread and a joy for many of his friends.

Campbell met his wife, the actor Prunella Gee, when she appeared in *Illuminatus!* They married in 1978, and although they subsequently divorced, they remained close. He is survived by Gee, their daughter Daisy, a writer and director, and two grandchildren, Dixie and Django.

---

*Kenneth Victor Campbell, actor, director, playwright, was born on 10 December 1941 in Ilford, Essex, and died in Epping Forest on 31 August 2009. At his bizarre burial, his own voice-over reminded mourners that 'funeral' was an anagram of 'real fun'.*

# Dilys Laye

*An effervescent star of the* Carry On *movies,*
*Dilys Laye was a formidable performer in*
*musicals and classic plays at the RSC.*

HERS WAS A FACE you were always glad to see in a *Carry On* movie, an old-style revue, a television series like *EastEnders* or — with her lifelong friend Sheila Hancock — *The Bed-Sit Girl*. Her range and talent were unconfined.

She would pop up all over the place: in a new play by Peter Barnes (who once wrote an exacting monologue as a belly-dancer for her), a revival of John Webster's Jacobean shocker *The White Devil* at the Lyric, Hammersmith, an Emlyn Williams drama in Clwyd, a new look at Stephen Sondheim's *Sweeney Todd* in Manchester.

The extraordinary career of Dilys Laye stretched, like that of Hancock and Maggie Smith, from intimate revue to the classical repertoire: she was the first Dulcie on Broadway in Sandy Wilson's *The Boy Friend* (she produced a curiously hoarse, and very funny, squeak in her voice, said Wilson), alongside Julie Andrews; she tried to seduce Dirk Bogarde as a married vamp in *Doctor At Large*; and she opened the new Wilde Theatre at Bracknell, Berkshire, as the eponymous Lady B in *The Importance of Being Earnest*.

Like all charismatic players, she attracted deep devotion on and off stage. During that debut Broadway season with *The Boy Friend* in 1954 she was dated by a handsome young actor called James Baumgarner. His career soon took off when he later changed his surname to Garner.

After returning to London, she worked with Joan Littlewood at Stratford East as 'the Redhead' in the 1959 saleroom musical comedy *Make Me An Offer* and became a regular in the unofficial company of great West End and television comediennes that included Hattie

Jacques, June Whitfield, Joan Sims and Annette Crosbie.

These thespians defined the sexual stratagems and appetites of a whole post-War generation in the comedy of the *Carry On* movies, the burgeoning world of television sit-com and radio surrealism. They were the proto-feminists before the day dawned. Laye scored a particular success opposite Ian Carmichael in the West End comedy *Say Who You Are* at the Her Majesty's in 1965.

There was a weaponry in Laye's acting, a cutting edge, that took her to the heart of an experimental writer like Peter Barnes, in whose amazing play *Bewitched*, directed by Terry Hands, she appeared with the RSC in 1975. This association continued in the mid-1980s when she graced an RSC *Romeo and Juliet* as the Nurse, Nick Dear's fantastic Hogarth play *The Art of Success* and a wonderful RSC and Opera North revival of Oscar Hammerstein and Jerome Kern's *Show Boat*, directed by Ian Judge.

As an undergraduate at Oxford in 1968, I took a vacation job as a stagehand on the Playhouse production by Minos Volonakis of Brecht's *Good Woman of Setzuan*. Peggy Ashcroft had scored a great personal success in the title role at the Royal Court; in Oxford, Sheila Hancock made that role her own, with support from Dilys as Mrs Shin.

During that high summer season, I spent many hours on the river, and in the local hostelries, with Dilys and an actor called Alan Lake, at that time married to Diana Dors. Dilys was a wise and perceptive, very sexy, woman, usually brunette, with more than a wry twinkle and knowing glance about her. I learned more about the theatre from her – some of it, classified information – than from anyone else I knew at that time. Plus, she never let me, or any other critic, down.

She was born in Muswell Hill, north London, adding an 'e' to her surname for the stage, and educated at St Dominic's Convent at Harrow on the Hill. 'Small but perfectly formed' ran a profile in *The Stage*: 'her smile is as warming as a log fire on a cold winter's night'. She made her stage debut in 1948 playing a boy in *The Burning Bush* at the New Lindsey and her screen debut in the same year playing a younger version of the popular star Jean Kent in *Trottie True*.

She was one of the few good things in the revival of Christopher Hampton's *Les Liaisons Dangereuses* starring Emily Fox and Jared Harris at the Playhouse in 2003 and her latter television appearances included a role in Lynda La Plante's two-part drama *The Commander*, with

Amanda Burton, and as Frankie Howerd's mother (Frankie was played, a bit too spookily, by David Walliams) in *Rather You Than Me*.

Her last stage appearance was in the three roles of Miss La Creevy, Mrs Gudden and Peg Sliderskew in the Chichester Festival revival of the RSC's *Nicholas Nickleby* in 2006. In rehearsals, she knew the cancer had returned, but told nobody. She was too ill to transfer with Philip Franks's and Jonathan Church's fine and spirited production to London. Mrs Gudden's moving farewell to the stage had been her own.

From her training at the Ada Foster stage school right through to her strong character roles on film with wimpy buffoons like Charlie Drake in *Petticoat Pirates* (1961) and Norman Wisdom in *On the Beat* (1962), Laye took a stand. She never wilted, never succumbed. In the late 1990s, she illuminated the Donmar Warehouse in *Nine* as the Fellini maternal figure and subsequently the brilliant 1998 revival by John Crowley and his designer brother Bob of Stephen Sondheim's *Into The Woods*.

She was married, briefly, to stuntman Frank Maher, and secondly to the actor Garfield Morgan. In 1972 she married her third husband, the actor and writer Alan Downer, who wrote scripts for *Coronation Street* and *Emmerdale Farm* on television, and *Waggoners' Walk* on radio.

Downer died in 1995, having been ill for some years after suffering a stroke, and it was not long before she was first diagnosed with bowel cancer. She spent her last years living on Ham Common and is survived by her and Alan's son, Andrew Downer, an agent for film crews. Feisty to the last, she outlived her doctors' predictions by six months, having ensured she would be alive to see her son married.

---

*Dilys Laye (Lay) was born on born 11 March 1934 and died of lung cancer aged 74 on 13 February 2009.*

# Natasha Richardson

*The cruelly truncated career of Natasha Richardson
nonetheless proclaimed an outstanding talent in the House of
Redgrave, the most prominent theatrical dynasty of our time.*

SHE WAS SO LIKE HER MOTHER it was almost unreal, and Natasha Richardson never played down the similarity, even going out of her way to both work with Vanessa Redgrave and take on some of her famous roles.

When she played Ellida, in Trevor Nunn's production of Ibsen's *Lady from the Sea* at the newly refurbished Almeida in 2003, it was like revisiting Vanessa in the role almost 30 years earlier.

There was a difference, though: whereas Vanessa's Ellida was a supercharged embodiment of 'the other life' in a performance of hyper intensity, Natasha lived her madness in the moment, with an edge around it, until she broke loose in a great explosion. Mother and daughter shared tremendous empathy with Ibsen's land-locked housewife answering the call of the deep from a mysterious, murderous sailor.

The same quality of emotional yearning informed her charismatic performance as Eugene O'Neill's Anna Christie, Greta Garbo's first speaking role, at the Young Vic in 1990. When she took the performance to New York in 1993, her sexual search was made real in the presence of Liam Neeson as the muscular stoker Mat Burke; she left her husband, the producer Robert Fox, and settled with Neeson, marrying him in 1994.

Although her parents, Vanessa and the charismatic director Tony Richardson, were divorced in 1967, Natasha made smooth progress through two private schools, the Lycée Français Charles de Gaulle in South Kensington and St Paul's Girls' School in Hammersmith, before training at the Central School of Speech and Drama.

She always said that her family connections opened doors but didn't guarantee work, although she made her film debut, aged four, in her film director father Tony Richardson's epic *The Charge of the Light Brigade* (1968). She made her stage debut in 1983 in out-of-town revivals of Caryl Churchill's *Top Girls* and Tom Stoppard's *On the Razzle*, followed by a season at the Open Air Theatre in London's Regent's Park, when she appeared in *A Midsummer Night's Dream* with Ralph Fiennes and Richard E. Grant.

Her West End debut was as Nina in Chekhov's *The Seagull* at the Queen's Theatre in 1985 – on the very stage where her mother had played the same role in her father's production in 1964; this time, Vanessa played the temperamental actress Arkadina.

Natasha exuded a wonderful freshness and spontaneity as Nina, suggesting a wild-eyed idealist whose eventual desolation cut pitifully deep. I declared that she had inherited the full expressive talent of the Redgrave dynasty along with the bony, slightly less generous facial features of her father.

By the time she appeared as Tracy Lord, the Grace Kelly role, in Richard Eyre's 1987 stage version of Cole Porter's *High Society*, she positively glowed with beauty and star quality. Vanessa shines a very strong beam on stage, Natasha irradiated more warmly.

In 1998, she played, and won a Tony, as Sally Bowles in Sam Mendes' revival of *Cabaret* on Broadway. The following year, she returned to Broadway in Patrick Marber's prophetic sex-on-the-internet comedy *Closer*, and in 2005 she appeared again with the Roundabout, this time as Blanche DuBois in a revival of Tennessee Williams's *A Streetcar Named Desire*, opposite John C. Reilly as Stanley Kowalski.

All the same, her stage career was disappointingly sporadic and she often made movies that were more interesting than really good, such as Ken Russell's *Gothic* (1987) in which she played Mary Godwin romping around with Byron and Shelley, or Volker Schlondorff's *The Handmaid's Tale* (1990) scripted by Harold Pinter from Margaret Atwood's bestseller, or Paul Shrader's *The Comfort of Strangers* (1991) adapted by Pinter from Ian McEwan.

After *Closer*, she played a bored housewife of an institutional gauleiter in Marber's script for David Mackenzie's *Asylum* (2004) and then embarked on two film projects with her mother: Merchant Ivory's last (and least good) collaboration *The White Countess* (2005), in which her Russian aristocrat was smitten by Ralph Fiennes's blind diplomat, and

Lajos Koltai's *Evening* (2007), in which Vanessa played a mother putting the domestic record straight for her daughters' benefit.

The split with Robert Fox, in the end, was amicable: Richardson and Neeson seemed meant for each other, and their domestic life in upstate New York with their two young boys apparently idyllic. It is shocking this has all come to an untimely end, with Natasha's unlucky fatal accident, as though the Redgrave dynasty is living out its own House of Atreus saga in accordance with the intervention of the gods and their own larger than life passions and instincts.

Natasha's grandfather Michael Redgrave died in 1985, a career wrecked by Parkinson's disease and illuminated in hindsight by the revelations of his 'secret' homosexual life. Vanessa herself has not been in the best of health these past few years.

Tony Richardson, father to Natasha and Joely, died of AIDS-related illnesses in 1991 and Vanessa's brother, Natasha's uncle, Corin Redgrave, suffered a heart attack while on the political stump in Billericay, Essex, four years ago, and has battled cancer for several years even as he grows into his kingdom as an actor, often playing roles made famous by his own father.

The tragedy of Natasha is not only a great loss to the world of movies and theatre, it is a devastating blow to a family that has had more than its fair share of grief already.

---

*Natasha Jane Richardson was born on 11 May 1963 in London and died on 18 March 2009 in New York after suffering a fall during a beginner's skiing lesson in Quebec, Canada.*

# Lynn Redgrave

*Though Lynn Redgrave was less politically
engaged than her older siblings, Vanessa and
Corin, she was no less a remarkable a talent.*

EVEN BY THE COLOURFUL STANDARDS of her own family's public profile and professional achievements, Lynn Redgrave was an exceptional personality. Her death seems particularly cruel after the loss of both her niece, Natasha Richardson, after a skiing accident last year, and her brother, Corin Redgrave, last month.

The third child of the actors Michael Redgrave and Rachel Kempson, Lynn was a gifted comedian who received her first Oscar nomination for a delightful, clownish performance in the title role of *Georgy Girl* (1966), one of the defining movies of the so-called swinging 60s. She went on to spend many years living and working in America.

Her 1991 television remake of *Whatever Happened to Baby Jane?* with Lynn and Vanessa in the Bette Davis and Joan Crawford roles respectively, is a collector's item. The sisters also starred together in a riotous and emotionally raw 1990 revival of Chekhov's *Three Sisters* at the Queen's Theatre, directed by Robert Sturua of the Rustaveli theatre in Tbilisi, Georgia. Vanessa played Olga, and the sisters' niece Jemma Redgrave (Corin's daughter) played Irena. Lynn's Masha was an unforgettable, frustrated bundle of nervous energy seeping through her cigarette smoke, musical wails and sudden cries.

In her touring solo show, *Shakespeare for My Father* (1994-96), she exorcised her feelings of distance from the imperious Michael Redgrave by relating how she reached him only by becoming an actor herself. The lonely, lumpy child was transformed by her talent, and the evening, full of wonderful vignettes and speeches, reached a moving climax in the reconciliation scene of Lear with Cordelia.

She turned her attention to her mother's life in a 2001 play for seven actors, *The Mandrake Root*. In her later one-woman show *Nightingale*, which won the LA Drama Critics Circle award for best solo performance, she again explored the life of her mother, as well as her maternal grandmother, and also touched upon her own failed marriage.

Lynn's legal battles and marital upheavals were the stuff of soap opera. In 1967 she married John Clark, a former child actor who played the title role in *Just William* on BBC radio. She settled happily in California in 1974, with Clark as her manager.

In 1981 she sued Universal Television for wrongful dismissal and claimed that she was not allowed to breast-feed her third child, Annabel, in her dressing-room during the filming of the CBS sitcom *House Calls*. The litigation lasted 13 years; she lost the suit and was declared bankrupt.

Her marriage to Clark was dissolved in 2000, two years after he revealed that he had had an affair with her personal assistant, Nicolette Hannah, and that Lynn's supposed grandson Zachary was in fact Clark's own son by Hannah, who had married (and subsequently divorced) their son Benjamin.

Lynn battled with her weight and was a spokesperson for Weight Watchers in the 1980s. She was diagnosed with breast cancer in 2002, had a mastectomy the following year and wrote a journal of her recovery with photographs by her daughter Annabel.

Like Vanessa before her, Lynn attended Queen's Gate school, Kensington, and the Central School of Speech and Drama. Her first job was at the Royal Court in *A Midsummer Night's Dream* (1962). The director Tony Richardson (Vanessa's then husband) told her to play Helena 'as a giraffe'.

She was one of the original 12 contract artists in Laurence Olivier's National Theatre, tragic as the daughter Kattrin in *Mother Courage* and hilariously dim as the gormless flapper Jackie Coryton in Noël Coward's own 1964 revival of *Hay Fever* – the one which had a cast, Coward said, that could play the Albanian telephone directory. (Her co-stars were Edith Evans, Robert Lang, Maggie Smith, Robert Stephens and Derek Jacobi.)

Before she left for California, she appeared in the West End transfer of David Hare's *Slag* in 1971 and at Greenwich in 1973 with Dave King in Garson Kanin's *Born Yesterday*. But her career, to British eyes at least, became unfocused. None of her films really matched the charm of early work in *Tom Jones* (1963) with Albert Finney; *The Girl With*

*Green Eyes* (1964) with Rita Tushingham and Peter Finch; and, of course, *Georgy Girl*, with Alan Bates and Charlotte Rampling.

There was the odd sighting on Broadway, ranging from Peter Shaffer's *Black Comedy* with Michael Crawford in 1966 to Alan Bennett's *Talking Heads* in 2003. A London visit in 2001, when she took over Patricia Hodge's role as Dotty Otley in a revival of Michael Frayn's sensationally funny backstage farce *Noises Off*, reminded audiences of her zany brilliance.

Lynn played Dotty, the fast-fading rep actress, in a floral housecoat, like some ridiculous parody of Gloria Swanson in Ashton-under-Lyne, refusing grandly to speak when constrained by a neck brace and dark glasses, or cutting loose maniacally in a symphony of hilarious postures and stricken pretensions, bearing plates of sardines around the stage as if they were the crown jewels. No Dotty was ever dottier, or funnier.

She appeared on Broadway in 2005 at the same time as both Natasha (in *A Streetcar Named Desire*) and Vanessa (in *Hecuba*), receiving rave reviews for her performance as Mrs Culver in Somerset Maugham's *The Constant Wife* at the Roundabout theatre. 'Every night, for a couple of hours,' she said, 'I wasn't a person with cancer. You almost feel like yourself when there's so much evidence, mainly the mirror, to show you aren't. It was true "Doctor Theatre".'

She was appointed OBE in 2002. Lynn is survived by her children Ben, Pema and Annabel, sister Vanessa and six grandchildren.

---

*Lynn Rachel Redgrave was born in London on 8 March 1943 and died of breast cancer, aged 67, on 2 May 2010, in Kent, Connecticut. She was buried in St Peter's Episcopal Cemetery in Lithgow, New York, alongside her mother Rachel Kempson and her niece Natasha Richardson.*

# Pete Postlethwaite

*Salt-of-the earth actor Pete Postlethwaite trained to be*
*a Roman Catholic priest before opting for a life in the*
*theatre. Stephen Spielberg called him 'the best actor in the*
*world' after directing him in his slave ship movie* Amistad.

AFTER TRAINING AT THE BRISTOL OLD VIC school, Peter Postlethwaite (as he was known for the first decade of his career) joined the Liverpool Everyman under the direction of John McGrath and then Alan Dossor.

That period in the early 1970s still shines like a distant beacon of engaged repertory theatre, producing new plays of local interest – by McGrath, C.G. Bond, Willy Russell, Alan Bleasdale, Mike Stott – with a crack troupe of brilliant new actors. Dossor had been a fine actor himself; he had a real eye for new and socially committed talent.

Postlethwaite stood out, first among equals, in such good company: Julie Walters, Alison Steadman, Kate Fahy, Jonathan Pryce, Nick Stringer, Bill Nighy, Antony Sher, Trevor Eve, Bernard Hill. Of course, he was always described as potato-faced, bloke-ish, searingly truthful and blissfully funny. But he had an edge, an ambiguity, and a gleaming maniacal quality, too.

He played the lead in Brecht's version of *Coriolanus* in a Japanese-style production by Geoffrey Reeves, transmitting a most unusual and appealing naivety as 'this thing of war' and flying at the peasants in a boiling, eye-popping rage; the heat of a battle was his sole, animating incentive.

You simply couldn't imagine anyone else playing the hen-pecked Syd in Russell's *Breezeblock Park*, or the obstreperous salesman in Stott's *Funny Peculiar*. Both were wonderful, affectionate portraits of put-upon suburban flummery. In the latter, a farce about fellatio in the Pennines, Postlethwaite engaged with Richard Beckinsale in a slapstick battle of cream puffs.

Back in the Shakespeare groove, he forged a significant relationship with director Adrian Noble at the Bristol OldVic in a 1978 chamber (of horrors) *Titus Andronicus*, playing the villainous and tragically bereaved Aaron opposite Simon Callow's Titus and Gabrielle Drake's Lavinia.

Again for Noble, he played a superb Antonio in an unforgettable *The Duchess of Malfi* (Helen Mirren, Bob Hoskins as Bosola) at the Royal Exchange in Manchester (later at the Roundhouse) in 1981. Instead of the usual dry old stick, he found new notes of decency and bubbling ambition in the steward-turned-lover role.

As Noble established himself at the RSC, he joined the company for five or six seasons, playing Cornwall to Michael Gambon's King Lear, Exeter to Kenneth Branagh's Henry V (both directed by Noble) and Hastings to Antony Sher's Richard III (directed by Bill Alexander), as well as Banquo to Bob Peck's Macbeth. He brought a quality and depth to these support roles more usually found in Russian companies.

Every RSC director, you felt, wanted his name on the team sheet. He was the perfect Ragueneau, the baker, in Derek Jacobi's glorious Cyrano de Bergerac, directed by Terry Hands, and he moved closer to centre stage as Bottom in Alexander's beautiful art deco-into-Narnia *A Midsummer Night's Dream*, finding his proper am-dram aspirations cruelly undermined by the other mechanicals going down the mime route in berets and polo necks.

And when Trevor Nunn opened the Swan in 1986, Postlethwaite was on hand to provide classic, rumbustious knockabout first as Captain Bobadil in John Caird's beautiful Ben Jonson revival, *Everyman In His Humour* (he played the role in a permanent state of helpless recovery from a hopeless hangover), and then as the loudmouth, rapacious Roughman in Nunn's own version of Thomas Heywood's *Fair Maid of the West*.

But he had to leave the RSC to play the leads elsewhere, giving a pacy, bloodcurdlingly haunted Macbeth back at Bristol for his old Liverpool mucker, George Costigan, in 1997 and a bewitching, valedictory Prospero for Greg Hersov at the Royal Exchange ten years later. At the National in 1992 he was in Sam Mendes' production of Jim Cartwright's *The Rise and Fall of Little Voice*, with Alison Steadman and Jane Horrocks, playing the sleazy talent agent Ray Say, far seedier than Michael Caine in the movie.

A highly successful collaboration with director Rupert Goold on Justin Butcher's *Scaramouche Jones* – as a dying clown re-living his colourful life as a last gasp over 90 minutes – led to his stage apotheosis as King Lear on the Liverpool Everyman stage where his career began. This was to mark Liverpool's year, in 2008, as European Capital of Culture.

The performance received mixed reviews, but the critically abhorred gimmicks seemed perfectly reasonable by the time the show fetched up at the Young Vic in London. Rather like Derek Jacobi – and here all comparisons end – Postlethwaite went down the route of splenetic crustiness rather than tyrannical grandeur.

The court greeted him in party hats with a chorus of 'For he's a jolly good fellow,' and he snatched back the microphone handed to his daughters to voice their devotion, briefly tempted to sing Paul Anka's 'My way' (and face the final curtain). The spirit of the Everyman was abroad. But the tragedy thickened, bristling with intelligent ideas and wonderful staging. Postlethwaite was, in the end, deeply touching in a housecoat and granny glasses, left out on the heath like some endangered relic from an old folks' home, cracked with madness, moving cheerlessly towards the inevitable.

---

*Peter William Postlethwaite was born in Warrington, Lancashire. on 7 February 1946 and died of pancreatic cancer, aged 64, in the Royal Hospital, Shrewsbury, on 2 January 2011.*

# John Wood

*Probably the best, least known actor of the last century,*
*John Wood's peculiar ferocity on stage was born of an*
*intellect powered by insatiable reserves of nervous energy.*

JOHN WOOD, WHO HAS DIED aged 81, was one of the greatest stage actors of the last century, especially associated with his roles in plays of Tom Stoppard. But a combination of his enigmatic privacy and low profile on film – he cropped up a lot without dominating a movie – means that he remained largely unknown to the wider public.

As with all great actors, you always knew what he was thinking, all the time. Wood was especially striking in the brain box department. Tall, forbidding and aquiline-featured, he was as much the perfect Sherlock Holmes on stage as he was the ideal Brutus. He exuded ferocious intelligence, and the twinkle in his eye could be as merciless as it was invariably amused.

As the Royal Shakespeare Company's Brutus in 1972, he was undoubtedly the noblest Roman of them all, with his severely etched profile, electrified presence and his impassioned argumentativeness.

This was his breakthrough performance, following a run of wonderful RSC appearances in Maxim Gorky's *Enemies*, James Joyce's *Exiles* (which he had first played in Harold Pinter's revelatory production at the Mermaid in 1970) and as the funniest and most fantastical Sir Fopling Flutter in George Etherege's glorious Restoration comedy *The Man of Mode*.

Wood's father was a surveyor, his mother from 'yeomen stock' and he was brought up in Harpenden and Derby. He was educated at Bedford School and Jesus College, Oxford, where he read law. He had seen John Gielgud as Angelo in Peter Brook's 1950 Stratford-upon-Avon production of *Measure for Measure*, 'and suddenly knew what I wanted to do'.

He did his national service with the Royal Artillery before Oxford, where he was president of the dramatic society, the OUDS, and played Malvolio – 'looking as lean, lanky and statuesque as Don Quixote', said the Oxford Mail – in a Mansfield College gardens production with Maggie Smith as Viola.

He joined the Old Vic company starring a young Richard Burton in 1954, playing a string of small roles over two years, before making his West End debut in 1957 as a self-fulfilling Don Quixote in Tennessee Williams's *Camino Real* at the Phoenix Theatre.

In leaner months, he was a reader of new plays at George Devine's new English Stage Company at the Royal Court and thought that John Osborne's *Look Back In Anger* was inferior to Pinero. He appeared at the Court in Nigel Dennis's *The Making of Moo* and returned to the West End in 1961 as Henry Albertson in the whimsical off-Broadway musical *The Fantasticks* at the Apollo.

He made an auspicious Broadway debut as Guildenstern in Tom Stoppard's *Rosencrantz and Guildenstern Are Dead* and, having warmed up as Sherlock Holmes in the 1974 RSC rediscovery of William Gillette's pot-boiler, he then took definitive possession of the role that Stoppard wrote specifically for him, Henry Carr, in *Travesties*. Wood was devastatingly funny as the British consular official who, stationed in Zurich towards the end of the First World War, takes part in an amateur production of *The Importance of Being Earnest* and falls into a legal wrangle with the business manager, a certain James Joyce, over the cost of a pair of trousers.

Wood revealed a unique knack of conveying Stoppard's cleverness as though it were contained within his own. He cemented his Stoppard association as the strangely afflicted Ivanov, who imagines he owns an orchestra, in Stoppard's zany political oratorio *Every Good Boy Deserves Favour*, directed by Trevor Nunn at the Royal Festival Hall in 1977. And his artistic conjunction with the playwright came full circle in 1997 when, in Richard Eyre's farewell to the National Theatre, Wood was literally spellbinding as the old classical scholar and poet, A.E. Housman, in Stoppard's *The Invention of Love*, managing to make intellectualism both heart-breaking and sexy.

For half an hour in that play, he sat stock still on a bench while his younger self, played by Ben Porter, poured out his dreams and fears, demonstrating that great acting needs few words, even though, of course, in Wood's case, the more words were also the merrier, for few actors have ever wrung more lucid inflections in a line, and as easily over vast tracts, as did Wood.

This coruscating, sulphurous presence ignited on the stage while he simultaneously backed modestly out of the limelight. We knew little about him and he never joined the celebrity throng at first nights, on red carpets or in fashionable restaurants. His real passion was architecture, which he rated the most important of all the arts.

While at Stratford, he acquired a Jacobean manor house in Chipping Campden, Gloucestershire, which had been remodelled in 1663. He said it was 'the most magical house in England', and when asked what he did when he stayed there for months on end, he replied, 'I look at it.' With his first wife (he was twice married) he raised four children there and paid for their education, and the house's upkeep, with frequent movie work in Hollywood and regular television appearances.

He played politicians and academics on screen, and was a notable detective once more in Jack Clayton's beautiful television film of Muriel Spark's spiky geriatric murder thriller, *Memento Mori*, in a stellar cast that also included Maggie Smith. He didn't disown his appearances in Woody Allen's *The Purple Rose of Cairo* (1972), nor his work alongside Jack Nicholson and Meryl Streep – both of whom he admired inordinately – in *Heartburn* (1986). He made notable appearances, too, in *Nicholas and Alexandra* (1971) and *Slaughterhouse Five* (1972).

But most of his film and television roles were ridiculously inferior to his talent, and he never really ventured decisively beyond the footlights, where he reigned supreme. There were long periods when he simply disappeared, rather like Eric Porter, another great, enigmatic actor, in an earlier time. His Prospero, directed by Nicholas Hytner (making his RSC debut) in 1988, struck me as the best I had ever seen – and I had seen Gielgud in the role, twice.

His Prospero was a demented stage manager on a theatrical island suspended between smouldering rage at his usurpation and unbridled glee at his alternative ethereal power. He bound the entire play to his wrecked view of experience and had no qualms about playing up and down the vocal register – in the dark backward and abysm of time we did indeed plummet several throaty fathoms deep. The critic Irving Wardle said that Wood lit up the text like an electric storm, and simply had no rival as a source of nervous energy on a stage.

A year later, his Solness in Ibsen's *The Master Builder*, opposite Joanne Pearce in an RSC production by Adrian Noble, confounded all memories of those who had seen both Redgrave and Olivier in the role. No one else conjured dreams and madness in such coruscating whispers. No one else dispensed sarcastic throwaways, or embarked on egotistical flights of vanity, with such force and energy.

Again, it was the sheer intensity of his ascent to madness in *King Lear*, directed at the RSC by Hytner in 1990, that made him unforgettable. Most Lears explode with anger at the start then find a way of making the rest of the play work in a sort of temperamental unravelling – Wood used that first scene to unlock his passage to his natural habitat of insanity.

It was a stylish, and shattering, performance. 'Make me not mad,' he declared, ambiguously, staring piteously at a wheelchair, his passport to the twilight zone of his own mighty fulfilment. Michael Billington, hailing the best King Lear since Paul Scofield's directed by Peter Brook 30 years earlier, said that Wood 'has the uncensored capacity of the very old to switch in a second from intemperate rage to sweet tenderness'.

In that same Stratford season he added a rare bonus of a vocally strangulated, tearfully regretful Don Armado in a beautiful Terry Hands production of *Love's Labour's Lost* – he was a spindle-shanked, decrepit remnant of the Spanish wars in a Napoleonic hat, finding unexpected lustful regeneration in the arms of a promiscuous wench (Alex Kingston played both Jacquenetta and Cordelia in the *Lear*).

Sightings had become even rarer in recent years, and an extraordinary appearance as an East End gangster in Philip Ridley's *Ghost from a Perfect Place* at the Hampstead Theatre in 1994, quivering with menace and vanity, said one critic, was a reminder of how small actors seemed when he wasn't around, and how puny.

His later films included Ian McKellen's fascist *Richard III* (1995) – ironic, as his own theatrical Richard III at the National in 1979 was a curious misfire – Nicholas Hytner's *The Madness of King George* (1994), scripted by Alan Bennett, and Christopher Riley's *Shadowlands* (1993).

He seemed to have grown smaller, and more bird-like, in his last stage appearance, ten years ago at the National, as the seedy old pot boy Spooner (another Gielgud role) in Pinter's *No Man's Land*. Darting anxious looks, and cawing like a crow, he stared in rapt admiration at Corin Redgrave's Hirst as he talked of making him a cuckold ('I'll never forget her way with my jonquils') – amazingly, he conveyed the idea that Hirst's adultery with his own wife was a thing of wonder, even beauty.

Not for the first time, I was dumbstruck at the brilliance and originality of this master craftsman of the mind, his transparent rapacity of thought, his insatiable intellectual curiosity. He was made CBE in 2007 and is survived by his second wife, Sylvia, and his sons, Sebastian and Rufus, and daughters, Ghislaine and Sibylla.

---

*John Wood was born in Derbyshire on 1 January 1930 and died aged 81 of natural causes in Gloucestershire on 6 August 2011.*

# Nicol Williamson

*John Osborne counted the mesmerising, unruly
Williamson the best actor since Marlon Brando, while
Samuel Beckett averred that he was touched by genius.*

NICOL WILLIAMSON WAS ARGUABLY the most electrifying actor of his generation, but one whose career flickered and faded like a faulty light fitting. Tall and wiry, with a rasping scowl of a voice, a battered baby face and a mop of unruly curls, he was the angriest of all modern Hamlets – a far cry from John Gielgud – though he scuppered his own performance at the Roundhouse, north London, one night in 1969, by apologising to the audience and walking off the stage. The experience was recycled in a 1991 Broadway comedy called *I Hate Hamlet*, in which he proved his point and fell out badly with his co-star.

Williamson's greatest performance was as the dissolute and disintegrating lawyer Bill Maitland in John Osborne's *Inadmissible Evidence* at the Royal Court theatre in 1964. It was a role from which he never really escaped, reviving it on the stage and making the 1968 movie. The play was seen again last year at the Donmar Warehouse, with Douglas Hodge in the leading role.

After a couple of chaotic performances in his own one-man show, and as the equally wild and unreliable actor John Barrymore in *A Night on the Town* at the Criterion theatre in London in 1994, Williamson was last sighted on the stage at the Clwyd Theatr Cymru, Mold, Flintshire, as King Lear in 2001.

Its director, Terry Hands, a one-time colleague at the Royal Shakespeare Company, allowed him free rein to wander through the play, but many of the speeches were misplaced. Like Eric Morecambe playing the piano, he knew all the notes, but not necessarily in the right order. Still, the performance was fretted with moments of gold dust and heartbreak, and you would not willingly have exchanged it for many a more competent or predictable performance.

Hands had taken the sensible precaution of cancelling the second-night performance as the first one was followed by the mother of all first-night parties, with Williamson banging out the jazz standards he loved to sing with a group of musicians including the film critic Ian Christie.

Williamson's talent for acting and lust for life were brilliantly recorded in a 1972 essay by Kenneth Tynan for the *New Yorker* which charted his haphazard preparation for a concert at the White House for President Richard Nixon. When it was published, warts and all, Williamson was furious and never spoke to Tynan again.

He was born in Hamilton, near Glasgow, the son of Mary (née Storrie) and Hugh Williamson. He trained for the stage at the Birmingham School of Speech and Drama and made his professional debut at the Dundee Rep in 1960. In the following year, he appeared as Flute in Tony Richardson's Royal Court production of *A Midsummer Night's Dream*.

He was at the Arts theatre in Thomas Middleton's *Women Beware Women* and in Henry Livings's *Nil Carborundum* in 1962. With Anthony Page directing – Page had first worked with him at the Dundee Rep, and directed *Inadmissible Evidence* – he played Vladimir at the Court in the first major London revival of Beckett's *Waiting for Godot*, partnered by Alfred Lynch as Estragon.

He took his performance of Bill Maitland to New York in 1965, where he was nominated for a Tony award and came to blows with the producer, David Merrick. Although his reputation for unpredictability grew, his talent was recognised in Bafta best actor nominations for his film performances in *Inadmissible Evidence*, Jack Gold's *The Bofors Gun* (1968), written by John McGrath especially for him, and a 1972 television film of Brecht's *The Resistible Rise of Arturo Ui*.

When Trevor Nunn presented a season of Shakespeare's Roman plays at Stratford-upon-Avon, and later at the Aldwych in London, in 1973, Williamson gave a coruscating performance as an unusually virulent and misanthropic Coriolanus. He returned to the Royal Shakespeare Theatre, Stratford, in 1974 as a sour-faced, vinegary Malvolio in *Twelfth Night* and a wolverine, prowling Macbeth. The following year Nunn took that production (Helen Mirren was Lady Macbeth) to London but cut out the Gothic excess in a journey with the play that took him to the defining chamber version of it at the Other Place, Stratford, in 1976 with Ian McKellen and Judi Dench.

Williamson was never as much a part of the RSC as some of his leading contemporaries, but he did 'muck in' with a small-scale production of Chekhov's *Uncle Vanya* at the Other Place, with his wife, Jill Townsend, in 1975. He had married Townsend when she appeared as his daughter in the Broadway production of *Inadmissible Evidence* (they divorced in 1977).

His best-known film roles included Sherlock Holmes in *The Seven-Per-Cent Solution* (1976, in which Watson, played by Robert Duvall, persuades Holmes to visit Sigmund Freud, played by Alan Arkin); and Merlin in John Boorman's *Excalibur* (1981, with Nigel Terry as Arthur and Helen Mirren as Morgana). 'I enjoyed playing Merlin,' Williamson told the *Los Angeles Times*. 'I tried to make him a cross between my old English master and a space traveller, with a bit of Grand Guignol thrown in.'

He had lived mostly in Amsterdam since 1970, but could sometimes be seen in various north London pubs, where he was quite happy to mind his own business and leave the pursuit of glamour and glory to other, less deserving performers. No one who saw him on stage will ever forget him, but it is difficult to see his career as anything but unfulfilled and disappointing. He is survived by his son with Jill, Luke Williamson.

---

*Thomas Nicol Williamson was born in Hamilton, Lanarkshire, on 14 September 1938 and died, after suffering from oesophagal cancer, in Amsterdam aged 73 on 16 December 2011.*

# Joyce Redman

*Vivacious Anglo-Irish comedienne who played opposite*
*Albert Finney, Laurence Olivier, Ralph Richardson,*
*Peter O'Toole and Ian McKellen.*

THE RED-HAIRED, VIVACIOUS and provocative actor Joyce Redman will for ever be remembered for her lubricious meal-time munching and swallowing opposite Albert Finney in Tony Richardson's 1963 film of *Tom Jones*.

Eyes locked, lips smacked, and jaws rotated as the two of them tucked into a succulent feast while eyeing up the afters. Sinking one's teeth into a role is one thing. This was quite another, and deliciously naughty, the mother of all modern mastication scenes.

Redman and Finney were renewing a friendship forged five years earlier when both appeared with Charles Laughton in Jane Arden's *The Party* at the New (now the Noël Coward) Theatre. Redman was not blamed by the critic Kenneth Tynan for making nothing of her role as Laughton's wife. 'Nothing, after all,' he said 'will come of nothing.'

But a great deal did come of her association with other titans of the day, especially Ralph Richardson and Laurence Olivier in their Old Vic and New Theatre seasons during and after the Second World War. She starred as Anne Boleyn opposite Rex Harrison in New York in *Anne of the Thousand Days* (1948) and was twice nominated for an Oscar as best supporting actress: first in *Tom Jones*, then as Emilia in the 1965 film of Olivier's *Othello*.

Redman was born in Northumberland and grew up in Newcastle, County Mayo, one of four sisters in an Anglo-Irish family. She was educated privately by a governess and trained for the stage at RADA in London, making her debut in 1935 as First Tiger Lily in *Alice Through the Looking Glass* at the Playhouse. She was established as a regular on the West End stage, and in the club theatres, by wartime. She was

George Bernard Shaw's Essie, 'a wild, timid-looking creature with black hair and tanned skin', in *The Devil's Disciple*, at the Piccadilly in 1940, followed in 1942 with Maria in *Twelfth Night* at the Arts Theatre and Wendy in *Peter Pan* at the Winter Garden.

Those Old Vic and New Theatre seasons were the defining period: an acclaimed Solveig in the Ralph Richardson production of Ibsen's *Peer Gynt*; Louka in Shaw's *Arms and the Man*; Lady Anne in the legendary *Richard III* of Olivier; Cordelia to the same actor's *King Lear*; Sonya in *Uncle Vanya*; and Doll Tearsheet in *Henry IV Part 2* (though James Agate, for some reason, thought her 'too small to play rampageous bawds').

Redman toured to the Comédie-Française in Paris, conquered Broadway, played the title role in Jean Anouilh's *Colombe*, directed by Peter Brook in 1951, then went to Stratford-upon-Avon in 1955 to play Helena in *All's Well That Ends Well* and Mistress Ford in *The Merry Wives of Windsor*. She could play light comedy and stern tragedy, as she demonstrated to many devoted gallery-ites during Olivier's exciting inaugural National Theatre seasons at the Old Vic in the early 1960s.

Her Emilia in *Othello*, playing that great bedroom scene with Maggie Smith's Desdemona, was indeed unforgettable, and she was a whirlwind as Elizabeth Proctor in Arthur Miller's *The Crucible* (directed by Olivier) and a heart-breaking Juno Boyle in Seán O'Casey's *Juno and the Paycock*.

Although she made a mark in Michael Powell and Emeric Pressburger's *One of Our Aircraft Is Missing* (1942), her film successes were limited to *Tom Jones* and *Othello*. A more topical departure came with the birth-control movie comedy, Ronald Neame's *Prudence and the Pill* (1968), starring Deborah Kerr and David Niven. Her character became pregnant when her daughter, played by Judy Geeson, stole some contraceptive pills and replaced them with aspirin, thus undermining her own mother's 'liberation'.

After several years away from the stage, Redman was enticed back to the National to play opposite Ralph Richardson in Tolstoy's *The Fruits of Enlightenment* in 1979. She joined a new touring company, Compass, directed by her old friend Anthony Quayle, to appear in *The Clandestine Marriage* on tour, and in the West End, in 1984. Three years later, she returned to Broadway as Mrs Higgins, mother to Peter O'Toole's irascible phonetician, in Shaw's *Pygmalion*.

Back in London, Richard Eyre, new boss at the National, cast her in 1990 as the Duchess of York in Ian McKellen's 1930s fascist *Richard III*.

She reminded one critic of the ancient Marie of Romania; another, of an Alan Bennett dowager about to throw on a third row of pearls. Eyre called on her again to play Evelyn, the mother-in-law of Esmé (Judi Dench), in David Hare's *Amy's View* (1997). She pottered around the stage sarcastically before being immobilised with Alzheimer's disease in the third act, death creeping in by inches. With Esmé's daughter Amy played by Samantha Bond, the 16-year span of the play also represented a dynamic dynasty of contemporary acting.

That was Redman's last stage role, and she completed a busy television career (which included spots in the 1990s in *Prime Suspect* and the Ruth Rendell mysteries) with an elderly Queen Victoria in *Victoria & Albert* in 2001.

She had retained her links with home when she bought the island of Beirtreach (three miles by three-quarters of a mile) off the Mayo coast in 1949. In the same year, she married Charles Wynne Roberts while appearing in New York. He predeceased her. She is survived by their three children and five grandchildren.

---

*Joyce Olivia Redman was born in Gosforth, Northumberland, on 7 December 1918 and died of pneumonia aged 96 in Pembury, Kent, on 9 May 2012.*

# Sophiya Haque

*Vibrant actor who achieved success in Bollywood films,
West End musicals and on* Coronation Street.

SOPHIYA HAQUE'S PERFORMANCE IN Peter Nichols's *Privates on
Parade*, which opened last month at the Noël Coward theatre, marked
a high point in the beautiful British Asian actor's West End career,
launched ten years ago with Andrew Lloyd Webber's presentation of
*Bombay Dreams*.

As the lustrous Welsh Eurasian Sylvia Morgan, Haque held her own
among the knobbly-kneed privates, led by Simon Russell Beale's
outrageous Captain Terri Dennis. However, illness forced her to
withdraw from the production before the end of the year and she has
died of cancer at the age of 41.

Haque was the youngest of three mixed race daughters. She was raised
by her British Jewish mother, Thelma, a divorced schoolteacher. She
attended Priory comprehensive school in Portsmouth and took dance
lessons from the age of two and a half at Mary Forrester's Rainbow
School of Dance before moving at the age of 13 to London, where she
lived with her Bangladeshi father, Amirul Haque, a restaurateur, and
his second wife, training full-time at the Arts Educational Schools. By
night, she wrote and recorded songs as the lead vocalist with the band
Akasa and this led to a record deal with WEA Records UK in 1988.

Akasa's music video *One Night in My Life*, directed by the great
cinematographer Jack Cardiff, attracted the attention of MTV Asia,
and Haque was employed as a presenter at Star TV in Hong Kong in
1992, becoming known as the first lady of music television, her daily
shows transmitted in 53 countries.

From 1994, she began appearing on TV in India and in 1997 she
moved to Mumbai full-time to work on the Channel V India service.

Her first Bollywood movie was *Khoobsurat* (1999), with the Indian star Sanjay Dutt, and she later made several more, including *The Rising* (2005), with Aamir Khan as a hero of the Indian mutiny of 1857.

She was a huge star by the time she returned to the UK in 2002 to appear in *Bombay Dreams* – at first in a minor part, understudying the lead role, Rani, knowing she would take over six months later. The show used music by A.R. Rahman, with a libretto by Meera Syal and lyrics by Don Black. Everyone had their favourite scenes: the exciting train-top sequence, the dance around the fountains leading to a crop of wet saris, or the irresistible number 'Shakalaka Baby'.

*Bombay Dreams* suggested a new, vibrant direction for the British Asian musical, but this initiative received a setback in Haque's next starring vehicle. In an adaptation of M.M. Kaye's British Raj blockbuster novel, *The Far Pavilions*, at the Shaftesbury in 2005, she played a wicked stepmother who seduces a maharajah with her dance routine. She was lovely. Shame about the show.

Haque segued into *Coronation Street* in 2008, appearing for six months as Poppy Morales, a barmaid in the Rovers Return who was responsible for sacking one of the show's most popular characters, the long-serving Betty Williams (Betty Driver). She also took a small supporting role in the movie *Wanted* (2008), starring Angelina Jolie, Morgan Freeman and James McAvoy.

Her musical theatre career was back on track in *Britain's Got Bhanghra* (2010) by Pravesh Kumar and Sumeet Chopra at the Theatre Royal, Stratford East, which charted the fortunes of an Indian immigrant and the rise of the Punjabi music genre in Britain over the past 30 years. She played a ruthless entrepreneur realising that bhangra means big bucks in what Michael Billington described as a 'blood transfusion' for the British musical.

Later that year, she popped up in *Gandhi and Coconuts* by Bettina Gracias, one of the last productions at the old Arcola theatre in Dalston, east London. She played a depressed and lonely housewife, escaping to the India of her imagination when Mahatma Gandhi and the Hindu deities Shiva and Kali turn up unannounced for tea.

In 2012 she returned to the forefront in *Wah! Wah! Girls* by Tanika Gupta (book and lyrics) and Niraj Chag (music), an exuberant, colourful dance show, produced by the Theatre Royal, Stratford East, with Sadler's Wells, directed by Kneehigh's Emma Rice at the Peacock theatre as part of the World Stages London festival. The musical registered the changing social and feminist dynamic in India as refracted through an East End of London storyline.

Haque was nothing short of sensational as Soraya, a dance club owner whose own act is one of intense erotic sensuality and blazingly proud defiance. The choreography took up where *Bombay Dreams* had left off, developing a new stage language of show routines and kathak disco dance.

*Privates on Parade*, a great success, was the first offering of the Michael Grandage Company in the West End, a project that is giving a facelift to London theatre with its reasonable ticket pricing, high production values and relentless star casting. The show runs until 2 March and the rest of the performances are dedicated to Haque's memory.

Haque is survived by her sisters and her partner, the musical director David White, with whom she had designed and built a houseboat over the past year.

*Syeda Sophiya Haque was born in Portsmouth on 14 June 1971 and died in a London hospital while undergoing tests, on 16 January 2013.*

# Richard Briers

*Popular, technically adroit rapid-fire actor whose
Hamlet was likened to a demented typewriter before
he found TV fame on* The Good Life.

WHEN HE PLAYED HAMLET as a young man, Richard Briers said he
was the first Prince of Denmark to give the audience half an hour in
the pub afterwards. He was nothing if not quick.

In fact, wrote the veteran critic W.A. Darlington, he played Hamlet
'like a demented typewriter'. Briers, always the most modest and self-
deprecating of actors, and the sweetest of men, relished the review,
happy to claim a place in the light comedians' gallery of his knighted
idols Charles Hawtrey, Gerald du Maurier and Noël Coward.

'People don't realise how good an actor Dickie Briers really is,'
said John Gielgud. This was probably because of his sunny, cheerful
disposition and the rat-a-tat articulacy of his delivery. 'You're a great
farceur,' said Coward, delivering another testimony, 'because you never,
ever, hang about.'

Although he excelled in the plays of Alan Ayckbourn and became
a national figure in television sitcoms of the 1970s and 80s, notably
*The Good Life*, he could mine hidden depths on stage, giving
notable performances in Ibsen, Chekhov and, for Kenneth Branagh's
Renaissance company, Shakespeare.

*The Good Life* defined his career, though he spent a lot of time
getting away from his television persona as the self-sufficient, Surbiton
smallholding dweller Tom Good in the brilliant series – 30 episodes
between 1975 and 1978 – written by John Esmonde and Bob Larbey.

Paired with Felicity Kendal as his wife, Barbara, and pitted against
their formidable, snobbish neighbour Margo Leadbetter (Penelope
Keith) and her docile husband, Jerry (Paul Eddington), he gave one
of the classic good-natured comedy sitcom performances of our time.

Briers was already an established West End star when he started in *The Good Life*. In the same year as the first series, he up-ended expectation as Colin in *Absent Friends*, Ayckbourn's bitter comedy about death, and the death of love, at the Garrick theatre. Like the playwright, he proved once and for all that he 'did' bleak, too.

Briers was born in Raynes Park, south-west London, and educated at schools in Wimbledon. He described his bookmaker father, Joseph, as a feckless drifter. His mother, Morna Richardson, was a pianist. Richard's cousin was the gap-toothed film star Terry-Thomas.

While doing his national service with the RAF, Briers attended evening classes in drama. He then worked as an office clerk before taking a place at RADA, where he won the silver medal. He won a scholarship to the Liverpool Rep for the season of 1956-57 and was never out of work thereafter. At Liverpool he met Ann Davies, whom he married in 1957; they spent most of their married life in Chiswick, west London, in a house they bought around 10 years later.

Seasons in Leatherhead and Coventry were followed by a London debut in 1959 at the Duke of York's as Joseph Field in Lionel Hale's *Gilt and Gingerbread*. He played in Harold Pinter's *A Slight Ache* at the Arts theatre and went on tour as Gerald Popkiss in Ben Travers's *Rookery Nook*, before giving an irresistible Roland Maule, the importunate playwright from Uckfield, in Coward's *Present Laughter*, at the Vaudeville in 1965.

He was back at the Duke of York's in Ayckbourn's first London hit, *Relatively Speaking*, in 1967, forming a wonderful quartet with Celia Johnson, Jennifer Hilary and Michael Hordern, who inadvertently trod on a garden rake that sprang up to hit him on the nose ('What hoe?!').

He was Moon, the stand-in critic, in Tom Stoppard's *The Real Inspector Hound* at the Criterion in 1968 ('a performance of sharp hopelessness and vindictiveness', said Helen Dawson), and played several roles in Michael Frayn's *The Two of Us*, with Lynn Redgrave, at the Garrick in 1970. He took over from Alan Bates in Simon Gray's *Butley* in 1972 and proceeded, he said genially, to empty theatres all over Britain in the leading role of *Richard III* on tour.

He regained his equilibrium, and his comedy momentum, as Sidney Hopcroft in Ayckbourn's *Absurd Person Singular* (set on three separate Christmas Eves) at the Criterion in 1973. So, he was well-established by the watershed year of 1975 and *The Good Life*.

His first leading television role had been in 1962 as a young barrister in *Brothers in Law*, scripted by Frank Muir and Denis Norden. He followed that with five series of *Marriage Lines* (1963-66) by Richard Waring, in which he was a lowly clerk, George Starling, married to Prunella Scales as Kate.

*The Good Life* launched him on a much more varied theatre diet, including Ibsen's *The Wild Duck* at the Lyric, Hammersmith, in 1980; George Bernard Shaw's *Arms and the Man* (his was a richly nuanced, physical performance as the battle-weary Bluntschli) in 1981; Ray Cooney's *Run for Your Wife* (as a bigamous taxi driver, with Bernard Cribbins as his 'cover' and 'apologist') in 1983; and Sir John Vanbrugh's *The Relapse* at Chichester in 1986, as the hilarious chatterbox Lord Foppington.

John Sessions was also in *The Relapse*, and his friend Branagh came to see it. This led directly to Briers working with Branagh on many subsequent projects: as a perhaps too likeable Malvolio ('My best part, and I know it,' he said) in an otherwise wintry *Twelfth Night* at the Riverside Studios, Hammersmith, in 1987, and on a world tour with the Renaissance company as a ropey King Lear (the set really was a mass of ropes, the production dubbed 'String Lear') and a sagacious, though not riotously funny, Bottom in *A Midsummer Night's Dream*.

He was much more successful as Uncle Vanya, directed by Branagh in 1991, in which his body, said one critic, seemed to be in a state of permanent civil war between his adoration of Yelena and a simmering outrage about his treatment at the professor's hands.

Briers's television work in the mid-to-late 1980s was concentrated on two hit series: *Ever Decreasing Circles*, again written by Esmonde and Larbey for the BBC, in which he played Martin Bryce, a well-organised fusspot obsessed with law and order; and *All in Good Faith*, written by John Kane for Thames TV, in which he excelled as the Rev. Philip Lambe, a caring vicar in a wealthy rural parish, pining for the inner-city hubbub.

Reunited with Eddington, who was by then very ill with skin cancer, he played Jack in David Storey's *Home* in 1994 at Wyndham's, a moving display of forced grins and competitive come-backs. Collaborating with a new generation of theatre-makers, he was a crabbed and susceptible Scrooge in a chorus of black-garbed, quick-changing carollers in Neil Bartlett's version of *A Christmas Carol* at the Lyric, Hammersmith, in 1996.

Even more significantly, he and Geraldine McEwan played the nonagenarian couple in Eugène Ionesco's *The Chairs*, directed by Simon McBurney for the Royal Court (relocated at the Duke of York's during refurbishment). He was magnificent as the mouldy old white-haired janitor, master of the mop and bucket, supervising an invisible gathering to hear the very last message for humanity.

He owed his late-flourishing film career to Branagh, appearing in a string of his movies: as Bardolph in *Henry V* (1989), Leonato in *Much Ado About Nothing* (1993), the old blind man in Mary Shelley's *Frankenstein* (1994), a cantankerous old thespian in *A Midwinter's Tale* (1995), Polonius in *Hamlet* (1996) and Sir Nathaniel in the musical *Love's Labour's Lost* (2000).

His bond with the British public was renewed in the highly successful upmarket BBC soap *Monarch of the Glen* (2000-05): he was Hector MacDonald, best chum of Julian Fellowes as Lord Kilwillie, but was blown up trying to train his dog; he returned in a later series as a ghost.

The Ayckbourn connection was cemented in 2002 in a fine revival of *Bedroom Farce* at the Aldwych, with June Whitfield as his stage wife. In classic Briers fashion, he entered beaming with a cup of cocoa at entirely the wrong moment.

At such moments, the Briers visage was like a sky full of swiftly moving clouds, changing from light to grey, querulousness to sorrow, silly ass to lovable child. What was so refreshing about this revival of a solid gold Ayckbourn classic – 27 years after it was presented at the National Theatre – was the way in which Briers and Whitfield led a younger cast of terrific actors (including Samantha Spiro, Jason Watkins and Jasper Britton) through a simultaneous farcical minefield of four marriages in three bedrooms.

Briers seemed to bid farewell to the stage as a touring Prospero in *The Tempest* in 2003 which coincided with a Prospero from Derek Jacobi at the Sheffield Crucible under Michael Grandage. It was an interesting contrast in style, Jacobi a master of verse and subtle sadness, Briers ruling his melancholy island roost with sudden irate surges and fractious asides. Oddly enough, Jacobi's Prospero, clad in green waistcoat and gardening trousers, bore a startling resemblance to Tom Good in *The Good Life*, while Briers gallantly, maybe doggedly, flew in the face of his own reputation as a light comedian.

Having broken his staff and drowned his books, he returned

unexpectedly in 2010 as the military relic Adolphus Spanker in Nicholas Hytner's mellow National Theatre revival of Dion Boucicault's *London Assurance*, alongside Fiona Shaw and Simon Russell Beale. It was sheer delight to be reminded of his natural comic vitality as he rambled on and on, the sound of gunshot still ringing in his ears from the sack of Copenhagen in 1807.

Briers became quietly disillusioned with contemporary television comedy and the cult of celebrity and reality shows, noting that people used to be magical because they were on television and that, now, 'nobody's magical because everyone's on television'.

He wrote several pleasant, light-hearted volumes, including *Coward and Company* (1987), *A Little Light Weeding* (1993) and, with his wife, *A Taste of the Good Life* (1995). He was made OBE in 1989 – 'And I suppose you're getting this for making people laugh?' said the Queen, a great fan of *The Good Life* – and CBE in 2003. He is survived by Ann and their daughters, Lucy and Kate.

---

*Richard David Briers was born 14 January 1934 and died of a lung condition, aged 79, on 17 February 2013.*

# Paul Bhattacharjee

*Elegant and meticulous actor whose work*
*ranged from Shakespeare to* EastEnders
*and whose life ended tragically.*

PAUL BHATTACHARJEE WAS one of the country's leading British
Asian actors, a key member of Jatinder Verma's Tara Arts, a regular at
the Royal Shakespeare Company – he was in the West End last year,
playing Benedick opposite Meera Syal in the RSC's *Much Ado About
Nothing* – and a popular television and film actor whose roles included
Inzamam in the BBC soap *EastEnders*; an immigration officer called
Mohammed in Stephen Frears's *Dirty Pretty Things* (2002); and cameo
roles in the Bond movie *Casino Royale* (2006) and John Madden's *The
Best Exotic Marigold Hotel* (2011).

He was tall, slim and naturally funny, always meticulous in his
movement and perfect in his articulation. He reminded me of an
elegant bird – a heron, perhaps, or a flamingo. His eyes twinkled as
much as they burned. He slowed things down, rather than speeded
them up, but his slowness and deliberation were always an exemplary
demonstration of good timing and manners as a performer.

In the mid-1970s, he was the go-to actor for Asian parts in new plays
in the Royal Court's Theatre Upstairs, and it was always a guarantee of
an element of class and distinction in the show that night if his name
was on the bill. Bhattacharjee was last seen on 10 July leaving a rehearsal
for a new play in the same building in Sloane Square, London, part of
the new artistic director Vicky Featherstone's Open Court weekly rep
season in which he had already played the president of Georgia. His
body was found two days later in East Sussex

He was the only son of Gautam Bhattacharjee, a software researcher
who was a member of the Communist party in India and was forced
to leave the country after his part in the naval mutiny of 1942. In

Britain, Gautam met Anne, who was herself from a migrant family of Russian Jews, and their son, Paul, was educated at state schools in Harrow, Middlesex.

In his teens, Paul was involved in anti-racist campaigns in London and met Verma, who became his great friend and mentor, in workshops they both attended in Southall. Verma recognised from the start a fellow spirit whose highly developed social conscience was linked to a remarkable artistic imagination.

Tara Arts, Britain's first Asian theatre company, was formed by Verma in 1977. Bhattacharjee was an actor and director with them over the next 10 years, notably in *Yes, Memsahib* (1979), which documented the formation of modern east Africa by colonial Indian 'coolie' labour; *Diwali* (1980), which he directed, an epic story set against the annual festival of lights; *Meet Me* (1983), which highlighted mental illness in the Asian community; and *The Little Clay Cart* (1984), a delightful adaptation by Verma of an 8th-century classic as a fable on poverty and revolution.

One of his most crucial roles was that of Gandhi in a play Verma wrote, and Anthony Clark directed, for the Edinburgh Festival fringe in 1982. Gandhi emerged in this play as the first modern Asian, Verma said, in the way we understand such a definition. The impression this experience made on Bhattacharjee never left him and informed his entire subsequent career.

He showed up tellingly in *Murmuring Judges*, the second of David Hare's 'state of the nation' trilogy, at the National Theatre in 1991, but gravitated more naturally towards the RSC, where he played leading roles in John Marston's *The Malcontent*, the disputed Shakespearean history *Edward III* and Philip Massinger's *The Roman Actor* in the Swan, Stratford-upon-Avon, season of 2002 which Thelma Holt and Bill Kenwright later presented in the West End.

In the next two years he gave major leading performances as the dyspeptic, limping paterfamilias in a brilliant 2003 Young Vic revival of Harold Brighouse's *Hobson's Choice*, relocated to modern day Salford by Tanika Gupta and director Richard Jones, and as a very funny Malvolio in a 2004 West End *Twelfth Night* set in Kerala in southern India.

But perhaps his most unusual and remarkable performance was in Complicite's ensemble production, directed by Simon McBurney, of *A Disappearing Number* (2007), in which the mystery of maths at the highest level turned out to be a thing of real beauty. The hinge of the dramatic dissertation was the friendship, around the time of the First World War, between the Cambridge mathematician G.H. Hardy, who believed that mathematicians were only makers of patterns, like poets and painters, and the Brahmin vegetarian autodidact Srinivasa Ramanujan. The air of magical contrivance was sustained by encasing this friendship in the expositions of a narrator physicist – played by Bhattacharjee – and a Hardy disciple many years later.

Having toured with this highly acclaimed production to festivals in Vienna and Amsterdam, in 2008 he plunged into two years of *EastEnders*, before returning to the RSC in Dominic Cooke's *Arabian Nights* (2009) and the *Much Ado* with Syal which, in its modern Mumbai setting and gorgeous colouring, was an update, perhaps, on the famous 1976 RSC production (Judi Dench and Donald Sinden) set in the last days of the Indian Raj.

In the past decade he had appeared regularly, also, at the Tricycle theatre in Kilburn in Nicolas Kent's series of verbatim documentary dramas, notably as Moazzam Begg, one of the detainees of the US military in *Guantanamo* (2004), and in *The Great Game: Afghanistan* (2009) cycle of short plays and the two-part meditation on the nuclear threat, *The Bomb* (2012).

Bhatacharjee was declared bankrupt in the High Court three days before his body was found at the foot of Splash Point cliffs in Seaford. The East Sussex coroner later declared his death a suicide while severely depressed. He was divorced and is survived by his mother and his son, Rahul.

---

*Gautam Paul Bhattacharjee was born in London on 4 May 1960 and was found dead of multiple injuries in East Sussex aged 53 on 12 July 2013.*

# Gerard Murphy

*Passionate actor who commanded the stage at*
*Glasgow's Citizens theatre and the RSC.*

GERARD MURPHY WAS A RARE sort of full-hearted actor, always on
the front foot. He could flood a theatre with passion and squeeze the
juice out of the most recalcitrant prose. Barrel-chested and large- (but
not big-) headed, he looked and sounded like a rampaging farmer,
with his distinctive carrot-coloured hair and stinging, musical, sardonic,
Northern Irish vocal inflections.

He once said that acting was like a drug and that doing it was an
'inexplicable fusion of need and possession'. The ferocity of his acting
was all part of his intellectual valour; he loved debating at school and
university, and could stand up and argue with anyone, usually having
the last word.

He made several films, including *Waterworld* (1995) and *Batman
Begins* (2005), and appeared in lots of television, most recently in the
BBC's *Spooks*. However, his province was the stage, where his flame
burned with magnificent intensity over four decades, from the Glasgow
Citizens theatre and the Royal Shakespeare Company, where he was
an associate artist, to the Royal Exchange in Manchester, the West End
and the Almeida in Islington.

A key figure for several years in the Citizens company, alongside
such remarkable peers as Ciarán Hinds, David Hayman, Suzanne
Bertish, Siân Thomas, Gary Oldman and Rupert Everett, he then
switched successfully, and unusually, to the RSC – the Citizens was
temperamentally and artistically opposed to everything the RSC stood
for. He opened the new Barbican theatre as Prince Hal in *Henry IV,
Parts 1 and 2*, in 1982 and appeared in the first RSC season at the Swan
theatre, Stratford-upon-Avon, four years later.

The eldest of three children, Murphy was born and raised in Newry, County Down. His father, Peter, served in the merchant navy, and his mother, Dympna, was a teacher and librarian. Murphy was educated at the Abbey Christian Brothers' Grammar School in Newry and Queen's University Belfast, where he studied music, psychology, literature and anthropology.

In Belfast, he hung around the Lyric theatre. He had already appeared in school and amateur productions in Newry, and he always played piano and guitar. He walked on in the RSC's *Coriolanus*, with Nicol Williamson, directed by Trevor Nunn at the Aldwych, and took a small role in David Rudkin's *Cries from Casement*, starring Colin Blakely, in an RSC production at the Place in London.

But he emerged most powerfully at the Citizens between 1974 and 1977, as Piraquo in a spaghetti western kitsch version of *The Changeling* by Thomas Middleton and William Rowley; in the British premiere of Mikhail Lermontov's *Maskerade* (the rewriting of 'Masquerade' was deliberate), a salon world of fops and gamblers updated to the 1890s with lashings of Rachmaninov; and as a touching Miss Prism in an all-male *The Importance of Being Earnest*.

The Citizens in this period under Giles Havergal, Philip Prowse and Robert David MacDonald, was the most exciting, most 'European' theatre in the land, slashing and re-energising the classics with style, verve and sexy actors, a very long way from most British theatre and the bourgeois earnestness of the founding father of the Citizens, the playwright James Bridie.

Their credo was articulated in MacDonald's *Chinchilla* (1977), directed by Prowse, in which Murphy played the Russian impresario Sergei Diaghilev (known as 'Chinchilla' because of a white flash in his dark, satiny hair), hunched and dying in a fur coat on the Venice Lido, while replacing Nijinsky with Massine in his personal and professional affections at the Ballets Russes.

On a bare white stage with waves lapping, music playing and boys dancing, this was the most beautiful aesthetic presentation of an aesthetic statement imaginable. Murphy's Diaghilev spoke for the Citizens itself in his 'passion for reform, passion for power, passion for beauty, a thirst to show, a lust to tell, a rage to love'.

*Chinchilla* was revived, with Murphy still as Diaghilev, at the 1979 Edinburgh international festival. In the same year in Glasgow, he played

Macbeth opposite Hayman as Lady M in a stripped-back, spartan version of Shakespeare's tragedy, one of Murphy's finest (and favourite) performances.

In almost the last RSC season at the Aldwych in 1980, he was Johnny Boyle opposite Judi Dench in Nunn's exquisite naturalistic revival of Seán O'Casey's *Juno and the Paycock*; and in the Barbican *Henry IV* in 1982 his Falstaff was Joss Ackland and his father, Henry IV, was Patrick Stewart (their deathbed scenes were electrifying).

He teamed once more with Prowse and MacDonald, as director and translator respectively, on *Phedra*, in true-to-Racine rhyming alexandrines, at the Old Vic in 1984; he was a grizzled, growling Theseus to Glenda Jackson's stupendous, sex-raddled incestuous queen. When Prowse directed a season at Greenwich theatre in the same year, he was a blood-curdling, murderous Brachiano in *The White Devil* by John Webster.

Staying with his predilection for extravagant roles and theatre, he went on to play Oberon, Petruchio and Oedipus in RSC productions in Stratford-upon-Avon, London and on tour, and directed not only a double bill of Jean Genet plays in the Pit of the Barbican, but also Simon Russell Beale as Marlowe's Edward II at the Swan in 1990.

He completed a transition into comic bombast two years ago, playing Sir Lucius O'Trigger in Peter Hall's revival of *The Rivals* at the Theatre Royal, Bath, and the Haymarket in London.

Last year, suffering acutely with a spinal cord compression from prostate cancer, he returned to the main stage of the Citizens in Beckett's *Krapp's Last Tape*, with all the enthusiasm, said one critic, of a man still clinging to life even though he knows the game is up. His mighty frame hovered above a tiny, illuminated desk and he padded back and forth in the pitch darkness beyond.

Murphy, always a free spirit, lived mostly in London but moved eight years ago to Cambridge, near his sister, Deirdre. She and his brother Brian survive him.

---

*Eamon Gerard Murphy was born in Newry, County Down, on 14 October 1948 and died of prostate cancer, aged 64, in Cambridge on 26 August 2013.*

# Barbara Hicks

*Stage and screen eccentric stalwart known for playing battle-axe aunts, village gossips and servants.*

WHEN MEL BROOKS VISITED the film set of *Up at the Villa* (2000), in which his wife, Anne Bancroft, was starring, he proclaimed Barbara Hicks, who has died aged 89, the funniest woman he had ever met. This stalwart character actor, always lodged some way down any cast list as if to prove the truth of Stanislavski's dictum that there are no small parts, only small actors, was a fund of stories, many of them unprintable. And Hicks, though slight of build, with a long face and asymmetrical features, was certainly not a small actor.

As another admirer, Alan Bennett, once told her wistfully: 'When you go, Barbara, there'll be a terrible hole in Spotlight.' And so there is, for since first appearing on television in 1962 playing Miss Print, a comedy sidekick to Richard Hearne's popular Mr Pastry, she had cornered the market in battle-axe aunties, village gossips and critical serving staff in pinnies and housecoats.

Although she was associated with the early periods of both the English Stage Company at the Royal Court and the National Theatre at the Old Vic (and, later, on the South Bank), she was best known on television in Dickens and other classic serials, and in films as varied as *Sailor, Beware!* (1956) and Terry Gilliam's *Brazil* (1985), Merchant/Ivory's *Howard's End* (1992) and Philip Haas's *Up at the Villa* (2000), her last film, in which, as Lulu Good, she teamed up with old friends and shared experiences of late, fulfilling motherhood with Bancroft who, like her, had given birth to a son in her mid-40s.

Hicks was born in Wolverhampton, the youngest of three daughters of an iron and steel merchant, William 'Copper' Hicks, and his wife, Hester Woolley, a formidable suffragist. She was educated at Adcote

School for Girls in Shrewsbury, Shropshire, where she appeared as the Duke of Gloucester in *Richard of Bordeaux* and as Bottom in *A Midsummer Night's Dream* ('Barbara's Bottom was truly remarkable,' said a school report), and served as a land girl in Wales during the war.

On graduating from the Webber Douglas School in London in 1947, she made her debut in *Written for a Lady* at the Royal Court in Liverpool, transferring to the Garrick in the West End. She worked in repertory theatres in New Brighton, near Liverpool, and at the King's, Hammersmith, and married a stage manager, Robert Loblowitz, in 1951. She made an impression in 1957 in *The Tunnel of Love* starring Ian Carmichael at Her Majesty's and in *Miss Pell is Missing* with Yvonne Arnaud and Wilfrid Hyde-White at the Criterion in 1962.

In between, she made her mark at the Royal Court in Noël Coward's *Look After Lulu*, starring Vivien Leigh, Wole Soyinka's *The Invention* and Christopher Logue's *The Lily White Boys*, starring Albert Finney and directed by Lindsay Anderson, who became a firm friend.

She then joined the National at the Old Vic and appeared in George Farquhar's *The Recruiting Officer* (with Maggie Smith and Laurence Olivier), Pinero's *Trelawny of the Wells*, Congreve's *Love for Love*, and as Clara the maid in Coward's own famous 1964 revival of *Hay Fever* with Edith Evans, Smith, Robert Stephens and Derek Jacobi; she extended her range as a harsh, accusatory Goody Putnam (who has laid seven unbaptised babies in the earth) in Olivier's production of Arthur Miller's *The Crucible*.

Her life now changed completely. She had separated from Loblowitz after 10 years and in 1966 met Lieutenant-Colonel Peter Taylor, twice awarded the MC during the Italian campaign in the war, at a dinner party in Highgate, north London. Taylor, who was estranged from his wife, had retired and gone to live on the island of Elba, where Hicks now joined him. She opted out of her career for 10 years to raise her only child, Giles, and they married in 1970.

Her one job in this period was on Tony Richardson's movie *The Charge of the Light Brigade* (1968), in which she once again belied her status by playing a maid. The family returned to London in the mid-1970s and she returned to the National in 1977 to appear in Harley Granville Barker's *The Madras House*, directed by William Gaskill, with Paul Scofield in the leading role. She also joined the company of her local rep on the Essex and Suffolk borders, the Mercury at Colchester, where she appeared in *Under Milk Wood* and Alan Ayckbourn's *Just Between Ourselves* in 1978.

Ten years later, at the National, she was in Ayckbourn's company to play in his rewrite of the old farce *Tons of Money* and his own 'state of the nation' masterpiece, *A Small Family Business*, in which, as Yvonne Doggett, she insinuated herself into the affections of the head of the failing firm, Ayres and Graces.

She made her last stage appearance at the National in 1995 in Anthony Page's blistering revival of Rodney Ackland's *Absolute Hell* (she had also appeared in the television version) with Judi Dench, another great friend. Peter died in 2010, and she is survived by Giles, currently a member of the Royal Shakespeare Company.

---

*Barbara Purser Hicks was born in Wolverhampton on 12 August 1924 and died on 6 September 2013.*

# Donald Sinden

*Formidable, fruity-voiced actor who embraced
tragedy and farce, stage and screen, and wore historic
mementoes onstage.*

'TO HEAR HIM IN FULL SPATE is not unlike being shot between the
eyes by the world's largest plum,' said the journalist and author John
Preston of Donald Sinden, who has died aged 90. The remark was
applicable to the actor's vocal delivery both on stage and off.

No review was ever penned without 'fruity' appearing somewhere
near 'voice' in the text. Judi Dench, who played a notable Beatrice
to his Benedick in *Much Ado About Nothing* in 1976, said he had 'a
Christmas pudding of a voice, soaked in brandy', while the director Peter
Hall, who played a very big part in his career, likened it to a bassoon
that could be terribly tragic, terribly moving – and extremely funny.
Physically, too, Sinden was both imposing and endlessly, sometimes
outrageously, inventive.

In all, Michael Billington averred, he was a critic's dream, because
he always gave you so much to write about. He became nationally
renowned as a Rank contract artist in the 1950s, appearing in notable
films such as *The Cruel Sea* (1953) with Jack Hawkins, *Mogambo* (1953),
directed by John Ford, with Clark Gable and Ava Gardner, and *Doctor
in the House* (1954) and *Doctor at Large* (1957), with Dirk Bogarde and
James Robertson Justice, and from the 1960s onwards in TV sitcoms.

Nonetheless, Sinden was unashamedly theatrical. He rarely went on
stage without an item of historical significance: a pair of Henry Irving's
boots, Fred Terry's eyeglass or John Martin Harvey's hat. He lived and
breathed the traditions of his trade and bent the technique he sought
out from his elders – he learned about listening and timing from Baliol
Holloway – to the service of both tragic and comic gods.

He was a notable Shakespearean at Stratford-upon-Avon either side of his early film stint, playing a booming, militaristic King Lear ('Let me not stay a jot for dinner … dinner, ho, dinner!' has never sounded so heartfelt) in the same season as Benedick and, soon after, less successfully, a blacked-up Othello.

He characteristically said that Lear became nice and easy after three acts, whereas Othello started quietly and just got harder and harder. Like one of his heroes, David Garrick, he believed that tragedy was easier than comedy: 'The expertise you need for farce,' he said, 'is far greater than for Shakespeare, though with him there has to be greater intellectual awareness.'

Sinden on the back foot, exposed and flummoxed in comedy, was one of the sights of the age. His great jowls would sag in a mask of stricken gravity, his eyes fixed wide open, and he would rake the stalls with baleful stares, reducing his audience to a state of gleeful hysteria.

The second of three children, he was born in Plymouth, the son of Alfred, a chemist, and Mabel (née Fuller), and grew up in Ditchling, East Sussex. He suffered from asthma from an early age and attended a series of private schools before going to Hassocks primary. He failed the 11-plus, went on to Burgess Hill secondary and, at the age of 15, was apprenticed in carpentry and attended evening classes in draughting, with aspirations to become an architect and surveyor.

His workplace was in nearby Brighton, where he fell into amateur dramatics and was given a chance by the director of the Theatre Royal, Charles F. Smith, who invited him to join his Mobile Entertainments Southern Area company, with his first professional appearance coming in 1942. His asthma kept him out of wartime action, and he continued with MESA and in joinery. Smith, who had seen Irving act, introduced him to the leaders of his new profession – John Martin Harvey, Irene Vanbrugh, Marie Tempest – and the critic James Agate.

In the 1944 volume of his diaries published as *The Selective Ego*, Agate records how he muttered, 'Stick to your fretwork, young man,' before asking Don Sinden to recite Wolsey's farewell from *Henry VIII* and finding evidence of promise: 'Enough height, an attractive head, something of the look of young [Henry] Ainley, a good resonant voice, vowels not common, manner modest yet firm.'

Later that year, after four years of modern comedies and one-night stands for the forces, Sinden embarked on two terms of training at the Webber Douglas School, before making his regional debut at the

Leicester Rep, moving on to the Stratford-upon-Avon Memorial theatre in 1946 for two seasons; his roles included Dumaine in *Love's Labour's Lost*, Lorenzo in *The Merchant of Venice* and Paris (also understudying Romeo) in Peter Brook's *Romeo and Juliet*.

His contract with Rank followed seasons at the Old Vic in both London and Bristol. By 1960 Sinden was anxious to resume his place on the stage. He was an ideal Captain Hook (doubled with Mr Darling) in *Peter Pan* opposite Julia Lockwood at the old Scala, but Hall, he said, 'rescued' him at the RSC, where he played Mr Price in Henry Livings's surreal comedy *Eh?* and the Duke of York in the legendary *Wars of the Roses* history play cycle at Stratford and the Aldwych in London for two years and shown on BBC television in 1965.

In the latter, Peggy Ashcroft as the 'she-wolf' Queen Margaret wiped his face with a rag soaked in the blood of his murdered son, and their brutish stand-off, ending in York's torture and death, was a highlight of the cycle. Still, he maintained a wider public profile in the popular television comedy series *Our Man at St Mark's* (1964-66), where he succeeded Leslie Phillips as a country vicar kept in check by Joan Hickson's sarcastically overbearing housekeeper.

He consolidated his RSC status, and was made an associate of the company, with his Lord Foppington in Vanbrugh's *The Relapse*, a feast of frippery and ('Stap me vitals') asides. Sinden based his make-up on that of Danny La Rue, but went even further with the rouge, the ribbons, the giant poodle wig and the flutter of silk kerchiefs.

He was in full sail and added three more great performances in the 1969-70 season: a comically puritanical, granite-featured Malvolio (his model was the Graham Sutherland portrait of Somerset Maugham) opposite Dench's exquisite Viola in *Twelfth Night*; a four-square Henry VIII based on Holbein; and another knockout fop, Sir William Harcourt Courtly, in Boucicault's *London Assurance*.

In between, he somehow threaded long West End runs in two hit farces: Terence Frisby's *There's a Girl in My Soup* (1966), in which he executed a celebrated piece of 'business', breaking two eggs (he played a celebrity chef) while seducing Jill Melford's 'dolly bird'; and Ray Cooney and John Chapman's *Not Now, Darling* (1968), weaving a web of deceit and adultery in a fantastic double act with another great farceur, Bernard Cribbins.

Still refusing to erect barriers between the subsidised and commercial stages – at a time when others were busy doing so – he played in Terence Rattigan's *In Praise of Love* (originally *After Lydia*) opposite Joan Greenwood at the Duchess theatre in 1973 and in Ibsen's *An Enemy of the People* ('The strongest man in the world is he who stands alone') at Chichester in 1975.

His last hurrah at the RSC was that wonderful *Much Ado* (directed, as was their *Twelfth Night*, by John Barton), he and Dench dicing with love and the onset of middle age in the last-chance saloon of a colonial Indian sunset. Sinden's technique of embracing the audience in his confidence while building a complex character was breath-taking. His Benedick, the best I have seen, was hilarious and heart-breaking, vain, masculine, silly and romantically efflorescent.

He segued into his second big television series, *Two's Company* (1975-79), playing a Jeevesian butler to Elaine Stritch's acerbic, best-selling American author who had moved to London. Bill McIlwraith's scripts capitalised on both actors' gifts for laconic comedy, rife with misunderstanding and affronted dignity. The result was high-calibre warfare between two proud thoroughbreds.

Another compelling sitcom partnership, full of barely concealed or completely open outrage, came with Windsor Davies in *Never the Twain* (1981-91). The rivalry between the two antique dealers was in no way assuaged by the love and marriage of their respective offspring.

He struck gold twice in this decade: first, as Dick Willey MP, a lascivious Home Office minister, in Ray Cooney's *Two Into One* (1984) at the Shaftesbury, raking the house with his trademark battery of stricken *oeillades* when caught with his trousers, as it were, down; then as Sir Percy Blakeney in Nicholas Hytner's sumptuous 1985 revival of *The Scarlet Pimpernel*, which transferred from Chichester to the Haymarket.

He teamed with Hall, yet again, as a definitive, baffled Mr Hardcastle, the country squire who is mistaken for an innkeeper in *She Stoops to Conquer* ('I no longer know me own house!') and as a growling, highly political Polonius to Stephen Dillane's taciturn Hamlet, the inaugural production at the newly named Gielgud theatre (formerly the Globe). His last West End appearance came in Ronald Harwood's *Quartet* at the Albery (now the Noël Coward) in 1999, playing an operatic has-been in an old folk's home, stalking the stage with Ralph Richardson's walking stick.

In later years, he toured abroad, indefatigably and heroically, in both the RSC's *The Hollow Crown*, John Barton's entertainment about English monarchs, and his own compilation of poetry and reminiscences. He served on many committees, notably the Arts Council and the Theatre Museum, and was a highly visible and participatory member of the Garrick Club.

His television work continued, notably as the father of the ex-wife of Judge John Deed (2001-07): of his own full-of-himself character he said, 'He cannot understand why the series is not called Judge Joseph Channing.'

Sinden was made CBE in 1979, but his 'old actor laddie' public persona, exuding an air of fulsome ingratiation, made him a sitting target for *Spitting Image*, the television satire show, where his florid, fawning puppet yearned for further recognition. The knighthood duly arrived in 1997.

His appetite for absorbing, and preferably relating, theatrical anecdotes was unquenchable, and he produced two delightful volumes of autobiography, *A Touch of the Memoirs* (1982) – which contains a lovely account of a Sussex childhood – and *Laughter in the Second Act* (1985), an invaluable, idiosyncratic document in the history of the RSC and the West End.

He was a great lover of architecture, the countryside and its churches, producing *The English Country Church* (1988) alongside two other collections, *The Everyman Book of Theatrical Anecdotes* (1987) and *The Last Word* (1994), featuring put-downs, final utterances and epitaphs.

Sinden married the actor Diana Mahony in 1948 and they were inseparable until her death in 2004. Their first son, the actor Jeremy, died in 1996. He is survived by their second son, Marc, also an actor, as well as a director and producer, and by his brother Leon, another actor.

---

*Donald Alfred Sinden was born in Plymouth, Devon, on 9 October 1923 and died at home in Wittersham on the Isle of Oxney, Kent, on 11 September 2014.*

# Billie Whitelaw

*Her compelling presence inspired new works by Samuel Beckett and made her a chilling nanny in* The Omen.

'I COULD EASILY HAVE become a nun, or a prostitute, or both,' said Billie Whitelaw. Instead, she claimed that acting had allowed her to use both these sides of herself in a career that included theatre, films, television – and a special place in the affection and inspiration of Samuel Beckett.

By the time the playwright died in 1989, Whitelaw had established herself as one of his favourite interpreters and most trusted confidantes. Her voice had as big an effect on Beckett as that of the Irish actor Patrick Magee. When he saw her in his work *Play* in a National Theatre production at the Old Vic in 1964 – occupying one of three urns alongside Rosemary Harris and Robert Stephens – he determined to write especially for her.

The result was *Not I*, a 16-minute monologue for a jabbering mouth picked out in a dark void. Although Jessica Tandy played the first performances in New York in 1972, Whitelaw's pell-mell, pent-up words of a lifetime were a sensation at the Royal Court theatre in London the following year. She called the experience 'the most telling event of my professional life'.

Beckett then directed her in the premiere of *Footfalls* (1976), a rapt dialogue for a woman and her unseen mother; also, in a revival of *Happy Days* (1979) – in which the post-nuclear Winnie is seen buried up to her waist, then her neck – both at the Royal Court. When Winnie sang her love song to the waltz of *The Merry Widow*, she did so just as Beckett had sung it to her, in a frail and quavering voice.

*Rockaby*, which Whitelaw first performed in New York in 1981, and in the following year at the National in London, was an entirely submerged Winnie, a gaunt human relic in a black dress covered in jet sequins, rocking herself to oblivion while listening to a recording of her own voice.

Billie Whitelaw was born in Coventry, on a housing estate owned by the General Electric Company, to Perceval, an electrician, and Frances (née Williams). A shadowy 'Uncle Len' lived in the same house, with Billie's mother and her elder sister, Constance.

In her autobiography, *Billie Whitelaw … Who He?* (1995), Whitelaw said that she always had two men in her life: two fathers, then husband and lover, later husband and son.

Her parents came from Liverpool, where Billie and the family (she had an elder sister) lived at the start of the Second World War before they moved to Bradford in 1941. There, she went to Thornton Grammar School and the Grange Grammar School for girls.

In 1943 she was sent to the Bradford Civic Playhouse, then run by J.B. Priestley and the formidable Esmé Church, in an attempt to rectify her stutter. She was soon playing children's roles on the radio and met Joan Littlewood and Ewan MacColl at the BBC in Manchester.

When Billie was 16, Littlewood asked her to join her acting group, but her parents would not let her. Instead, she joined Harry Hanson's company in Leeds in 1948 and played in repertory theatres in Dewsbury, New Brighton and Oxford, where she worked with Peter Hall and Maggie Smith. She became one of the most familiar faces on television drama in the next two decades, usually cast as a battling working–class figure in either kitchen-sink dramas or what she called 'trouble up at t'mill' plays.

Through John Dexter, who directed her in *England, Our England* (1962), a West End revue by Keith Waterhouse and Willis Hall, she came to the attention of Laurence Olivier, and she joined his illustrious first company at the National in 1963, sharing a dressing room with Joan Plowright, Maggie Smith and Geraldine McEwan. Her time there included playing Desdemona to Olivier's Othello.

In 1983, she returned to the National as Hetty Mann, dipsomaniac wife of the novelist Heinrich Mann, in Christopher Hampton's brilliant account of wartime European literary émigrés in Tinsel Town, *Tales from Hollywood*. The cast list of characters included the movie stars Johnny Weissmuller, Chico and Harpo Marx, Greta Garbo, and dramatists Ödön von Horváth and Bertolt Brecht. Whitelaw upstaged them all by entering a party bearing a birthday cake and wearing just a white mini-pinny.

Her last stage appearance – apart from her unceasing cycle of Beckett solo shows and readings – came in Edward Albee's *Who's Afraid of Virginia Woolf?* at the Young Vic (1986), where she was a full-on slatternly Martha opposite Patrick Stewart's intimidated, bespectacled George. In her autobiography she recounts how she was mysteriously struck by stage fright and struggled to complete the run.

She married the actor Peter Vaughan, nine years her senior, in 1952, and started a relationship with the writer and critic Robert Muller as the marriage failed; it ended in divorce in 1966. The following year she married Muller, and they had a son, Matthew.

Whitelaw's film career was patchy. She made a more consistent mark on television, starting as a maid in an adaptation of Frances Hodgson Burnett's *The Secret Garden* (1952) and as Mary Dixon, daughter of the police constable played by Jack Warner in the first series of *Dixon of Dock Green* (1955). She took the role of Countess Ilona in two episodes of *Supernatural* (1977), written by Muller, and her TV work continued until the start of the new century.

Film appearances included Alfred Hitchcock's *Frenzy* (1972); *The Omen* (1976), as the chilling nanny Mrs Baylock; *The Krays* (1990), as Violet, the mother of the East End gangster brothers; and the police comedy *Hot Fuzz* (2007). She was at her vibrant, blowzy best in two early films with Finney, *Charlie Bubbles* (1967) and *Gumshoe* (1971). In 1991 she was appointed CBE.

Whitelaw divided her time between a flat in Hampstead and a cottage in Suffolk, and never quite believed her luck: 'When I wake up at dawn, and that grey cloud of work anxiety is there, I only have to get up and open the window to feel so free and happy that I think I'm going to go off pop.'

---

*Billie Honor Whitelaw was born in Coventry on 6 June 1932 and died in a nursing home in Hillingdon, Greater London, following a bout of pneumonia on 21 December 2014.*

# Geraldine McEwan

*Brilliant, kittenish (with claws) and fascinating*
*exponent of high comedy and darkest drama.*

GERALDINE MCEWAN COULD PURR like a kitten, snap like a viper and, like Shakespeare's Bottom, 'roar you as gently as any sucking dove'. She was a brilliant, distinctive and decisive performer whose career incorporated high comedy on the West End stage, Shakespeare at Stratford-upon-Avon, Laurence Olivier's National Theatre, and a cult television following in E.F. Benson's *Mapp and Lucia* (1985-86).

She was also notable on television as a controversial Miss Marple in a series of edgy, incongruously outspoken Agatha Christie adaptations (2004-09). Inheriting a role that had already been inhabited at least three times 'definitively' – by Margaret Rutherford, Angela Lansbury and Joan Hickson – she made of the deceptively cosy detective a character both steely and skittish, with a hint of lust about her, too.

This new Miss Marple was an open-minded woman of the world, with a back story that touched on a thwarted love affair with a married man who had been killed in the First World War. Familiar thrillers were given new plot twists, and there was even the odd sapphic embrace.

For all her ingenuity and faun-like fluttering, there remained an oddness about the performance; McEwan was no more successful in the part than was Julia McKenzie, her very different successor.

Although she was not easily confused with Maggie Smith, she often tracked her stylish contemporary, succeeding her in Peter Shaffer roles (in *The Private Ear* and *The Public Eye* double bill in 1963, and in *Lettice and Lovage* in 1988) and emulating Smith as both Millamant and Lady Wishfort in Congreve's masterpiece *The Way of the World* in 1969 and 1995.

And a decade after Smith won her Oscar for *The Prime of Miss Jean*

*Brodie*, McEwan scored a great success in the same role on television in 1978; the novelist Muriel Spark herself said that McEwan was her favourite Miss Brodie in a cluster that also included Vanessa Redgrave and Anna Massey.

McEwan was born in Old Windsor, where her father, Donald McKeown, was a printers' compositor who ran the local branch of the Labour party in a Tory stronghold; her mother, Nora (née Burns), came from a working-class Irish family. Geraldine was always a shy and private girl who found her voice, she said, when she stood up in school and read a poem.

She had won a scholarship to Windsor County Girls' School, but she felt out of place until she found refuge in the Windsor Rep at the Theatre Royal, where she played an attendant fairy in *A Midsummer Night's Dream* in 1946.

After leaving school, she joined the Windsor company for two years in 1949, meeting there her life-long companion, Hugh Cruttwell, a former teacher turned stage manager, 14 years her senior, whom she married in 1953, and who became a much-loved and influential principal of the Royal Academy of Dramatic Art in 1965.

Without any formal training, McEwan went straight from Windsor to the West End, making her debut in *Who Goes There?* by John Deighton (Vaudeville, 1951), followed by an 18-month run in *For Better, For Worse...* (Comedy, 1952) and with Dirk Bogarde in *Summertime*, a light comedy by Ugo Betti (Apollo, 1955).

*Summertime* was directed by Peter Hall and had a chaotic pre-West End tour, Bogarde's fans mobbing the stage door every night and in effect driving him away from the theatre for good. McEwan told Bogarde's biographer, John Coldstream, how he was both deeply encouraging to her and deeply conflicted over his heartthrob star status.

Within a year she made her Stratford-upon-Avon debut as the Princess of France in *Love's Labour's Lost* and played opposite Olivier in John Osborne's *The Entertainer*, replacing Joan Plowright as Jean Rice when the play moved from the Royal Court to the Palace.

Like Ian Holm and Diana Rigg, she was a key agent of change in the transition from the summer Stratford festival – playing Olivia, Marina and Hero in the 1958 season – to Peter Hall's new Royal Shakespeare Company; at Stratford in 1961, she played Beatrice to Christopher Plummer's Benedick and Ophelia to Ian Bannen's Hamlet.

Kittenish and playful, with a wonderful gift for suggesting hurt innocence with an air of enchanted distraction, she was a superb Lady Teazle in a 1962 Haymarket production of *The School for Scandal*, also starring John Gielgud and Ralph Richardson, that went to Broadway in early 1963, her New York debut.

She returned to tour in the first, disastrous, production of Joe Orton's *Loot*, with Kenneth Williams, in 1965, and then joined Olivier's National at the Old Vic, where parts over the next five years included Raymonde Chandebise in Jacques Charon's landmark production of Feydeau's *A Flea in Her Ear*, Alice in Strindberg's *Dance of Death* (with Olivier and Robert Stephens), Queen Anne in Brecht's *Edward II*, Victoria ('a needle-sharp gold digger' said one reviewer) in Somerset Maugham's *Home and Beauty*, Millamant, and Vittoria Corombona in *The White Devil*.

Back in the West End, she formed a classy quartet, alongside Pat Heywood, Albert Finney and Denholm Elliott, in Peter Nichols's *Chez Nous* at the Globe (1974), and gave a delightful impression of a well-trained, coquettish poodle as the leisured whore in Noël Coward's broken-backed adaptation of Feydeau, *Look After Lulu*, at Chichester and the Haymarket.

In the 1980s, she made sporadic appearances at the National, now on the South Bank, winning two Evening Standard awards for her fresh and youthful Mrs Malaprop in *The Rivals* ('Men are all Bavarians,' she exclaimed on exiting, creating a brand new malapropism for 'barbarians') and her hilariously acidulous Lady Wishfort; and was a founder member of Ray Cooney's Theatre of Comedy at the Shaftesbury theatre.

In the latter part of her stage career, she seemed to cut loose in ever more adventurous directions, perhaps through her friendship with Kenneth Branagh, who had become very close to Cruttwell while studying at RADA.

She was surprise casting as the mother of a psychotic son who starts behaving like a wolf, played by Will Patton, in Sam Shepard's merciless domestic drama, *A Lie of the Mind*, at the Royal Court in 1987. And in 1988 she directed *As You Like It* for Branagh's Renaissance Theatre Company, Branagh playing Touchstone as an Edwardian music-hall comedian.

The following year she directed Christopher Hampton's under-rated *Treats* at the Hampstead theatre. This was in the middle of three sensationally re-imagined comedy classics by Congreve, Ionesco and Noël Coward in the last five years of the 20th century. In these performances, more than in any others, McEwan demonstrated that old plays are best treated with intelligent irreverence.

The characters in the National's new *The Way of the World*, directed by Phyllida Lloyd, did not congregate, as in Congreve, in St James's Park, but in a stark white art gallery showing large red abstracts. London was in the height of a rebel, punk fashion era, the girls in puffed up satin dresses, the sardonic *raisonneur* Witwoud done up to resemble the punk pop impresario Malcolm McLaren.

The cherry on the cake of this alignment of the narcissism, bitchiness, dandyism and casual promiscuity of Restoration comedy with the punk culture of the 1970s was McEwan's Lady Wishfort, that 'old peel'd wall', usually played as a sedate old prune. She entered looking like an ostrich, said Sheridan Morley, 'which has been crammed into a tambourine lined with fresh flowers'.

By the end of the play, her brutally powdered white face suggesting an unholy alliance of Barbara Cartland and Lindsay Kemp as designed by Vivienne Westwood, she was fluffed up in a rose tutu and reaching for the cherry brandy before collapsing outside her own front door on a pile of bin bags.

McEwan then formed a fantastical nonagenarian double act with Richard Briers in a Royal Court revival, directed by Simon McBurney, of Ionesco's tragic farce *The Chairs*, her grey hair bunched on one side like superannuated candy floss.

She was hosting a dumb orator's last message for humanity to an audience of unoccupied chairs. Those chairs formed a fearsome avalanche at the end amid a wild clanging of bells, a surreal tango of impersonal stage activity.

She was just as brilliant as fading stage pin-up Judith Bliss in Noël Coward's *Hay Fever* (1999), directed as a piece of Gothic absurdism at the Savoy by Declan Donnellan; McEwan tiptoed through the thunderclaps and lightning like a glinting harridan, a tipsy bacchanalian with a waspish lust and highly cultivated lack of concern ('My husband's not dead; he's upstairs.')

Other television successes included *Oranges Are Not the Only Fruit* (1990), playing Jeanette Winterson's mother, and an adaptation of Nina Bawden's tale of evacuees in Wales, *Carrie's War* (2004). Her occasional movie appearances included Cliff Owen's *The Bawdy Adventures of Tom Jones* (1975), two of Branagh's Shakespeare adaptations – *Henry V* (1989) *and Love's Labour's Lost* (2000) – as well as *Robin Hood: Prince of Thieves* (1991); Peter Mullan's devastating critique of an Irish Catholic education, *The Magdalene Sisters* (2002), in which she played cruel, cold-hearted Sister Bridget; and *Vanity Fair* (2004).

McEwan was rumoured to have turned down both an OBE and a damehood, but never confirmed this. Hugh died in 2002. She is survived by their two children, Greg and Claudia, and seven grandchildren.

---

*Geraldine McEwan (McKeown) was born in Old Windsor, Berkshire, on 9 May 1932 and died, aged 82, in Charing Cross Hospital, Hammersmith, after suffering a stroke three months earlier, on 30 January 2015.*

# Alan Howard

*One of the leading heroic actors of his generation, whose*
*clarion voice would reverberate to the RSC's rafters.*

WHEN THE GREAT SHAKESPEAREAN ACTOR Alan Howard, who has died aged 77, returned to the stage after a five-year absence in 1990, all of his special qualities came into focus, ironically, in a piece of Victorian hokum by Henry Arthur Jones. The occasion of this revival of *The Silver King* at Chichester was a reminder that the history of British theatre is, in the first place, written by its actors.

Howard had played almost every Shakespearean king (and Coriolanus) for the Royal Shakespeare Company over 16 years from 1966, as well as the double of Oberon and Theseus in Peter Brook's legendary 1970 production of *A Midsummer Night's Dream* set in an all-white gymnasium; Howard as Oberon scornfully surveying the muddled lovers while swinging languidly on a trapeze is an indelible image of the RSC in this period.

More usually, he was attired in cloaks and leathers and, as in his preferred director Terry Hands's version of *Henry V*, isolated in a spotlight. His clarion voice, the most distinctive (with Ian Richardson's) of his generation, would reverberate to the rafters, his myopic demeanour – his face was studded, it seemed, with eyes like currants either side of a banana nose – seeking refuge in an audience's sympathy. Solitude was his mindset, grand spiritual debauchery his inclination.

Howard's silver king at Chichester was an innocent dissolute in the criminal underworld, implicated in the murder of his wife's former admirer, pronounced dead and reborn in America to redeem both his impoverished family and his reputation.

Striking lucky as a miner in Nevada, hence the silver king tag, he returned home in mysterious splendour, oscillating between haunted angularity and aristocratic poise. He cowered like a holy fool on his uppers and dreamed himself into the oblivion from which, like a venerably restored chieftain in snakeskin boots and silver-sleek hair, he magnificently awoke to achieve retribution.

It was as fantastical a performance as any of his Shakespearean monarchs, or his star turn as Carlos in Peter Barnes's *The Bewitched* (1974), culminating in a King Lear for Peter Hall at the Old Vic in 1997 in which his trumpet-tongued voice invoked goose bumps on his cry of 'O reason not the need.'

Alongside Ian McKellen, Howard was the leading heroic actor of his generation, someone whose voice, even in a misfired 1993 National Theatre *Macbeth* (known as the 'gas-ring' *Macbeth* on account of some circular ground level lighting of blue flames), thrillingly encompassed, said the critic Irving Wardle, a sardonic croak, a lyrical caress, a one-man brass section and a whinnying cry of horror.

His Hamlet was a model of melancholic introspection without a jot of sentiment or self-pity, his Benedick (opposite Janet Suzman as Beatrice) in *Much Ado* a genuinely funny and self-deluded popinjay, his Achilles in a famous *Troilus and Cressida* the most sensual and riveting in RSC history.

Howard was of impeccable theatrical pedigree, the only son of the comic actor Arthur Howard and his wife Jean Compton (Mackenzie). His uncle was the film star Leslie Howard, his great-uncle, with whom he spent most of his childhood in the Hebrides, was the novelist Sir Compton Mackenzie, and the Compton side of the family boasted five generations of actors and producers, including the venerable Fay Compton. Alan acted while at school at Ardingly College in Haywards Heath, West Sussex, and during national service in Germany.

He did not train at drama school but started sweeping the stage at the Belgrade in Coventry when that theatre opened in 1958. He appeared in Arnold Wesker's trilogy – *Roots, Chicken Soup with Barley* and *I'm Talking About Jerusalem* – directed by John Dexter and came with those plays to the Royal Court in London the next year. He first impressed as a classical actor in Tony Richardson's revival of *The Changeling* at the Court in 1961 and made a West End debut alongside Wendy Hiller in *The Wings of the Dove* by Henry James at the Haymarket in 1963.

He played in rep with Judi Dench and John Neville at the Nottingham Playhouse and started quietly at the RSC with a melodious, virtually sung, Orsino in *Twelfth Night* before exploding as an outrageous, vile Lussurioso in Trevor Nunn's black-and-white revival of *The Revenger's Tragedy* in 1966.

This launched him into the repertoire of Jaques in *As You Like It*, Edgar in *King Lear*, followed in the 1970s with his sequence of kings (Hands's *Henry VI* trilogy was the first time these plays had been performed uncut in the modern theatre), his glorious Jack Rover in the landmark rediscovery of John O'Keefe's 18th-century comic melodrama *Wild Oats*, and his only serious RSC failure, opposite Glenda Jackson, in Peter Brook's surprisingly flat *Antony and Cleopatra* in 1978.

Sightings in the theatre over the past decade – Howard suffered with diabetes and eventually had one leg amputated – were rare and treasurable: a lewd and satanic Dr Schoning with Anna Friel in Wedekind's *Lulu* at the Almeida, directed by Jonathan Kent, in 2001; a terrifying and daringly intoned blind prophet Tiresias with Ralph Fiennes in *Oedipus* at the National in 2008; and, in 2011, a semi-immobilised but still magnificent Sir Peter Teazle in Deborah Warner's Barbican Centre revival of Sheridan's *The School for Scandal*, a masterclass in how to do style and stillness in high comedy.

He was appointed CBE in 1998. He regretted not having more film work, but appreciated the ownership one had in theatre, relishing the room to manoeuvre a good director would leave him with, he said, a degree of leeway and moments of discovery every night.

Quiet and reflective away from the stage, he was happiest in his house on the Isle of Barra in the Outer Hebrides, where his great-uncle had written *Whisky Galore*. His first marriage, to the actor and scenic designer Stephanie Hinchcliffe Davies, ended in divorce.

He met his second wife, the novelist Sally Beauman, when she interviewed him for the *Sunday Telegraph*; she subsequently wrote a fine history of the RSC. He is survived by Sally, whom he married in 2004, and their son, James.

---

*Alan Mackenzie Howard was born in Croydon, Surrey, on 5 August 1937, and died of pneumonia in Hampstead, London, on 14 February 2015. He is buried, alongside Sally Beauman (who died a year later), in Highgate Cemetery.*

# Alan Rickman

*Languorous actor as renowned on stage as in popular movies such as* Robin Hood: Prince of Thieves, Harry Potter *and* Love Actually.

THE WORLD BECAME FULLY AWARE of the sly, languid and villainous charms of Alan Rickman, who has died aged 69 of cancer, as the self-parodying Sheriff of Nottingham pitted against Kevin Costner in *Robin Hood: Prince of Thieves* (1991). However, the actor had already established himself as a star name at the Royal Shakespeare Company in the mid-1980s and as the hilarious German terrorist, Hans Gruber, in the action thriller *Die Hard* (1988) with Bruce Willis.

Rickman appeared as the cello-playing, dearly departed ghost in Anthony Minghella's sensual, taut and wonderfully muted *Truly, Madly, Deeply* (1990), with Juliet Stevenson as his grieving partner.

At the RSC, he had been sensational as the predatory, dissolute Vicomte de Valmont in *Les Liaisons Dangereuses*, Christopher Hampton's brilliant adaptation of Choderlos de Laclos's 18th-century epistolary novel that started small in the RSC's Other Place in Stratford-upon-Avon and trailed clouds of glory to the West End and Broadway in 1987. Rickman was a pivotal figure in a company that included, at that time, and in that production, Lindsay Duncan, Stevenson and Fiona Shaw.

Having first trained and worked as a graphic designer, Rickman was a late starter as an actor, attending RADA between 1972 and 1974, and winning the Bancroft gold medal, before working in rep and the RSC in small roles at the end of the 1970s. He began making waves as Anthony Trollope's devious chaplain Obadiah Slope in BBC television's *The Barchester Chronicles* in 1982.

Then he was, for a new generation entirely, the sinister potions master Severus Snape in the eight Harry Potter movies, for a decade from 2001. Snape had secrets, and this inner life infused one of the outstanding performances in the series as he stalked the corridors and back passages at Hogwarts like the ghost in *Hamlet*, smelling a rat at every turn, his noble face contorted with mysterious loathing and curious motivation.

However, it would be wrong to typecast Rickman as a villain. He was an outstanding Hamlet at the Riverside Studios and on tour in 1992, a mature student whose rampant morbidity masked an intense, albeit perverse, zest for life. And in *Antony and Cleopatra* at the National Theatre in 1998, he was fabulous opposite Helen Mirren's voluptuous serpent of old Nile – shambolic, charismatic, a spineless poet of a warrior. It was his misfortune to have both these great classic performances displayed in productions that met with considerable critical hostility and public indifference.

Tall, commanding, extremely funny when required, he was never above sending himself up either on stage or in the movies. He had talent to burn, a glorious voice that sometimes blurred in slack-jawed articulation, if only because everything he did seemed to come so easily to him.

He was a central figure in the life of the little Bush theatre on the London fringe, at the Royal Court in the Max Stafford-Clark era of the 1980s, as well as at Trevor Nunn and Terry Hands's RSC, and he was a continual source of inspiration, and practical support, to his colleagues. He proved also to be a fine stage director, and directed two films. In the second of them, *A Little Chaos* (2014), a handsome 17th-century costume drama of love among the landscape artists at the newly constructed palace of Versailles, Rickman himself presided in his bewigged pomp as Louis XIV, the Sun King.

The son of a factory worker, Bernard (who died when Alan was eight), and his wife, Margaret (née Bartlett), he was of Irish and Welsh descent, raised on a council estate in Acton, west London, with three siblings (he was the second child), and educated at Derwentwater Primary School in Acton, a Montessori school, and Latymer Upper. He studied graphic design at Chelsea School of Art – where he first met, aged 18, his future life partner, Rima Horton – and the Royal College of Art. With three friends, he ran a graphic design studio for three years in Notting Hill before going to RADA at the age of 26.

Rickman made his first impact with the Birmingham Rep, the first regional company to visit the new National Theatre's home on the South Bank, when he played the upright Wittipol, disguised as a Spanish lady, in Ben Jonson's *The Devil Is an Ass* in 1976, and also at the Edinburgh Festival.

Small parts in the RSC season of 1977-78 were followed, in 1980, by leading roles as a distraught sponsor of a pop concert in Stephen Poliakoff's *The Summer Party* at the Crucible in Sheffield, with Brian Cox and Hayley Mills, and in Dusty Hughes's anatomy of the Trotskyite left in *Commitments*, at the Bush. Rickman was a lifelong Labour party activist, while Rima, an economist, with whom he lived from 1977, was a Labour councillor in Kensington and Chelsea for 20 years from 1986.

In the early 1980s, he was an ideal, doggedly English Trigorin in Thomas Kilroy's otherwise Irish version of Chekhov's *The Seagull* at the Royal Court; a coruscating Grand Inquisitor in Richard Crane's adaptation of Dostoevsky's *The Brothers Karamazov* at the Edinburgh Festival; and a cheerfully stoned pragmatist on a Californian dope farm in Snoo Wilson's *The Grass Widow*, also at the Royal Court, laying bare the capitalism of the drugs world as a sort of displaced Howard Marks, alongside Ron Cook and Tracey Ullman.

Everything about his acting came into sharp focus in the 1985-86 RSC season, when *Les Liaisons Dangereuses* was in repertory with three other plays. In *As You Like It*, he was the perfect 'Seven ages of man' Jaques with Stevenson as Rosalind and Shaw as Celia; in Troilus and Cressida, Achilles never sulked so mightily as Rickman in his tent; and in Ariane Mnouchkine's superb version of Klaus Mann's *Mephisto*, translated by Timberlake Wertenbaker, he nailed the dilemma of a creative artist in the censorious climate of the Third Reich: 'What can I do? I'm only an actor.' He took the next big job.

He was both rooted in his own theatre world and internationally curious. Guided by the producer Thelma Holt, he played a reclusive, abandoned actor in a derelict cinema in Kunio Shimizu's *Tango at the End of Winter*, a beautiful poetic drama of memory and illusion directed by the Japanese maestro Yukio Ninagawa, at the Edinburgh Festival in 1991; and buckled down to *Hamlet* with Robert Sturua, the great director of the Rustaveli theatre in Georgia who had lately made waves in western Europe.

In the earlier part of his career, Rickman had supervised several shows with the comedian Ruby Wax, whom he had met at the RSC, and had recommended a play by Sharman Macdonald to the Bush. He expanded his directing work with Wax into a new play he commissioned from Macdonald, *The Winter Guest* (1995, West Yorkshire Playhouse and the Almeida in London), a tone poem in a Scottish seaside town, with no plot, for the superb quartet of Phyllida Law, Sheila Reid, Sian Thomas and Sandra Voe; he also directed a film version (1997) with an overlapping cast.

But film had begun to take precedence, *Robin Hood* leading to big roles and billing in Tim Robbins's satirical *Bob Roberts* (1992), about a right wing folk singer running for the US Senate; as Colonel Brandon in Ang Lee's fine version of Jane Austen's *Sense and Sensibility* (1996), with a screenplay by Emma Thompson; and as Eamon de Valera in Neil Jordan's *Michael Collins* (1996), starring Liam Neeson as the IRA founder.

Even with the Harry Potter franchise under way, Rickman managed a triumphant return in 2001 to the West End and Broadway in Noël Coward's *Private Lives*, displaying what the New York Times called a virtuosity of disdain as the squinting, wounded egomaniac Elyot Chase opposite Lindsay Duncan's blonde ice queen of an Amanda Prynne.

Too much in love to like each other very much, Rickman and Duncan pickled their performances in their many years of friendship and collaboration. Theirs was the epitome of a messy modern marriage relaunched on the sea of bitter experience. Here was the real texture of Coward's elliptically expressed sexual skirmishing, and the best pairing in the roles since Robert Stephens and Maggie Smith 30 years earlier.

Rickman released Coward in an entirely new idiom, playing Elyot's vanity like some heroic adventure, squinting at everyone through a veil of delighted disapproval. The second act sofa fight was a logical collusion to deep-seated affection, the sort that breeds real hate over trivialities. Rickman impressed his fans with an impressive display of mock gamesmanship, and the fashion pundits with a truly fetching pair of black silk pyjamas.

His last stage roles, both critically acclaimed, were as Ibsen's John Gabriel Borkman at the Abbey in Dublin (with Duncan and Fiona Shaw) in 2010 and as a celebrity teacher in a writing workshop in Theresa Rebeck's *Seminar* on Broadway in 2011.

In between, he directed *My Name Is Rachel Corrie* at the Royal Court, the West End, the Edinburgh Festival and on Broadway in 2005-06. He compiled the show with Katharine Viner [now editor-in-chief of the *Guardian*] from the writings and emails of the American activist Corrie, who was killed by a bulldozer operated by the Israeli army in Gaza in 2003 while protesting against its occupation. This sense of political justice and civic responsibility informed his life as a citizen, too.

Rickman will be remembered latterly as Thompson's husband in Richard Curtis's *Love Actually* (2003), the voice of Marvin the paranoid android in *The Hitchhiker's Guide to the Galaxy* (2005), as Judge Turpin in Tim Burton's wacky movie version of Stephen Sondheim's *Sweeney Todd* (2007) and as (another voice) Absalom the Caterpillar in Burton's *Alice in Wonderland* (2010).

He was a committed vice-chairman of RADA, a patron of the charity Saving Faces, dedicated to helping those with facial disfigurements and cancer, and honorary president of the International Performers Aid Trust, which works to alleviate poverty in some of the world's toughest areas. He married Rima in 2012. She survives him, as do his siblings, David, Michael and Sheila.

---

*Alan Sidney Patrick Rickman was born in London on 21 February 1946 and died aged 69 in London on 14 January 2016, four days after David Bowie, also 69 and also, like Bowie, from a cancer only his closest family knew about.*

# Anita Reeves

*Vivacious actor who was a favourite of
the Dublin stage and ideal exponent of
Seán O'Casey and Brian Friel.*

SPEECHES WERE MADE FROM every stage in Dublin on the night
Anita Reeves died, a mark of the popular affection in which the actor
was held. Small, vivacious and red-haired, she was as much a musical
theatre star as she was a leading exponent of Seán O'Casey and Brian
Friel. When she played the long-deceased adoptive mother in Hugh
Leonard's autobiographical *Da*, the author said she was the closest to
the real-life Maggie Tynan as anyone had ever been in the role.

Her acting personality was imbued with the warmth and generosity
she displayed in everyday life. Her family came first – she did not, for
instance, go to Broadway with Friel's great hit *Dancing at Lughnasa*
in 1991 because of family commitments – but she had a terrier-like
devotion to a new play, however small or uncommercial, if it engaged
her mind and spirit. She would travel with a piece such as Elaine
Murphy's *Little Gem* (2008) – a litany of love, sex and death for three
generations of women speaking in a dense northside Dublin idiom –
on tour in Ireland and to Edinburgh, London, New York, Australia.

The youngest daughter of Jack Reeves, a sergeant in the Dublin police
force, and his wife, Kay, Anita was educated at St Louis High School,
Rathmines, and trained as an actor for four years at the Brendan Smith
Academy in Dublin, having worked briefly as a vet's assistant and in an
old people's care home.

She appeared as a principal boy in pantomime in a small theatre
in Dún Laoghaire owned by the gas company, several pantomimes at
the Gaiety with Eamon Morrissey and, in 1966, in a mass pageant of
students celebrating the 50th anniversary of the Easter Rising in Croke
Park, hallowed home of Gaelic football.

She became a favourite in the Dublin revues of the mid-1960s, many of them written and produced by Fergus Linehan and starring his wife, another fabled Dublin star, Rosaleen Linehan. This prepared her for such later triumphs as Mme Thénardier in the Dublin premiere of *Les Misérables* in 1993, or a bewitching Mrs Lovett in Stephen Sondheim's *Sweeney Todd* at the Gate in Dublin in 2007. She chilled the audience's collective marrow, too, in a musical moment in Joe Dowling's 2012 production of James Joyce's *The Dead*, adapted for the stage by Frank McGuinness, at the Abbey.

Dowling had first directed Reeves in the Irish premiere of Alan Ayckbourn's *Absurd Person Singular* at the Gate in 1974 and, although she had many successes at both the Abbey and the Gate, she remained a non-aligned employee. She was a quintessentially Dublin actor and defied all other categories.

*Dancing at Lughnasa* (1990), first directed by Patrick Mason, is Friel's magical, mystical memory play about his mother and aunts during the long hot summer of 1936, and Reeves embodied the spirit and tenacity of those 'five Glenties women' as Maggie, the good-natured family clown; the scene of them all dancing around the kitchen is securely lodged in Irish theatre folklore.

The play came to the National Theatre in London and transferred to the West End. Over the following five years, Reeves revisited the West End in two Dowling productions of O'Casey political classics: in the Gate revival of *Juno and the Paycock* at Wyndham's in 1993 (with Niall Buggy and Mark Lambert), she was surely the definitive Juno Boyle; and in a touring revival of *The Plough and the Stars* at the Garrick in 1995 she was in bustling, comical form as Jinnie Grogan the charwoman, lamenting her marriage while excavating ear wax.

She adorned one of Nicholas Hytner's first productions as artistic director of the National Theatre in London when, with Dearbhla Molloy, she played one of the chatty aunts in the grocery store in Martin McDonagh's extraordinary *The Cripple of Inishmaan* (1997) and returned in the following year to play a figure of comparative rectitude, a landlady, in the Almeida theatre's version of Pirandello's *Naked* starring Juliette Binoche – who drew a fine caricature of Reeves as a first night gift.

She was back in Dublin as Mrs O'Kelly in a well-remembered revival of Dion Boucicault's *The Shaughraun* (2005) and toured to the

Edinburgh Festival and New York in 2013 with Deirdre Kinahan's two-hander *These Halcyon Days* in which, opposite Stephen Brennan as a former actor, she played a retired primary schoolteacher in a nursing home with her customary grace and large, watery eyes.

Her last stage appearance was as Juno again, directed by Dowling in his farewell production in charge of the Guthrie theatre in Minneapolis last summer. She had, said Dowling, grown even greater in the role, bringing an added elegance and finesse to the spirited mouthpiece of the Dublin tenements during the nationalist schisms of 1922.

Reeves's films included Neil Jordan's remarkable debut, *Angel* (1982), as well as the same director's *The Miracle* (1991) and *The Butcher Boy* (1997), Mike Newell's *Into the West* (1992) and Alan Archbold's *The Life of Reilly* (1995).

She was briefly married to (and divorced from) the actor Barry McGovern and lived for more than 30 years with Julian Erskine, the executive producer of Riverdance, whom she married in 2000. She is survived by Julian, their two children, Gemma and Danny, and her siblings, Maureen, Tom and John.

---

*Anita Reeves was born in south Dublin on 24 June 1948 and died of cancer, aged 68, in the same city, on 7 July 2016.*

# John Hurt

*Hurt could do no harm, he could do anything, including
Quentin Crisp in the television film* The Naked
Civil Servant, *the Elephant Man and the petulant,
debauched emperor Caligula in* I, Claudius.

FEW BRITISH ACTORS of recent years have been held in as much affection
as John Hurt. That affection is not just because of his unruly lifestyle –
he was a hell-raising chum of Oliver Reed, Peter O'Toole and Richard
Harris, and was married four times – or even his string of performances
as damaged, frail or vulnerable characters, though that was certainly a
factor. There was something about his innocence, open-heartedness
and his beautiful speaking voice that made him instantly attractive.

As he aged, like a good port, his face developed more creases and
folds than the old map of the Indies, inviting comparisons with the
famous 'lived-in' faces of W. H. Auden and Samuel Beckett, in whose
reminiscent *Krapp's Last Tape* he gave a definitive solo performance
towards the end of his career. One critic said he could pack a whole
emotional universe into the twitch of an eyebrow, a sardonic slackening
of the mouth. Hurt himself said: 'What I am now, the man, the actor, is
a blend of all that has happened.'

For theatregoers of my generation, his pulverising, hysterically funny
performance as Malcolm Scrawdyke, leader of the Party of Dynamic
Erection at a Yorkshire art college, in David Halliwell's *Little Malcolm
and His Struggle Against the Eunuchs*, was a totemic performance of
the mid-1960s; another was David Warner's Hamlet, and both actors
appeared in the 1974 film version of *Little Malcolm*. The play lasted only
two weeks at the Garrick Theatre (I saw the final Saturday matinée),
but Hurt's performance was already a minor cult, and one collected by
the Beatles and Laurence Olivier.

He became an overnight sensation with the public at large as Quentin
Crisp – the self-confessed 'stately homo of England' – in the 1975

television film *The Naked Civil Servant*, directed by Jack Gold, playing the outrageous, original and defiant aesthete whom Hurt had first encountered as a nude model in his painting classes at Saint Martin's School of Art, before he trained as an actor.

Crisp called Hurt 'my representative here on Earth', ironically claiming a divinity at odds with his low-life louche-ness and poverty. But Hurt, a radiant vision of ginger quiffs and curls, with a voice kippered in gin and as studiously inflected as a deadpan mix of Noël Coward, Coral Browne and Julian Clary, in a way propelled Crisp to the stars, and certainly to his transatlantic fame, a journey summarised when Hurt recapped Crisp's life in *An Englishman in New York* (2009), ten years after his death.

Hurt said some people had advised him that playing Crisp would end his career. Instead, it made everything possible. Within five years he had appeared in four of the most extraordinary films of the late 1970s: Ridley Scott's *Alien* (1979), the brilliantly acted sci-fi horror movie in which Hurt – from whose stomach the creature exploded – was the first victim; Alan Parker's *Midnight Express*, for which he won his first Bafta award as a drug-addicted convict in a Turkish torture prison; Michael Cimino's controversial western *Heaven's Gate* (1980), now a cult classic in its fully restored format; and David Lynch's *The Elephant Man* (1980), with Anthony Hopkins and Anne Bancroft.

In the last-named, as John Merrick, the deformed circus attraction who becomes a celebrity in Victorian society and medicine, Hurt won a second Bafta award and Lynch's opinion that he was 'the greatest actor in the world'. He infused a hideous outer appearance – there were 27 moving pieces in his face mask; he spent nine hours a day in make-up – with a deeply moving, humane quality. He followed up with a small role – Jesus – in Mel Brooks's *History of the World: Part 1* (1981), the movie where the waiter at the Last Supper says, 'Are you all together, or is it separate checks?'

Hurt was an actor freed of all convention in his choice of roles, and he lived his life accordingly. He was the youngest of three children of a Church of England vicar and mathematician, the Reverend Arnould Herbert Hurt, and his wife, Phyllis (née Massey), an engineer with an enthusiasm for amateur dramatics.

After a miserable schooling at St Michael's in Sevenoaks, Kent (where he said he was sexually abused), and the Lincoln Grammar School (where he played Lady Bracknell in *The Importance of Being Earnest*), he rebelled as an art student, first at the Grimsby Art School where, in 1959, he won a scholarship to Saint Martin's, before training at RADA for two years from 1960.

He made a stage debut that same year with the Royal Shakespeare Company at the Arts, playing a semi-psychotic teenage thug in Fred Watson's *Infanticide in the House of Fred Ginger* and then joined the cast of Arnold Wesker's national service play, *Chips with Everything*, at the Vaudeville. Still at the Arts, he was Len in Harold Pinter's *The Dwarfs* (1963) before playing the title role in John Wilson's *Hamp* (1964) at the Edinburgh Festival, where the critic Caryl Brahms noted his unusual ability and 'blessed quality of simplicity'.

This was a more relaxed, free-spirited time in the theatre. Hurt recalled rehearsing with Pinter when silver salvers stacked with gins and tonics, ice and lemon, would arrive at 11.30 each morning as part of the stage management routine. On receiving a rude notice from the distinguished *Daily Mail* critic Peter Lewis, he wrote, 'Dear Mr Lewis, Whooooops! Yours sincerely, John Hurt' and received the reply, 'Dear Mr Hurt, Thank you for short but tedious letter. Yours sincerely, Peter Lewis.'

After *Little Malcolm*, he played leading roles with the RSC at the Aldwych – notably in David Mercer's *Belcher's Luck* (1966) and as the madcap dadaist Tristan Tzara in Tom Stoppard's *Travesties* (1974) – as well as Octavius in Shaw's *Man and Superman* in Dublin in 1969 and an important 1972 revival of Pinter's *The Caretaker* at the Mermaid. But his stage work over the next 10 years was virtually non-existent as he followed *The Naked Civil Servant* with another pyrotechnical television performance as Caligula in *I, Claudius*; Raskolnikov in Dostoevsky's *Crime and Punishment* and the Fool to Olivier's King Lear in Michael Elliott's 1983 television film.

His first big movie had been Fred Zinnemann's *A Man for All Seasons* (1966) with Paul Scofield (Hurt played Richard Rich), but his first big screen performance was an unforgettable Timothy Evans, the innocent framed victim in Richard Fleischer's *10 Rillington Place* (1970), with Richard Attenborough as the sinister landlord and killer John Christie.

He claimed to have made 150 movies and persisted in playing those he called 'the unloved … people like us, the inside-out people, who live their lives as an experiment, not as a formula'. Even his

Ben Gunn-like professor in Steven Spielberg's *Indiana Jones and the Kingdom of the Crystal Skull* (2008) fitted into this category, though not as resoundingly, perhaps, as his quivering Winston Smith in Michael Radford's terrific *Nineteen Eighty-Four* (1984); or as a prissy weakling, Stephen Ward, in Michael Caton-Jones's *Scandal* (1989), about the Profumo affair; or again as the lonely writer Giles De'Ath in Richard Kwietniowski's *Love and Death on Long Island* (1997).

His later, sporadic theatre performances included a wonderful Trigorin in *The Seagull* at the Lyric, Hammersmith, in 1985 (with Natasha Richardson as Nina); Turgenev's incandescent idler Rakitin in a 1994 West End production by Bill Bryden of *A Month in the Country*, playing a superb duet with Helen Mirren's Natalya Petrovna; and another memorable match with Penelope Wilton in Brian Friel's exquisite 70-minute doodle *Afterplay* (2002), in which two lonely Chekhov characters – Andrei from *Three Sisters*, Sonya from *Uncle Vanya* – find mutual consolation in a Moscow café in the 1920s. The play originated, as did that late *Krapp's Last Tape*, at the Gate theatre in Dublin.

His last screen work included, in the Harry Potter franchise, the first, *Harry Potter and the Philosopher's Stone* (2001), and last two, *Harry Potter and the Deathly Hallows Parts One and Two* (2010, 2011), as the kindly wand-maker Mr Ollivander; Rowan Joffé's 1960s remake of *Brighton Rock* (2010); and the 50th anniversary television edition of *Dr Who* (2013), playing a forgotten incarnation of the title character.

Because of his distinctive, virtuosic vocal attributes – was that what a brandy-injected fruitcake sounds like, or peanut butter spread thickly with a serrated knife? – he was always in demand for voiceover gigs in animated movies: the heroic rabbit leader, Hazel, in *Watership Down* (1978), Aragorn/Strider in *Lord of the Rings* (1978) and the Narrator in Lars von Trier's *Dogville* (2004). In 2015 he took over the Peter O'Toole stage role in *Jeffrey Bernard is Unwell* for BBC Radio 4. He had foresworn alcohol for a few years – not for health reasons, he said, but because he was bored with it.

Hurt's sister was a teacher in Australia, his brother a convert to Roman Catholicism and a monk and writer. After his first marriage to the actor Annette Robinson (1960, divorced 1962) he lived for 15 years in London with the French model Marie-Lise Volpeliere Pierrot. She died in a riding accident in 1983.

In 1984 he married, secondly, a Texan, Donna Peacock, living with her for a time in Nairobi until the relationship came under strain from his drinking. They divorced in 1990. With his third wife, Jo Dalton, whom he married in the same year, he had two sons, Nick and Alexander ('Sasha'); they divorced in 1995.

In 2005 he married the actor and producer Anwen Rees-Myers, with whom he lived in Cromer, Norfolk. Hurt was made CBE in 2004, given a Bafta lifetime achievement award in 2012 and knighted in the New Year's honours list of 2015. He is survived by Anwen and his sons.

---

*John Vincent Hurt was born in Chesterfield, Derbyshire, on 22 January 1940 and died of pancreatic cancer in Cromer, Norfolk, on 27 January 2017.*

# Tim Pigott-Smith

*Stage and screen actor who belied a mild*
*temperament with villainous performances, notably*
*in the TV series* The Jewel in the Crown.

THE ONLY UNEXPECTED THING about the wonderful actor Tim Pigott-Smith, who has died suddenly, was that he never played Iago or, indeed, Richard III. Having marked out a special line in sadistic villainy as Ronald Merrick in his career-defining, award-winning performance in *The Jewel in the Crown* (1984), Granada TV's adaptation of Paul Scott's *Raj Quartet* novels, he built a portfolio of characters both good and bad who were invariably presented with layers of technical accomplishment and emotional complexity.

He emerged as a genuine leading actor in Shakespeare, contemporary plays by Michael Frayn – in Frayn's *Benefactors* (1984) he was a malicious, Iago-like journalist undermining a neighbouring college chum's ambitions as an architect – and Stephen Poliakoff, American classics by Eugene O'Neill and Edward Albee, and as a go-to screen embodiment of high-ranking police officers and politicians, usually served with a twist of lemon and a side order of menace and sarcasm.

He played a highly respectable King Lear at the West Yorkshire Playhouse in 2011, but that performance was eclipsed, three years later, by his subtle, affecting and principled turn in the title role of Mike Bartlett's *King Charles III* (soon to be seen in a television version) at the Almeida, in the West End and on Broadway, for which he received nominations in both the Olivier and Tony awards. The play, written in Shakespearean iambics, was set in a futuristic limbo, before the coronation, when Charles refuses to grant his royal assent to a Labour prime minister's press regulation bill.

The interregnum cliff-hanger quality to the show was ideal for Pigott-Smith's ability to simultaneously project the spine and the jelly of a character, and he brilliantly suggested an accurate portrait of the future king without cheapening his portrayal of him.

Although not primarily a physical actor, like Laurence Olivier, he was aware of his attributes, once saying that the camera 'does something to my eyes, particularly on my left side in profile', something to do with the eye being quite low and 'being able to see some white underneath the pupil'.

It was this physical accident, not necessarily any skill, he modestly maintained, which gave him a menacing look on film and television, 'as if I am thinking more than one thing'.

Tim was the only child of Harry Pigott-Smith, a journalist, and his wife Margaret (née Goodman), a keen amateur actor, and was educated at Wyggeston Boys' School in Leicester and – when his father was appointed to the editorship of the *Herald* in Stratford-upon-Avon in 1962 – King Edward VI Grammar School, where Shakespeare had been a pupil.

Attending the Royal Shakespeare Theatre, he was transfixed by John Barton and Peter Hall's *Wars of the Roses* production, and the actors: Peggy Ashcroft, with whom he would one day appear in *The Jewel in the Crown*, Ian Holm and David Warner. He took a part-time job in the RSC's paint shop.

At Bristol University he gained a degree in English, French and drama (1967), and at the Bristol Old Vic theatre school he graduated from the training course (1969) alongside Jeremy Irons and Christopher Biggins as acting stage managers in the Bristol Old Vic company.

He joined the Prospect touring company as Balthazar in *Much Ado* with John Neville and Sylvia Syms and then as the Player King and, later, Laertes to Ian McKellen's febrile first Hamlet.

Back with the RSC he played Posthumus in Barton's fine 1974 production of *Cymbeline* and Dr Watson in William Gillette's *Sherlock Holmes*, opposite John Wood's definitive detective, at the Aldwych and on Broadway. He further established himself in repertory at Birmingham, Cambridge and Nottingham.

He was busy in television from 1970, appearing in two *Doctor Who* sagas, *The Claws of Axos* (1971) and *The Masque of Mandragora* (1976), as well as in the first of the BBC's adaptations of Elizabeth Gaskell's *North and South* (1975, as Frederick Hale; in the second, in 2004, he played Hale's father, Richard).

His first films were Jack Gold's *Aces High* (1976), adapted by Howard Barker from R.C. Sherriff's *Journey's End*, and Tony Richardson's *Joseph Andrews* (1977). His first Shakespeare leads were in the BBC's Shakespeare series – Angelo in *Measure for Measure* and Hotspur in *Henry IV Part One* (both 1979).

A long association with Hall began at the National Theatre in 1987, when he played a coruscating half-hour interrogation scene with Maggie Smith in Hall's production of *Coming in to Land* by Poliakoff. He was a Dostoeyvskyan immigration officer, Smith a desperate, and despairing, Polish immigrant.

In Hall's farewell season of Shakespeare's late romances in 1988, he led the company alongside Michael Bryant and Eileen Atkins, playing a clenched and possessed Leontes in *The Winter's Tale*; an Italianate, jesting Iachimo in *Cymbeline*; and a gloriously drunken Trinculo in *The Tempest* (he played Prospero for Adrian Noble at the Theatre Royal, Bath, in 2012).

The Falstaff on television when he played Hotspur was Anthony Quayle, and he succeeded this great actor, whom he much admired, as director of the touring Compass Theatre in 1989, playing Brutus in *Julius Caesar* and Salieri in Peter Shaffer's *Amadeus*.

When the Arts Council cut funding to Compass, he extended his rogue's gallery with a sulphurous Rochester in Fay Weldon's adaptation of *Jane Eyre* (1993) on tour and at the Playhouse, in a phantasmagorical production by Helena Kaut-Howson, with Alexandra Mathie as Jane; and, back at the NT, as a magnificent, treacherous Leicester in Howard Davies' remarkable revival of Schiller's *Mary Stuart* (1996) with Isabelle Huppert as a sensual Mary in a very red dress and Anna Massey a bitterly prim Elizabeth.

In that same National season, he teamed with Simon Callow (as Face) and Josie Lawrence (as Doll Common) in a co-production by Bill Alexander for the Birmingham Rep of Ben Jonson's trickstering, two-faced masterpiece *The Alchemist*; he was a comically pious Subtle in sackcloth and sandals.

He pulled himself together as a wryly observant Larry Slade in one of the landmark productions of the past 20 years: O'Neill's *The Iceman Cometh* at the Almeida in 1998, transferring to the Old Vic, and to Broadway, with Kevin Spacey as the travelling salesman Hickey revisiting the last chance saloon where Pigott-Smith propped up the bar with Rupert Graves, Mark Strong and Clarke Peters in Howard Davies' great production.

But something's happened, and it was an almost unrecognisable Pigott-Smith as the bar-room philosopher Larry Slade who led the nervous interrogation as a sort of sardonic chorus. Hickey is in quiet, confessional mode for once, not drowning his sorrows on one of his periodic benders.

The time for truth-telling, not the iceman, hath cometh. Hickey's expiation of guilt acts as a kind of faith-healing for the others, all expertly delineated in an excellent cast, none more so than Pigott-Smith's disillusioned, perceptive former anarchist. Critical comparisons with the poetic richness of Gorky's journey through the underworld in *The Lower Depths* were neither fatuous nor unjust.

He and director Davies combined again, with Helen Mirren and Eve Best, in a monumental NT revival (designed by Bob Crowley) of O'Neill's epic *Mourning Becomes Electra* in 2003. Pigott-Smith recycled his ersatz 'Agamemnon' role of the returning civil war hero, Ezra Mannon, as the real Agamemnon, fiercely sarcastic while measuring a dollop of decency against weasel expediency, in Euripides' *Hecuba* at the Donmar Warehouse in 2004.

In complete contrast, his controlled but hilarious Bishop of Lax in Douglas Hodge's 2006 revival of Philip King's *See How They Run* at the Duchess suggested he had done far too little outright comedy in his career. In the third, increasingly chaotic final act, Pigott-Smith, dressed in his ecclesiastical striped pyjamas, issued a command that rang out like a pistol shot: 'Sergeant, arrest most of these vicars!'

The sergeant, suitably non-plussed, tried to comply: 'Which one of you lot is the vicar 'ere?' There were vicars 'ere, there and everywhere, as well as an escaped German prisoner, a bendy-limbed spinster who had been hitting the sherry and an innocent housemaid accused of being an accelerator before the fact.

Television roles after *The Jewel in the Crown* included the titular chief constable, John Stafford, in *The Chief* (1990-93) and the much sleazier chief inspector Frank Vickers in *The Vice* (2001-03).

On film, he showed up with Anthony Hopkins in *The Remains of the Day* (1993); in Paul Greengrass's *Bloody Sunday* (2002), a harrowing documentary reconstruction of the protest and massacre in Derry in 1972; as Pegasus, head of MI7, in Rowan Atkinson's *Johnny English*

(2003); and as the foreign secretary in the Bond movie *Quantum of Solace* (2008).

In the last decade of his life he achieved an amazing roster of stage performances, including a superb Henry Higgins, directed by Hall, in *Pygmalion* (2008); the avuncular, golf-loving entrepreneur Ken Lay in Lucy Prebble's extraordinary *Enron* (2009), a play that proved there was no business like big business; the placatory Tobias, opposite Penelope Wilton, in Albee's *A Delicate Balance* at the Almeida in 2011; and the humiliated George, opposite his Hecuba, Clare Higgins, in *Who's Afraid of Virginia Woolf*, at Bath.

At the start of this year he was appointed OBE. His last television appearance came as Mr Sniggs, the junior dean of Scone College, in Evelyn Waugh's *Decline and Fall*, starring Jack Whitehall. He had been due to open as Willy Loman in *Death of a Salesman* in Northampton prior to a long tour.

The director of *King Charles III*, Rupert Goold, who had known Pigott-Smith since childhood, said that he was a funny mix, really bright, very educated, with a silly, playful, mischievous side. An example was a decades-long prank Pigott-Smith had played with Judi Dench, in which each tried to slip a black glove into productions featuring the other.

Pigott-Smith was a keen sportsman, loved the countryside and wrote a memoir, and four short books, three of them for children. In 1972 he married the actor Pamela Miles. She survives him, along with their son, Tom, a violinist, and two grandchildren, Imogen and Gabriel.

---

*Timothy Peter Pigott-Smith was born in Rugby, Warwickshire, on 13 May 1946 and died while rehearsing* Death of a Salesman *in Northamptonshire on 7 April 2017. His tombstone in Highgate cemetery quotes Horatio in Hamlet: 'Good night, sweet prince...'*

# Bruce Forsyth

*A tap-dancing TV presenter and entertainer who began his career in variety and became an enduringly popular audience-participation compere on* The Generation Game *and* Strictly Come Dancing.

BRUCE FORSYTH, WHO HAS DIED aged 89, was associated with some of the most successful shows in television history, from *Sunday Night at the London Palladium* in the late 1950s to *The Generation Game* in the 1970s and, for a decade from 2004, *Strictly Come Dancing*, a light-entertainment phenomenon that attracts a third of the viewing audience to BBC1 on a Saturday night.

As a compere, game-show host and fleet-footed comedian, he was in a class of his own, providing an authentic link between the old days of variety, where he started as a youthful sensation during the Second World War, and the new craze for audience participation and reality television.

He had appeared in variety (and indeed on the golf course) with the great Max Miller, admiring the way Miller put his foot on the footlights to lean over and reach out to the audience, but his real idol (and good friend) was Sammy Davis Jr, and he aspired to the same distinction as an all-rounder on the variety stage.

His flashing, sometimes tetchy-seeming, personality and distinctive 'edge' paradoxically endeared him to audiences – he wasn't lovable, or 'cuddly' like Ronnie Corbett, for instance; he used the game-show participants or the celebrity dancers on *Strictly* to feed his own performance and impeccably timed double-takes (expressions of mock disbelief or patronising, po-faced quasi-pity), to the camera, in the style of Eric Morecambe.

Forsyth sometimes expressed regret at being side-tracked by game shows, but his stage career never really took off, and his films were few. His resilience as a personality on television, however, was remarkable.

He bounced back from the disappointment of being moved to the afternoon schedules by television executives at ITV; there was a huge bust-up in 2000 when he left *Play Your Cards Right* and denounced David Liddiment, the new controller, as someone who had stripped him of his dignity.

But having launched a comeback as an unlikely guest host on the BBC's satirical flagship *Have I Got News for You* in 2003, he regained his place in the national affection with *Strictly*, and in 2011 was knighted following a noisy public campaign.

He retained a trim, dapper appearance – his trademark Rodin's Thinker pose in silhouette dates from *The Generation Game* – with his skateboard chin and natty moustache, and a hairstyle that had been remodelled over the years from tidy teddy boy quiffs at the Windmill Theatre to a more carefully structured coiffure of corn-coloured thatch.

And he displayed a true vaudevillian's talent for catchphrases. As Tommy Trinder (whom he succeeded on *Sunday Night at the London Palladium*) had 'You lucky people,' or Arthur Askey 'I thangk-yeaow,' so Forsyth patented 'I'm in charge' at the Palladium followed by 'Nice to see you ... to see you, nice!' and 'Didn't he do well?' on *The Generation Game*.

In a 2011 interview with Mick Brown in the *Daily Telegraph*, he attributed his longevity, and extraordinary energy, to his experience in variety: 'This other person turns up, and thank goodness I've never known him to be late. He just gets into me, and I go and perform, and that's what I do.' In 2013, at the age of 85, he became the oldest performer to appear at the Glastonbury Festival, in the same year that the Rolling Stones also made a belated debut there.

Forsyth, who was born in Edmonton, north London, was the third child and second son of John Forsyth-Johnson, a relatively prosperous garage owner, and his wife, Florence (née Pocknell), both Salvation Army members. He was educated at Latymer Grammar School, Edmonton, but left without any qualifications, having become obsessed with tap dancing after seeing Fred Astaire movies at the local Regal cinema. He made a BBC television debut in 1939 on the Jasmine Bligh talent show.

On the outbreak of war, he was evacuated to Clacton-on-Sea in Essex, but insisted on coming home after just three days, continuing his dance lessons with Tilly Vernon and even running his own classes in one of his father's garages. He launched his career as Boy Bruce, the

Mighty Atom, at the Theatre Royal, Bilston, in Staffordshire, in 1942, wearing a satin suit made by his mother and playing the accordion, ukulele and banjo.

There followed a long, hard slog of 16 years of variety halls and summer shows around the country, interrupted only by two years of national service with the RAF in Warrington and Carlisle after the war (in which his older brother, John, was killed on an RAF training exercise in Scotland in 1943; his body was never found).

Forsyth, who led a busy and sometimes complicated private life, with a penchant for showgirls, singers and beauty queens, made his Windmill theatre debut in 1953, performing impressions of Tommy Cooper (already a cult figure); he also married one of the Windmill dancers, Penny Calvert, and they formed a song-and-dance double act.

During a third summer season at Babbacombe in Devon in 1957, another dance act recommended Bruce to their agent, Billy Marsh, and this contact with a key figure in the all-powerful Bernard Delfont organisation led to a booking on a television show, *New Look*, followed by the breakthrough *Sunday Night at the London Palladium* gig in September 1958.

In black and white, and always broadcast 'live' on ATV, Forsyth demonstrated his genius for improvisation and ad-libbing as he shuffled and chivvied the audience participants in physical competitions and word games in the show's Beat the Clock segment.

On that first show, he also hosted the comedy act of Jimmy Jewel and Ben Warriss, the singers Anne Shelton and David Whitfield, and a fellow Windmill alumnus, Peter Sellers; a contract for three weeks was stretched to three years, and at Christmas he headlined the Palladium pantomime, *Sleeping Beauty*, alongside Charlie Drake, Bernard Bresslaw and the singer Edmund Hockridge.

By 1961 he was compering what he called the best ever Royal Variety Show – Kenny Ball, Morecambe and Wise, Arthur Haynes, Shirley Bassey, George Burns, Jack Benny, Sammy Davis, Frankie Vaughan and Maurice Chevalier. Forsyth read out a poem written by A.P. Herbert for the Queen Mother – and he was earning a then-enormous salary of £1,000 a week.

His jazz piano playing, influenced by George Shearing and Bill Evans, was better than competent, and his high level of versatility was fully apparent in 1964 when he made a cabaret debut at the new Talk of the Town (his impressions included Nat King Cole, Frank Sinatra, Anthony Newley and Frank Ifield, as well as Davis) and starred in *Little Me*, his one West End musical, at the Cambridge.

*Little Me*, with a book by Neil Simon, songs by Cy Coleman and Carolyn Leigh, and choreography by Bob Fosse, involved Forsyth in seven roles and 29 costume changes as he played the various lovers of an old movie star, Belle Poitrine ('Real Live Girl' is the best known song). The show had starred the great Sid Caesar on Broadway but Bruce made the roles his own – they ranged from a virginal doughboy and goose-stepping movie director to a scaly old miser and billionaire newspaper baron. He scored a success with the critics, but the show only ran for ten months.

A film debut followed in Robert Wise's *Star!* (1968) with Julie Andrews as Gertrude Lawrence – Bruce played her father and did a music hall turn with Beryl Reid as her mother – and Daniel Massey as Noël Coward, and then he stalled badly in Newley's self-indulgent autobiographical fantasy *Can Heironymus Merkin Ever Forget Mercy Humppe and Find True Happiness?* (1969) with Joan Collins and Milton Berle. He showed up to better effect as a vivid spiv in the Disney film *Bedknobs and Broomsticks* (1971), which starred Angela Lansbury and David Tomlinson.

By now he was established on *The Generation Game*, an early evening 'hook' (attracting a peak audience of 21m viewers) for the BBC's now-legendary Saturday stay-at-home night of *Doctor Who*, Morecambe and Wise, *The Duchess of Duke Street*, *Match of the Day* and Michael Parkinson's chat show.

'Let's meet the eight who are going to generate,' said Brucie, after encouraging his gorgeous blonde assistant, Anthea Redfern, to 'give us a twirl'. (Redfern became his second wife; he had met her at a Miss Lovely Legs competition in a London nightclub.) The contestants (an older and a younger member in each of the four family duos) played for prizes they had to memorise as they passed by on a conveyor belt laden with kitchen appliances, fondue sets and cuddly toys.

During this decade, Forsyth also toured with his one-man show and realised a lifelong ambition in taking it to Broadway in 1979. The *New York Times* raved but other reviews were mixed and Forsyth never really recovered from being branded a Broadway flop with jokes older than Beowulf.

He was always uneasy with the press, which had relished his colourful private life. After his first wife, Penny, and one daughter sold stories to the tabloids, he instigated a ten-year ban on talking to them and made a digest of selected favourable commentary in the programme for his show when he reprised it at the Palladium, under the heading 'Some Reviews You Might Not Have Heard About'.

In 1983 he married for the third time, Wilnelia Merced – a model and beauty queen whom he had met as a fellow judge on the 1980 Miss World contest. He maintained his popularity throughout sundry ITV game shows in the 1980s before returning to *The Generation Game* in 1990 for four more years, with a new assistant, the singer/dancer Rosemarie Ford.

A lifelong golf fanatic, Forsyth lived in a house on the Wentworth Estate in Surrey from 1975; he could walk from his back garden straight on to the first tee of the golf course. In 2010 he appeared on the BBC's *Who Do You Think You Are?* programme and was grimly affected – though he never shed a tear; he didn't 'do' crying – to discover that his great-grandfather, a landscape gardener, had deserted two families and died in poverty.

He was voted BBC TV Personality of the Year in 1991, and was made OBE in 1998, CBE in 2006, a fellow of Bafta in 2008 and knighted in 2011. He is survived by Wilnelia, and their son, Jonathan Joseph, or JJ; by three daughters, Debbie, Julie and Laura, from his first marriage, which ended in divorce; two daughters, Charlotte and Louisa, from his second marriage, which ended in divorce; and by nine grandchildren.

---

*Bruce Forsyth (Bruce Joseph Forsyth-Johnson), entertainer and comedian, was born in Edmonton, north London, on 22 February 1928, and died aged 89 at home in Virginia Water, Surrey, on 18 August 2017.*

# Rosemary Leach

*Rosemary Leach, admired as Helene Hanff in*
84 Charing Cross Road *and as Mrs Honeychurch in*
*the 1985 film* A Room with a View, *thought she was*
*as good as Judi Dench. She probably was.*

THE TALENTED AND ACCOMPLISHED actor Rosemary Leach reminded an interviewer in 2012 that she had never been invited to appear with either the National Theatre or the Royal Shakespeare Company. 'I'm as good as Judi Dench, I'm sure I am,' she added, before saying how lucky she had been to have had such an extensive and all-consuming career on television.

Viewers had warmed to her expansive features, beautifully modulated voice and emotionally truthful acting on screen since the mid-1960s. She appeared in such notable series as *The Power Game* (1965-69), as the lover of a ruthless building tycoon (Patrick Wymark), *The Jewel in the Crown* (1984), as Aunt Fenny in the hit adaptation of Paul Scott's twilight-of-the-Raj quartet, and as the victimised widow who falls for a murderous conman and total cad (Nigel Havers) in *The Charmer* (1987), an acrid 1930s drama based on a Patrick Hamilton novel.

She moved effortlessly across the class and social divide, playing royalty – as a porcelain-voiced Queen Victoria in Claude Whatham's four-part *Disraeli* (1978) and as arguably the best of all Queen Elizabeth IIs, in three separate BBC dramas, *Prince William* (2002), *Tea With Betty* (2006) and *Margaret* (2009) – as well as 'ordinary' mums: luminous as Laurie Lee's mother in *Cider With Rosie* (1971) and heartily earthy as David Essex's in *That'll Be the Day* (1973).

Her true valour was rarely seen on stage though, when it was, she was unforgettable. In 1982, she won the Olivier best actress award for her performance as Helene Hanff, the eccentric Manhattan bibliophile, in *84 Charing Cross Road*, an enchanting two-hander, adapted and directed by James Roose-Evans, based on the transatlantic correspondence of Hanff and an antiquarian bookshop manager, who never met each other.

On the first night, Hanff – small, intense, bird-like – appeared on the stage of the Ambassadors theatre alongside her counterpart. Leach looked nothing like her but had brilliantly distilled the very essence of her charm and character, and made her story profoundly moving.

Rosemary was the second daughter of teachers, Sidney and Mary (née Parker). Her father was headteacher (as well as organist and choirmaster) at the village school in Diddlebury, near Ludlow. Rosemary was educated at Oswestry Girls' High School, where she excelled in plays. After a brief spell selling shoes in the Reading branch of John Lewis, she went to London, aged 18, to train at RADA.

She graduated in 1955 and immediately plunged into the dying days of small regional repertory companies in Amersham, Buckinghamshire, then Coventry, for two years. Her roles grew bigger at the larger reps in Liverpool and Birmingham, where she worked with Bernard Hepton (a lifelong friend and colleague) and Derek Jacobi.

But while the National and the RSC were getting under way in the early 60s, Leach was establishing herself as a permanent member of what she described as 'a sort of television rep', making her debut in two episodes of the police series *Z Cars* in 1962.

The TV die was cast – and she would be nominated, in all, five times for a Bafta award, never winning one – when she signed up for *The Plane Makers* in 1963 with Wymark and Barbara Murray. It was a prequel to *The Power Game*, set in a fictional aircraft factory with trade union struggles, an infighting management and political and personal chicanery at every turn. These were significant TV dramas, and the six years of them ended only because Wymark died in 1970.

From this point, Leach was in demand. She was Laura, the amenable wife to pint-sized ('male chauvinist piglet') Ronnie Corbett in *No, That's Me Over There* (1967), *Now Look Here ...* (1971) and *The Prince of Denmark* (1974), with scripts by Barry Cryer, Graham Chapman and Eric Idle. She figured prominently, as lover and mistress, respectively, in Zola's *Germinal* (1970), which charted the brutal suppression of a miners' strike in northern France, and Sartre's *Roads to Freedom* (also 1970), a ground-breaking 13-part series set in the period around the start of the Second World War.

She returned to the stage in the mid-1970s, playing a (then) fashionably be-denimed journalist, a hilariously unlikely amalgam of Jilly Cooper and Jill Tweedie, in Don Taylor's Chekhovian *Out on the Lawn* at the Watford Palace (with marvellous performances, too, from T.P. McKenna, Dinah Sheridan and Edward Hardwicke). She joined the founding company in 1976 at George Murcell's St George's Theatre, Tufnell Park, which stuttered on for a decade, with a programme devoted to Shakespeare; the opening season comprised *Twelfth Night, Romeo and Juliet* and *Richard III*.

Her next (and last) brush with Shakespeare came as Emilia in Jonathan Miller's richly textured BBC television *Othello* in 1981, with Anthony Hopkins 'blacking up' in the lead, just about before it became impossible to do so, Bob Hoskins as her husband, Iago, and Penelope Wilton as Desdemona.

A good example of her prominence in television films of the day was a full-blown, big budget BBC Play of the Month in 1973, *The Adventures of Don Quixote* starring Rex Harrison as the deluded caballero and Frank Finlay as his grouchy, long-suffering Sancho Panza.

Leach was the idealised princess 'Dulcinea' – 'I see her as I would have her be' exclaimed the Don of his slatternly peasant woman, Aldonza – and Leach's inner glow irradiated both personifications, so much so that the *New York Times* said that the film could have done with a lot more of her in it. The idealisation of Aldonza was a conscious reflection of the cult of the Blessed Virgin, her gentleness an alternative to the forbidding Christ of the Inquisition.

Harrison gave one of his more relaxed and befuddled performances, but there was no shirking in other departments. Hugh Whitemore's text from a standard translation of Cervantes was highly literate and witty, the direction of Alvin Rakoff well judged especially in the evocative Spanish locations, the score of Michel Legrand a work of atmospheric artistry in its own right.

Just as prestigious, but a total disaster, was a British–Italian remake of David Lean's *Brief Encounter* in 1974, scripted by John Bowen, which gloriously miscast Richard Burton (a last-minute replacement for Robert Shaw) and Sophia Loren in the Trevor Howard/Celia Johnson roles, with Leach one of several good British actors in support roles – Jack Hedley and John Le Mesurier among them.

Probably her most notable film was Merchant Ivory's star laden *A Room With a View* (1985), in which she ticked off another notable mum, Mrs Honeychurch. This was the first of the Merchant Ivory E.M. Forster adaptations and an almost overwhelmingly sensual evocation of Edwardian society on the move in Tuscany and in the depths of the English countryside. Both Leach – who lends a fulsome, dignified Victorian elegance to her portrayal of parental propriety – and Judi Dench as the rackety novelist Eleanor Lavish were nominated as best supporting actress in the Bafta awards; Dench won.

She appeared in two television adaptations of Edith Wharton novels, *The Children* (1990), scripted by Timberlake Wertenbaker and directed by Tony Palmer, and *The Buccaneers* (1995) directed by Philip Saville, in which she made a marvellous meal of Selina Marable, snobbish Marchioness of Brightlingsea.

In between the Whartons, she materialised in Stuart Urban's *An Ungentlemanly Act* (1992) as Mavis Hunt, holding the fort in the Falklands during the invasion alongside her husband, the governor, Rex Hunt (later knighted), played by Ian Richardson.

There was more quality work in Jack Rosenthal's scripts for an early suburban sitcom with Hepton, *Sadie, It's Cold Outside* (1975); his adaptation of Stanley Houghton's *Hindle Wakes* (1976) for Laurence Olivier – the only television show Olivier ever directed; and *Day to Remember* (1986), on Channel 4, in which she struggled through Christmas with George Cole as her husband with dementia. Hepton was alongside, too, in *The Charmer*, as her 'white knight' admirer.

*Hindle Wakes*, in which Leach gave a masterly display of maternal charm and concern in the social crisis caused by her son seducing a lower-class mill girl on a works outing to Llandudno, was part of an anthology of classic stage plays produced by Granada Television under the banner, Laurence Olivier Presents. Again, she avoided any hint of coy 'mumsiness' as she and her self-made tycoon husband, superbly played by Donald Pleasence, wrestled with their own expectations of how the younger generation should behave.

The play was also a reminder of a glorious theatrical tradition at a time when the live theatre still supplied a hugely important strand of television drama. It was first produced in 1912 at the Gaiety Theatre in Manchester, Britain's first regional repertory company, and spawned two silent movie versions in 1918 and 1927, and two 'talkie' screen adaptations in 1931 and 1952, these featuring, respectively, Sybil Thorndike and Joan Hickson as the antagonistic, self-righteous mother of the mill girl on the other side of the pre-marital sex argument defended by Leach's character.

A full decade after *84 Charing Cross Road*, she returned to the West End in a superb revival by Peter Hall of Terence Rattigan's *Separate Tables* at the Albery, stretching the critical thesaurus to fully appreciate her magnificent Mrs Railton-Bell, righteous defender of public morality shading into bigotry. The Rattigan revival was safe in her hands, and those of Peter Bowles, Patricia Hodge, Ernest Clark and Miriam Karlin.

She toured in creaky revivals of Emlyn Williams and William Douglas-Home before joining one of the longest-running TV sitcoms of the new millennium, *My Family*, starring Robert Lindsay and Zoë Wanamaker, dropping in between 2003 and 2007 as Wanamaker's 'difficult' alcoholic mother. Her last movie was Stuart Urban's *may i kill u?* (2012), a low-budget black comedy in which a policeman is transformed into a vigilante killer on the night of the Tottenham riots of 2011.

Leach lived quietly with her husband, the actor Colin Starkey, whom she married in 1981, in Kew, near the river, and, later, in Teddington. After making *The Jewel in the Crown* without ever having visited India, she became a devoted traveller to that subcontinent thereafter. She is survived by Colin.

---

*Rosemary Anne Leach was born in Much Wenlock, Shropshire, on 18 December 1935 and died aged 81 after a short illness, in the Charing Cross Hospital on 21 October 2017.*

# Ken Dodd

*The irrepressible comedian with an endless desire to*
*make people laugh was known for his tickling sticks,*
*Diddymen and marathon stage performances,*
*offering will forms for the nervous.*

THE LAST GREAT 'FRONT-CLOTH' COMIC of our times, and the last standing true vaudevillian, Ken Dodd, who has died aged 90, was even more than that – a force of nature, a whirlwind, an ambulant torrent of surreal invention, physical and verbal, whose Liverpudlian cheek masked the melancholy of an authentic clown.

'This isn't television, missus,' he'd say to the front stalls, 'you can't turn me off.' And then he would embark on an odyssey of gag-spinning that, over five hours, would beat an audience into submission, often literally, banging a huge drum and declaring that if we did not like the jokes he would follow us home and shout them through the letter-box.

He entered the Guinness Book of Records in 1974 with a marathon mirth-quake at the Royal Court Liverpool lasting three hours, 30 minutes and six seconds. But his solo shows, in which he would perform three 90-minute-plus sets between magic acts, or a female trumpeter (the formidable Joan Hinde), or a pianist playing country music (his partner Anne Jones), frequently lasted much longer.

One good thing, he would say, was that you always went home in the daylight. And the sooner you laugh at the jokes, he would say, the sooner you can go home, as if we were in school. He admitted that his was an educational show – when you did get home, you would say to yourself, 'That taught me a lesson!'

The jokes went on: the usherettes would shortly be taking orders for breakfast, and will forms were under the seats. I was sitting in his dressing room before show time in High Wycombe when the house manager knocked on the door to tell him that a party of 76 pensioners would have to leave the theatre at 11pm precisely. 'What,'exclaimed a miffed Doddy,'before the interval?'

On another occasion I greeted him at the stage door in Bromley with the news that a full and expectant audience was gathering. 'You mean to say there are 2,000 pregnant women out there tonight?'

He had a gag for every occasion and would usually try out six new ones in each performance. He kept voluminous note books of jokes, and a record of how they had gone down, and where, and how long the laughter. There was nothing improvised or 'on the wing', the whole routine planned with military precision.

The placement of the songs (accompanied, in later years, by a moth-eaten duo in tuxedos on keyboard and drums – 'The Liverpool Philharmonic after Arts Council cuts'), was delivered in his Italianate tenor with a tear-inducing éclat; his throwback social world was of seaside boarding houses, funny foreigners, fearsome mothers-in-law and recalcitrant musicians.

His cheeky little men, the Munchkin-like Diddymen, were inspired by his own plump little Uncle Jack, who wore a bowler, and were played by children before the chaperoning and logistics became impracticable, on the road at least. The whole experience, as the Dodd aficionado Michael Henderson once wrote, was like plunging down a waterfall in a barrel, swept away on the tide of his boundless energy.

This never came across on television, where he appeared merely to be a crackpot zany. On stage, there was something deeply atavistic about his mastery of the revels, his physical appearance of Bugs Bunny teeth (the result of a childhood cycling accident), sticking-up hair like an astonished ice-cream cone, the gentle sway of his shoulders to encompass the house, the transformations from a one-man band (drum, horn, union flag and pig whistle) in khaki fig doing the old variety song 'On the Road to Mandalay', to the floor-length red Diddyman coat made from '28 moggies – all toms' (sniff, pong, funny face) that is whipped off to reveal a dazzling yellow jacket and smart dark trews for the next segment.

This outrageous Lord of Misrule's tickling stick, a red, white and blue feather duster, was the equivalent of the medieval jester's pig's bladder, laid as in a ritual at the front of the stage then thrust between his legs from behind: 'How tickled I am, under the circumstances. Hello, missus [stick a-tremble], have you ever been tickled under the circumstances?' The art of innuendo was his stock-in-trade, and he would use it to bemoan his fall from TV popular grace: 'Alternative comedy is where you're supposed to laugh at every other joke. I'm not in the top 100 lists anymore. In the last one, Dale Winton and Julian Clary were ahead of me. Mind you, I'm glad they weren't behind me!'

Dodd was one of three children of a coal merchant, Arthur Dodd, and his wife, Sarah; he continued to live in the 18th-century former farmhouse he was born in, a run-down double-fronted manse with adjoining cottages and a large garden in the suburb of Knotty Ash in Liverpool. The coal – 'sex is what posh people have their coal delivered in' – was stored on the premises, and accounted for his asthmatic cough, as distinctive a characteristic as the Judi Dench-like crack in his lyrical voice – which he turned to his advantage.

He was known for walking backwards to Holt High School and attending dance classes with his sister, June. He left school aged 14 and, with his elder brother, Billy, humped bags of coal for his father, a part-time saxophonist and clarinettist who gave Ken his first ventriloquist's dummy.

At the age of 19, he branched out as a self-employed salesman, knocking on doors with his own Kay-Dee brand of disinfectant while developing his ventriloquist act. He joined a juvenile concert party run by Hilda Fallon, who also 'discovered' Freddie Starr and Bill Kenwright, the actor turned theatre producer, and began performing in clubs and hotels around Liverpool and Birkenhead.

He extended his stomping ground to Manchester, having acquired an agent, David Forrester (he never signed a contract in the 19 years they stayed together), which led to more open doors through contact with Bernard Delfont and the Stoll Moss group.

He made his professional debut in September 1954 at the Empire theatre, Nottingham, on a bill with the singer Tony Brent and the jazz trumpeter Kenny Baker, adopting the persona of Professor Yaffle Chuckabutty, operatic tenor and sausage knotter, and driving around in a van on which was painted: 'Ken Dodd – the Different [printed upside down] Comedian.'

In the summer of 1955, he was on the Central Pier at Blackpool and then, for eight years, in variety and pantomime in venues from Blackpool and Great Yarmouth to Torquay and Bournemouth.

In those days, there was a distinct cultural divide between north and south – Max Miller, on being invited to play the Glasgow Empire, said he was a comic, not a missionary – and although two of Dodd's heroes, Arthur Askey and Ted Ray, both Scousers, were huge radio stars already, it was Dodd more than anyone who broke down the barriers.

His 42-week season at the London Palladium in April 1965, *Doddy's Here*, took him to the top of the pop charts ('Tears for souvenirs' dislodged the Beatles and stayed there for six weeks) and the Royal Variety Performance, and won him the Variety Club's showbusiness personality of the year.

And he always undercut the gravity of theatrical architecture ('This magnificent shed' was his phrase at the Palladium) while reinforcing the immediacy of theatrical experience. When he played the Open Air theatre in Regent's Park he marvelled at his predicament: 'Forty years in the business, and I'm standing in the middle of a field in a theatre that can't afford a roof.' In Croydon, he congratulated the audience on their new one-way system: 'They'll never find you now.'

In the 1980s, his television profile fading, there were fewer summer shows and pantos, many more one-night stands ('One night is all they can stand'). A cloud crossed over at the end of the decade when he faced charges of cheating the Inland Revenue and of false accounting. He was acquitted after a five-week trial, but the humiliation in his home city, where his grandmother had been Liverpool's first female magistrate, was hard to bear.

The image of a man who had never made a psychological separation from his parents in order to become an adult, and one who was innately stingy and kept his money in shoe-boxes under the bed ('I like to collect pictures of the Queen') as well as in offshore accounts, was initially tragic; but after paying his defence counsel, George Carman, £1m, and approximately the same amount to the Revenue, he bounced back with a stash of new material.

'Income tax was invented 200 years ago, at two pence in the pound. My trouble was I thought it still was ... so I've had problems, but nothing compared to those of the trapeze artist with loose bowels.' In a panto kitchen scene, Dodd's Idle Jack was asked by the Dame if he was kneading the dough. 'About a million quid,' he shot back.

In 2001, he was given the Freedom of the City of Liverpool. He was then voted the greatest Merseysider in a poll on local radio and in the *Liverpool Echo* (Lennon and McCartney were runners-up) and in 2009 his statue, complete with tickling stick – and that of the battling Labour

MP Bessie Braddock – were cast in bronze on Lime Street station.

Dodd was restored on television, to some extent, by two Audience with … programmes in 1994 and 2001, in which he refracted some of his act through a Q & A with a crowd of celebrities; they are wonderfully poignant, revealing programmes, and are often repeated.

In 1971 he had been an admired Malvolio in *Twelfth Night* at the Liverpool Playhouse – and he returned to Shakespeare as Yorick the jester in Kenneth Branagh's 1996 film of *Hamlet*; Yorick is only a skull in the play, but we see this peerless clown in full (though silent) stream with his flashes of merriment that were wont to set the table on a roar.

The most touching part of his act was always the expert and hilarious duet with his vent doll Dicky Mint, the Diddyman who was perhaps the little 'sonny boy' he never had in real life. And if his signature tune was 'Happiness', he would always leave you with a lament in 'Absent Friends' for loved ones and the departed music hall stars in whose wake he so gloriously trailed.

He really was the last in the line and acknowledged by his peers as one of the greatest ever. He was made OBE in 1982, an honorary fellow of John Moore University, Liverpool, in 1997, an honorary DLitt at Chester in 2009, and was knighted, after a sustained public campaign, last year.

He was a deeply private man, which is why the two court cases hurt him so much. There was no luxury lifestyle, and he usually drove home in the small hours after each show, wherever he was in the country, to save on hotel bills.

He had two successive fiancées: Anita Boutin, a nurse, from 1955 until her death from a brain tumour in 1977; and Anne Jones, who survives him, a former Bluebell dancer who often appeared in his shows as Sybie Jones, playing the piano and singing, in between running his affairs and stage management.

He married Anne last Friday, once he had returned to the Knotty Ash home where he had been born, after spending six weeks in hospital with a chest infection.

---

*Kenneth Arthur Dodd was born in his family home of Knotty Ash, Liverpool, on 8 November 1927 and died there, with his socks and pound notes in boxes under the bed, on 11 March 2018.*

# Fenella Fielding

*Best known for her femme fatale roles in the* Carry On *and*
Doctor *films, Fenella was a sly intellectual with a glorious voice.*

INIMITABLE, LUXURIANTLY BREATHY and slyly mellifluous, Fenella
Fielding, who has died aged 90, was a household name in the 1960s
when she graced and sidled across the West End stage and the television
screen, as well as appearing in the *Carry On* and *Doctor* films, usually
playing a vamp, or the femme fatale, alongside actors such as Kenneth
Williams, Sid James, Dirk Bogarde and James Robertson Justice.

There was always something exotic and possibly louche about
Fielding. You never felt that she had skimped on mascara, eyeshadow
or lipstick, or that her hair was necessarily all her own in its chaotic and
often strangely unkempt manifestation.

At the same time, she might appear in public, and occasionally on
television, on a chat show, or the popular word game *Call My Bluff*,
dressed in clothes of a distinctly severe line, with white collars back
and front, clasped with big jewellery, which gave her the appearance of
an unlikely modern nun on the run. No one ever had such a laughing
drawl, or haughtier, naughtier intonations.

And then she would be spied scuttling around the stacks in the
London Library, researching and reading, writing up her diary; as an
intellectual, she was no slouch. She was as clever as she was funny, the
emphatic articulation a sign of both the musical value she attached to
words and the precise weight and emphasis of their meaning.

A lot of gurgling and swooping went on, but years at the coal face
of cabaret and intimate revue ensured that Fielding's timing was never
out, her meaning never insecure, her indecision always final.

Her defining performance was that of Lady Parvula de Panzoust,
an outrageous, high fashion man-eater, in Sandy Wilson's *Valmouth*,

a brilliant musical version of Ronald Firbank's orchidaceous 1919 novelette.

Although *Valmouth* ran for only 84 performances at the Lyric, Hammersmith, in 1958, it was one of several remarkable British and American musicals that opened in London that year. They included *Expresso Bongo* by Wolf Mankowitz, Julian More, David Heneker and Monty Norman, about a new kind of Tommy Steele-type pop singer in Soho; *Irma La Douce* by Marguerite Monnot with More, Heneker and Norman again, directed by Peter Brook, with a knockout performance by Elizabeth Seal as a Parisian prostitute; and, from Broadway, *My Fair Lady* and *West Side Story*.

Even in this exalted company, Fielding enjoyed her finest hour as the unquenchably amorous centenarian Lady Parvula de Panzoust whose holiday in the southern English spa of the show's title saw her, rejoiced the musicals historian Kurt Gänzl, throw her bonnet over the windmill and a young shepherd into the hay.

On seeing the shepherd's thighs, Fielding abandoned all bodily purification intentions and launched into one of her two refulgent showpieces: 'Just once more I want to put my déshabillé on/ While I flutter round the room like some désorientée papillon/ Slapping on strategic rouge and spraying scent/ Where so much expensive scent already went.'

When the piece was revived by the director John Dexter at the Chichester festival theatre in 1982, Fielding returned to the role, as did her fellow original cast members, Bertice Reading and Doris Hare, to theirs. It was clearer than ever that instead of neutralising Firbank's high-flown Gothic camp, Wilson took the hothouse unreality of the fictional spa town and imposed upon it the comparatively real world of the musical comedy stage. Yet, once again, the composer's masterpiece failed to be a commercial hit.

Alas, by this time, Fielding's stage career was virtually over. Her utterly distinctive performance persona was both her chief calling card and her greatest handicap. The world of entertainment treasured a talent it found increasingly hard to accommodate.

In 1979, she had opened the restored Lyric Hammersmith's studio space with a solo show (with piano trio) that included poems by W.H. Auden, Fran Landesman and A.P. Herbert, as well as Broadway songs and an erotic sketch during which you heard her orgasmic moanings offstage before she marched on smartly to shoot the lover boy dead.

With her flounced auburn locks arrayed in startling bunches on either side of her face, and dressed in a chic rust trouser suit, she resembled a whacked-out Theda Bara with just enough juice to last the evening. She was gloriously funny and uncompromising.

Later in her career, certainly as Madame Arcati, the eccentric medium, in Noël Coward's *Blithe Spirit* at the Salisbury Playhouse in 1999, her magnificent weirdness was scuppered by a weakened technical assurance; nor could you imagine such a creature pedalling herself home for seven miles on a bicycle. Fielding's Arcati would only have contemplated a sedan chair fitted out with an abundance of cushions and custards, borne by two well-built local lads with a penchant for show tunes.

Fenella grew up in a mansion flat in Clapton, east London, with her parents, Philip and Tilly Feldman (both Jewish, he an immigrant Lithuanian, she originally Romanian), an elder brother, Basil (later Lord Feldman, a Tory peer), and a 'sort of nanny person' who took Fenella to dance classes on the Holloway Road. Philip was a cinema manager and boss of a ladies underwear factory, a prominent freemason and, according to his daughter, abusively violent towards her.

The family moved to Edgware in 1940 when Fenella was 13 and a pupil at the North London Collegiate School. She won a scholarship to RADA, but left after one year, pressured by her parents to 'get a proper job'. She took a secretarial course while studying at Saint Martin's School of Art (now Central Saint Martins) and worked for the actors' agent Al Parker, and in a beautician's parlour.

Still, she was determined to go on the stage. After a grounding in concert halls and club theatres around London, she left home, took a flat in Clarges Street, Mayfair, which she shared with a prostitute, and started making cameo appearances on the night club scene of the 1950s: at Churchill's in Bond Street, the Don Juan in Brook Street and in the Washington Mayfair hotel.

She was talent-spotted while appearing at the London School of Economics in a revue written by Ron Moody, and this led to her first West End professional engagement, in a 1954 revue, *Cockles and Champagne*, at the Saville. So she was a comparatively late starter, but she made up for lost time as an exotic vamp, Luba Tradjejka, in *Jubilee Girl* (1956) at the Victoria Palace.

She was acquiring a following, and the producer Michael Codron cast her first in *Valmouth* and then in a revue, *Pieces of Eight* (1959), at the Apollo co-starring Williams – with whom she soon fell out, noting that he wanted her to be good, but not too good – which featured sketches written by Peter Cook and Harold Pinter.

Her earliest films included *Doctor in Distress* (1963), with Bogarde at his smoothest and sprightliest as Simon Sparrow, and Ken Hughes's *Drop Dead Darling* (1966) in which, as a wealthy object of Tony Curtis's attentions, she was treated to a ride out in the country, where she jumped over a hedge Curtis had artfully placed on the edge of a cliff.

She also played Valeria the vampire in *Carry on Screaming* (1966), a very funny spoof of the Hammer horror films, in which she curled up on a sofa and exhaled the line, 'Do you mind if I smoke?' after which vapour billowed out from beneath her body; the phrase served as the title of her chatty 2017 autobiography, written with Simon McKay.

She could be perfect in Feydeau farces, and was just that in Sardou's *Let's Get a Divorce* at the Mermaid in 1966 and as the aptly named Lady Eager in another Mermaid classic, *Lock Up Your Daughters* (1969), an updated musical version by Keith Waterhouse and Willis Hall, with music by Laurie Johnson, of both Henry Fielding's *Rape Upon Rape* and Vanbrugh's *The Relapse*, with Christopher Plummer as Lord Foppington leading a cast including Georgia Brown, Glynis Johns and Roy Kinnear.

The Chichester Festival Theatre was another regular haunt; she was Mrs Sullen in *The Beaux' Stratagem* there in 1967, and an imperious duchess in *Look After Lulu*, adapted by Coward from Feydeau, in 1978. Even Ibsen held no fear for her, and there were glowing reports of her Hedda Gabler in Leicester in 1969 and her Nora in *A Doll's House* at the Gardner Centre in Brighton in 1970.

She moved in 1966 into a top-floor flat in Connaught Mews, near Marble Arch, which cost her just £13 a week. She had a knack for landing on her feet in her personal life that perhaps evaded her professionally later on. She did not marry, but said that for 20 years she kept two lovers on the go, one of them married, without either knowing of the other's existence, as befits a Feydeau specialist.

In her memoir she described the men who had behaved badly in the workplace: Tony Hancock was 'drunk', Warren Mitchell simply 'horrible' and Norman Wisdom (with whom she filmed *Follow a Star* in 1959) prone to on-set lechery: 'His hand up your skirt first thing in the morning was not a lovely way to start a day's filming,' she said.

Critics loved her and hated most of the things she was in. When she played Kaa the rock snake in *The Jungle Book* at the Adelphi in 1984, she wrapped herself around a pole in a manner that reminded Michael Billington of Hermione Gingold in a Medea parody clinging to a phallic pillar with a cry of 'This is my personal column!,' while another scribe said of her Lady Fidget in a vile production of *The Country Wife* at the Mermaid in 1990 that she 'pouts like a tulip in a field of potatoes'.

Fielding continued working past her 90th birthday, making radio programmes, recording poetry and voiceovers and rarely going anywhere without her spider-like eyelashes, eyelashes Dusty Springfield once acknowledged as the model for her own. She was not immune to the appeal of drink, drugs and psychotherapy, but survived all these brushes to come out fighting, and as huskily cheerful and optimistic as ever. She was appointed OBE in the Queen's birthday honours in June. She is survived by her brother.

---

*Fenella Marion Fielding (Feldman), was born in Hackney, London, on 17 November 1927 and died aged 90 in Hammersmith, London on 11 September 2018.*

# Thomas Baptiste

*Breakthrough actor and singer whose roles ranged*
*from Coward and Shakespeare to* Coronation Street.

LIKE SO MANY AFRICAN-CARIBBEAN ACTORS of his generation, Thomas Baptiste, who has died aged 89, straddled two career horses: token casting, and radical breakthrough. He invested both streams of work with pride and dignity.

He appeared on TV in the *Dick Emery Show* and as a doctor when Warren Mitchell's Alf Garnett in *Till Death Us Do Part* turned up for treatment after initiating a racist punch-up at a football match. But he also played for two years in Noël Coward's *Nude With Violin* (1956) – in Dublin and then the West End – with John Gielgud, Patience Collier and Kathleen Harrison.

In the 1960s he subversively, and prophetically, occupied roles such as the dustman Doolittle in Shaw's *Pygmalion* and, at the Connaught in Worthing, Edward Albee's benighted academic George opposite Isabelle Lucas's black Martha in *Who's Afraid of Virginia Woolf?*

More obviously, he could play Shakespearean roles such as Orsino in *Twelfth Night*, Caliban in *The Tempest*, the Prince of Morocco in *The Merchant of Venice*, and Othello. He had great success in Eugene O'Neill's *The Emperor Jones* as a deranged African despot at the short-lived Dark and Light theatre in Brixton in 1973, and on film he imposingly embraced the outer lineaments of a pipe-smoking secret agent in *The Ipcress File* (1965), a corrupt African military dictator in *The Wild Geese* (1978) and the operating surgeon engulfed in a coup against Milton Obote in *The Rise and Fall of Idi Amin* (1981).

Baptiste was born in Georgetown in British Guiana (now Guyana), one of the many children of a wealthy landowner who rented parts of his estate to tenant farmers. He was not close to his father, but at the age of 21 persuaded him to allow him to leave for Britain to study agriculture. On arrival in London in 1950, where his mother, Pearl, joined him later, he took a factory job, enrolled at Morley College to study the rudiments of music and began mixing with artistic types.

Thanks to Baptiste's social graces and good looks, allied to a chance encounter with Tom Driberg, the gadfly journalist and Labour MP, he was swept into the salon cultural life of London, consorting with Driberg's chums about town, who included Nye Bevan, Jennie Lee and Joan Littlewood. He also maintained a close friendship with the designer Oliver Messel and a place at the centre of Princess Margaret's Mustique 'set' in the Caribbean.

Like his hero, Paul Robeson, Baptiste started his professional life as a baritone singer. Eventually he joined Littlewood's Theatre Workshop and lived communally with the company in Edinburgh before it found its creative home at the Theatre Royal in Stratford, east London.

During that time he entered the Richard Tauber international singers' competition, came third, got noticed and studied with Joan Cross. He won a scholarship to the Royal Academy of Music, London, but sensing little opportunity for black baritones in the opera world as then constituted, plumped for a dramatic role in Eric Maschwitz's *Summer Song* (1956), based on Dvořák's composition of the New World symphony, starring Sally Ann Howes and Edric Connor.

After *Nude with Violin* it was mainly drama, but he maintained his singing career while moving more certainly into theatre and television. In the early 1960s he co-founded an African-Asian committee of the actors' union Equity; in 1992, however, he said that black actors in Britain found more difficulty beginning their careers than he had experienced 40 years previously.

Baptiste was in O'Neill's *The Iceman Cometh* at the Bristol Old Vic, then Harold Pinter invited him to join the first professional production of his first play, *The Room*, in 1960, at Hampstead theatre club. He played Riley, the blind black man who lurks in the basement, a messianic figure who gets beaten up for his pains. When the play transferred to the Royal Court on a double bill with another short Pinter, *The Dumb Waiter*, Michael Caine joined the cast – five years before he worked with Baptiste again on *The Ipcress File*.

In 1963 Baptiste became the first black character in *Coronation Street*, appearing in several episodes as a bus conductor, Johnny Alexander, who was sacked as a result of a racist altercation with Len Fairclough (Peter Adamson). Several important BBC plays also marked his television career: John Hopkins' *Fable* (1965) prompted Baptiste to play a Nelson Mandela figure in a fantasy totalitarian state with the white population as social underdogs; Alun Owen's *Pal* (1971) paired him with Robin Phillips to play across the racial prejudice divide; and in Barrie Keeffe's *King* (1984), the celebrations of his Lear-like potentate on returning home did not quite go to plan.

Other screen highlights included a notable cameo in John Schlesinger's *Sunday Bloody Sunday* (1971) with Glenda Jackson, and appearances in many of the 15 episodes of *Empire Road* (1978), the first all-black TV soap. In 1978, on stage, at the Birmingham Rep and the Mayfair in London, he played Robeson, in *Are You Now or Have You Ever Been*, Eric Bentley's dramatised transcript of the McCarthy hearings of 1950.

Baptiste led a life rich in friends and colleagues (and he had 14 godchildren), enjoying his longest and closest relationship with Francis Rutland, a solicitor, who died in the 90s. From that decade onwards he had a home in St Lucia in the Caribbean, but he spent the last ten years of his life in Hove, East Sussex.

---

*Thomas Baptiste, actor and singer, born 17 March 1929 and died 6 December 2018.*

# Albert Finney

*Finney was hailed as the new Olivier, the most exciting
young actor to emerge since the war and made his
name playing classical leads and working-class heroes.*

ONE OF THE NEW-STYLE working-class heroes and shooting stars of
the 1960s, Albert Finney enjoyed a rich and varied career that never
quite fulfilled its early promise. Like Richard Burton before him and
Kenneth Branagh after him, he was expected to become the new
Laurence Olivier, the leader of his profession, on stage and on screen.

That this never quite happened was no fault of Finney's. He worked
intensely in two periods at the National Theatre, was an active film
producer as well as occasional director, and remained a glowering,
formidable presence in the movies long after he had been nominated
five times for an Oscar (without ever winning).

Although a stalwart company member – Peter Hall paid heartfelt
tribute to his leadership and to his acting at the National – he led his
life, personal and professional, at his own tempo.

From middle age onwards – and he was only 47 when he gave one
of those Oscar-nominated performances, the fruity old actor defying
the blitz, Donald Wolfit-style, in Peter Yates's *The Dresser*, written by
Ronald Harwood – he assumed a physical bulk and serenity that
bespoke a life of ease, far from the madding crowd, in good restaurants
and on Irish racecourses. He never courted publicity.

His unusual, cherubic face, slightly puffy and jowly, but with high
cheekbones, the face of an unmarked boxer, was always a reminder
of his sensational breakthrough in two signature British films, Karel
Reisz's *Saturday Night and Sunday Morning* (1960) – his line as the
Nottingham bruiser Arthur Seaton, 'What I want is a good time; the
rest is all propaganda,' could serve as a professional epitaph – and
Tony Richardson's *Tom Jones* (1963), a lubricious historical romp that

imparted a metaphorical mood of the swinging 1960s.

Finney was the new roaring boy of that high-spirited, colourful decade – cheeky, northern and working-class. Born in Salford, he was the son of Albert Finney Sr, a bookmaker, and his wife, Alice (née Hobson); as it happens, also born on the very same day, was another northern 'new wave' actor, Glenda Jackson.

Young Albert attended Tootal Drive Primary School and Salford Grammar. He flunked his exams but played leading roles in 15 school plays and went south to London and RADA, where he was in a class that included Peter O'Toole, Tom Courtenay, Frank Finlay, John Stride and Brian Bedford.

While still a student, as Troilus in a modern play, he was spotted by Kenneth Tynan – the best-known critic of the day – who proclaimed a 'smouldering young Spencer Tracy ... who will soon disturb the dreams of Messrs Burton and Scofield'. And so it proved. His rise was instant and meteoric. He played Brutus, Hamlet, Henry V and Macbeth at the Birmingham Rep, and in 1956 made his London debut in the Old Vic's production of Shaw's *Caesar and Cleopatra*. In 1958 he played opposite Charles Laughton in Jane Arden's *The Party* at the Arts Theatre. This was, significantly, his West End debut and Laughton's last appearance on the London stage.

He followed Laughton to Stratford-upon-Avon in 1959, joining a stellar company under the direction of Glen Byam Shaw, and played Lysander in *A Midsummer Night's Dream* (Laughton was Bottom) and Cassio with Paul Robeson as Othello and Mary Ure as Desdemona. He also understudied (and went on for, to sensational effect) Olivier as Coriolanus.

Finney was a totemic modern actor not really destined, perhaps, for classical eminence. Much more his style was the insolence and daydreaming of *Billy Liar* by Keith Waterhouse and Willis Hall at the Cambridge theatre, though the role on film went to Tom Courtenay. At the Royal Court he took lead roles in a satirical musical, *The Lily White Boys*, directed by Lindsay Anderson, and in John Osborne's vitriolic, tumultuous *Luther* (the latter in the West End, later on Broadway); he made his film debut opposite Olivier in *The Entertainer* in 1960.

A pattern of oscillation between theatre and cinema was soon established, as he bookended his first major stint at the National, in the great Olivier company, with screen appearances in Reisz's 1964 remake of Emlyn Williams's psychological thriller *Night Must Fall* and Stanley Donen's delightful study of a disintegrating relationship, scripted by Frederic Raphael in flash back and fast forward, *Two For the Road* (1967). Finney's leading lady in the latter, Audrey Hepburn, was not the first nor last of his amorous work-and-pleasure intrigues.

His NT appearances in 1965 and 1966 were as a strutting Don Pedro in Franco Zeffirelli's Sicilian take on *Much Ado About Nothing* (with Maggie Smith and Robert Stephens), the lead in John Arden's *Armstrong's Last Goodnight*, a great double of the candescent upstart Jean in Strindberg's *Miss Julie* and the outrageous Harold Gorringe in Peter Shaffer's *Black Comedy*, topped off with the double-dealing, split-personality Chandebise in Jacques Charon's definitive production of Feydeau's *A Flea in Her Ear*.

Then he was off again, having founded Memorial films in 1965 with his great friend and fellow actor Michael Medwin, directing and starring in *Charlie Bubbles* (1968), written by his fellow Salfordian Shelagh Delaney (author of *A Taste of Honey*) and featuring Billie Whitelaw and Liza Minnelli. He co-produced Lindsay Anderson's savage public school satire *If ...* (1968) and bankrolled Mike Leigh's (another Salfordian) first feature film, *Bleak Moments* (1971).

He also gave Stephen Frears his movie-directing debut on *Gumshoe*, a brilliant homage to film noir as well as a good story (written by Neville Smith) about a bingo caller (Finney) in a trench coat with delusions of being Humphrey Bogart. He even had time to disguise himself totally as a wispily senile Scrooge in Ronald Neame's 1970 film of *A Christmas Carol*, with Alec Guinness as Jacob Marley and Edith Evans as the Ghost of Christmas Past.

An invitation to return to the Royal Court as an associate director (1972-75) resulted in one of his most blistering stage performances, opposite Rachel Roberts, in E.A. Whitehead's *Alpha Beta*. He directed Brian Friel's *The Freedom of the City* and a revival of Joe Orton's *Loot*, and appeared in David Storey's *Cromwell* and Samuel Beckett's *Krapp's Last Tape*.

The reminiscing Krapp unspooled his old Grundig on a double bill with Billie Whitelaw's hectic jabbering in *Not I*, and Finney confided in Whitelaw his lack of rapport with the playwright: 'You know the way I work, I take all the different paints out of the cupboard, I mix the colours together. If they're not right, I shove them all back and take out a new lot.' Whitelaw advised him to dispose of all the colours and retain the white, black and grey.

He was much happier unbuttoning in Peter Nichols's sharp West End comedy *Chez Nous* and embodying Agatha Christie's Hercule Poirot in Sidney Lumet's star-laden *Murder on the Orient Express* (1974). But he returned to the National under Peter Hall during the difficult transition period from the Old Vic to the South Bank.

Over six years from 1974, as striking technicians and unconvinced critics lined up to try and scupper the new building, Finney ploughed on as a bullish, tormented Hamlet, a lascivious Horner in *The Country Wife*, the perfect arriviste Lopakhin in *The Cherry Orchard* and a disappointing Macbeth. The centrepiece was his heroic, muscular and glistening Tamburlaine in Peter Hall's 1976 defiant staging of Marlowe's two-part mighty epic, twirling a curtle-axe to deadly effect.

This performance marked Finney's grandest, if not necessarily finest, hour on stage. He appeared at the Royal Exchange, Manchester, in 1977 to deliver beautifully modulated performances as Uncle Vanya and an ultra-credible woman-slaying Gary Essendine in Coward's *Present Laughter*. Another long absence from the theatre ended with a stunning performance as a roguish Chicago hoodlum in Lyle Kessler's *Orphans* at the Hampstead Theatre in 1986 (and a movie version a year later) and another great turn as a Catholic priest, held hostage and deprived of his faith, in Harwood's *JJ Farr* at the Phoenix.

Finney was now nearly a grand old man, but without the seigneurial distinction of either Olivier or Gielgud. He was delightful and dewy-eyed, eventually, as a bald Daddy Warbucks in John Huston's film of *Annie* (1982), but truly magnificent as the alcoholic British consul – 'a drunk act to end all drunk acts' said one critic – in Huston's *Under the Volcano* (1984), adapted from the novel by Malcolm Lowry.

That performance should have won the Oscar, perhaps, but he remained a near-miss nominee, as he had done in *The Dresser* (1983). On stage, the beautiful, bolshie boy had settled into ruminative, but always interesting, late middle age, notably in Harwood's ingeniously structured *Another Time* (1989), in which he played a bankrupt Jewish commercial traveller and, in the second act, his own musician son, 35 years later.

Another Harwood play, *Reflected Glory* (1992), allowed him to let rip as a breezy Mancunian restaurateur confronted with a critical family play written by his own playwright brother. His last stage appearance reunited him in 1996 with his old friend Courtenay in Yasmina Reza's *Art*, at Wyndham's, a play about friendship being threatened by the purchase of a white painting for a lot of money. Courtenay was the art-loving dermatologist, Finney hilarious and exasperated as an astronautical engineer appalled by the purchase.

His best, and now often elegiac, performances materialised sporadically on television: as Maurice Allington in *The Green Man* (1991), adapted from a Kingsley Amis novel; as Reggie in *A Rather English Marriage* (1998), alongside Courtenay; and as Churchill in *The Gathering Storm* (2002), written by Hugh Whitemore, with Vanessa Redgrave as his wife.

In Hollywood, he clocked in for Soderbergh's *Ocean's Twelve* (2004) and the third in a superb trilogy adapted from Robert Ludlum's spy action thrillers, starring Matt Damon, Paul Greengrass's *The Bourne Ultimatum* (2007). His last movie credits came in *The Bourne Legacy* and the Bond film *Skyfall* (both 2012), Sam Mendes directing the beautifully acted climactic scenes of the latter with Finney as the Scottish gamekeeper on the Skyfall estate and Judi Dench as M dying in Daniel Craig's arms.

Finney, always known as Albie, was rumoured to have declined both a CBE and a knighthood. In 1957 he married the actor Jane Wenham; they had a son, Simon, and divorced in 1961. His marriage to the French actor Anouk Aimée in 1970 ended in divorce eight years later. He then had a long relationship with the actor Diana Quick – the pair were for a while feared missing up the Amazon. In 2006 he married Pene Delmage, who survives him, along with Simon.

---

*Albert Finney, a lifelong supporter of Manchester United, was born on 9 May 1936 in Salford, Lancashire and died aged 82 of a chest infection in the Royal Marsden hospital, London, having battled kidney cancer for some years, on 7 February 2019.*

# Freddie Jones

*Veteran actor admired for his roles as 'Sir' on stage in*
*The Dresser, the freak-show owner in the 1980 film*
*The Elephant Man and Sandy Thomas in TV's Emmerdale.*

FREDDIE JONES WAS THE BEST SORT of old-fashioned actor, a comic tragedian, eccentric and full-hearted, with something of both Donald Wolfit and Dickens' Vincent Crummles about him.

Indeed, his most famous stage role was that of Ronald Harwood's affectionate near-portrait of Wolfit in *The Dresser* (1980), an old ham called 'Sir' who faces disaster in the mirror while preparing to play King Lear. And he memorably embodied the extravagant Crummles in a television *Nicholas Nickleby* of 1977.

If Jones sometimes emulated Wolfit, his real hero was Wilfrid Lawson, a bibulous character actor who could break your heart on the instant, and he always welcomed the comparison. Yet, to the general public, he was never a name in lights, his career was patchwork, and he suffered the indignity of outright failure in a role that should have been a triumph, Malvolio in *Twelfth Night*, when he returned to the Royal Shakespeare Company in 1991, three decades after his debut in 1962.

Instead, he achieved a recognition of sorts as Sandy Thomas, the estranged father of a vicar, in the long-running television soap *Emmerdale*, a role he unashamedly, and gratefully, enjoyed in the twilight of his years, from 2005 to 2018.

For an actor who could cry havoc and let loose the dogs of war with the best of them, he was surprisingly mild and unambitious, tall and courteous, bearded and ruddy-faced, one who declared that, 'My life springs from my wife, my family, my work and my whisky.'

He was born and raised in Dresden, Stoke-on-Trent, one of two sons of Charles Jones, an electrical porcelain thrower and his wife, Ida (née Godwin), and attended the nearby grammar school in Longton, which he hated. As a boy scout, he appeared in a show at the old Theatre Royal in Hanley.

On leaving school to work at Creda, the home appliances store, in Blythe Bridge, and then for ten years as a lab assistant at a chemical factory in Tamworth, he immersed himself in amateur dramatics at the old Shelton rep and other companies around Stoke.

So, he was well into his thirties by the time he trained at Rose Bruford and made his London debut with the RSC at the Arts Theatre in David Rudkin's *Afore Night Come* (1962) and at the Aldwych in Gorky's *Lower Depths* in 1964.

He was immediately one of the company's most distinctive character actors and appeared in Beckett's *Act Without Words*, as Pistol in *The Merry Wives of Windsor* and as Cucurucu in Peter Brook's landmark 1964 production of *The Marat/Sade* (released as a film in 1967) alongside Glenda Jackson, Ian Richardson and Patrick Magee.

No subsequent performance in *The Dresser* – not Albert Finney in the 1983 film, nor Anthony Hopkins on television in 2015, nor Ken Stott in the West End in 2016 – matched the rumbling thunder of Jones in Manchester and subsequently at the Queen's in London.

With the bombs dropping on a provincial town in 1942, he slumped into the dressing room, dispirited, starting in horror at the nightmare to come and collapsed in tears while Courtenay's dresser, Norman, leaning backwards while gliding forwards, launched poisonous glances back over his shoulder into Sir's make-up mirror.

His favourite screen role was Orlando, an intermittently drunk journalist in Fellini's *And the Ship Sails On* (1983), who is chronicling the journey of a party of hedonists committed to scattering the ashes of a dead opera singer whose on-board friends and admirers included Barbara Jefford, Janet Suzman, Peter Cellier and the German dancer/ choreographer Pina Bausch.

After appearing as Bytes, the bullying freak-show owner in David Lynch's *The Elephant Man* (1980) starring John Hurt, he collaborated further with Lynch on *Dune* (1984), *Wild at Heart* (1990) and in Lynch's bizarre three-part US television series *On the Air* (screened in Britain in 1993), in which he played a guest star on a live variety show having trouble with his voice and with a duck that is roasted in an electric chair and consumed by stage hands.

Jones played another celebrated thespian, Sir Giles Hampton, in an episode of *Just William* on TV in 1994, rescuing the little blighter's career in am-dram, while his gallery of actor-managers was vividly increased by another fruity cameo as Thomas Betterton, pride of the Restoration theatre, with Johnny Depp as the Earl of Rochester, in *The Libertine* (2005), adapted by Stephen Jeffreys from his own stage play.

And there were other performances to treasure such as Barkis ('is willin'') in Peter Medak's TV version of *David Copperfield* (2000); a rubicund fisherman in Charles Dance's delightful *Ladies in Lavender* (starring Judi Dench and Maggie Smith, 2004), with Jones's son, Toby Jones, popping in as a village postman; and as an Irish domestic bulwark on a slow burn in Finola Geraghty's *Come On Eileen* (2010).

He had nothing to prove on stage after *The Dresser*, but still, his continued absence was marked and regrettable. In the 1991 RSC season, the Malvolio misfire was in part compensated for by a dotty and hilarious performance as Sir Nicholas Gimcrack in Thomas Shadwell's 17th-century comedy *The Virtuoso*, directed by Phyllida Lloyd. Jones's Gimcrack was bent on a course of pointless scientific research – dissecting insects and lobsters, perfecting the art of swimming on dry land and collecting bottled air – in a superb display of gravely befuddled distraction.

It is hard to think of another great actor whose comic genius and tragic bravura were so under-used in the profession. His working-class childhood and early years had been hard and unhappy. 'Acting saved his life,' said his son Toby. 'Drama school was a reinvention, or an awakening of stuff he hadn't been allowed to show in his life.'

He took solace in his long marriage to the actor Jennie Heslewood, whom he married in 1965 and who survives him, as do their three sons, Toby, Rupert, a director, and Casper, also an actor.

---

*Frederick Charles Jones, a dyed-in-the wool Stoke City supporter, was born in Dresden, Stoke-on-Trent, on 12 September 1927 and died aged 91 in Bicester, Oxfordshire, on 9 July 2019.*

# Diana Rigg

*Founder member of the RSC and a West End star for
decades, tall and glamorous, Rigg shot to TV stardom
in the 1960s as Emma Peel in* The Avengers *and
found new fans in* Game of Thrones.

AMONG THE ICONIC FIGURES of the 1960s – the Beatles, Bobby
Moore lifting the World Cup and Sean Connery as James Bond –
must be counted Diana Rigg. Her role as the secret agent Emma Peel
in *The Avengers* on ITV, magnetically sexy in trademark black leather
jumpsuit, was truly a sign of the times.

Rigg often said she was unhappy on the series, claiming that her
only friends were Patrick Macnee, her co-star as the bowler-hatted
gentleman spy John Steed, and a television company chauffeur. But
the on-screen chemistry with Macnee was palpable, and Rigg drew a
scintillating portrait of a woman who knew her own mind as well as
her own strength.

She had succeeded Honor Blackman (as Cathy Gale) as Steed's
independent sidekick and appeared in three series of *The Avengers*
between 1965 and 1967, during which period she was also one of
the founding members of the Royal Shakespeare Company, playing
many lead roles at Stratford-upon-Avon and at the Aldwych theatre in
London between 1961 and 1966.

If Emma Peel was a career-defining role in the public eye, Rigg was
never seduced from her dedication to the stage, although she expressed
disappointment at a film career that never took off. Tall, elegant, vocally
mellifluous and often strikingly acerbic, she could play tart comedy
roles as easily as melting heroines, and in the latter part of her career
she revealed untold depths of savagery and resilience with a series of
award-winning performances in works by such masters as Euripides,
Edward Albee, Jean Racine and Tennessee Williams.

She renewed her television stardom when, between 2013 and 2017, to the rejoicing of a new legion of fans, she played the ruthless Lady Olenna Tyrell in *Game of Thrones*, a fearsome matriarch whose political machinations in the cause of keeping the House of Tyrell's legacy intact were of a Shakespearean malice and complexity. After completing the recording, she underwent heart surgery, and wryly remarked after her recovery that God must have said, 'Send the old bag down again, I'm not having her yet.'

She was born in Doncaster, South Yorkshire, but raised for the first eight years of her life in Jodhpur, India, where her father, Louis, was a railway engineer. She knew both the privileges of the British Raj and the hardship of living in reduced circumstances in post-war Leeds, where she returned with her older brother, Hugh, and her mother, Beryl (née Helliwell), in 1945. Her parents had been in India since 1925, and her father re-joined the family in 1948.

By then she was boarding at Fulneck Girls' School in Pudsey, where her aptitude for acting propelled her to London and RADA. She first appeared at the Theatre Royal, York, in a RADA production of Bertolt Brecht's *Caucasian Chalk Circle* and, after further seasons in York and Chesterfield, went straight to Stratford-upon-Avon in 1959, where Peter Hall was planning the launch of the RSC the following year.

Rigg made her London debut with the RSC in Jean Giraudoux's *Ondine* (playing second fiddle to Leslie Caron, then Hall's wife) in 1961, and over the next few years, as part of a brilliant nucleus of young actors that included Judi Dench, Ian Holm, Ian Richardson and Tony Church, she helped define the new RSC adventure in a series of dazzling performances.

These included a spirited, diaphanously clad Helena in *A Midsummer Night's Dream* (later filmed by Hall), Bianca in *The Taming of the Shrew*, Adriana in *The Comedy of Errors* (a thrown-together comedy riot that returned year after year to the repertoire), a sweet but determined Cordelia to Paul Scofield's titanic King Lear, directed by Peter Brook – the production toured many European cities – and a radiant, striding Viola in *Twelfth Night*, a shimmering androgyne and first cousin to Emma Peel.

Her West End 'commercial' debut followed in a lumpen 1970 retelling of the Abelard and Heloise story in which she starred opposite Keith Michell in both London and New York.

The National Theatre came calling in 1972 for the Old Vic premiere of Tom Stoppard's brilliant man-on-the-moon philosophical comedy *Jumpers*, in which Rigg was languorously draped across a crescent moon as Dottie Moore, the dissatisfied, romantic wife of Michael Hordern's dotty George Moore. The play was a sensational success, followed in 1973 by an equally stunning Célimène, the bitchy hostess in Tony Harrison's brilliant rhyming update of Molière's *The Misanthrope*.

Her tragic muse remained dormant at this time, despite a brave stab at Lady Macbeth opposite a curiously listless Anthony Hopkins (Old Vic, 1973), and she struck more comic sparks off Alec McCowen in a John Dexter revival of Shaw's *Pygmalion* in the West End in 1974. Dexter had accused her of being 'hard' and as easy to negotiate as the north face of the Eiger, but she always listened to his uncomfortably critical concerns.

After scoring another hit with Harrison in his Racine rewrite, *Phaedra Britannica*, in the last season of the National at the Old Vic in 1975, and giving birth to a daughter in 1977, she cut all ties with the two subsidised monoliths and appeared in the West End as Ruth Carson in Tom Stoppard's *Night and Day* (1978) at the Phoenix ('I'm with you on the free press. It's the newspapers I can't stand,' was Ruth's languidly pleasant view in the play's discussion of journalistic ethics); in an all-star *Heartbreak House* with Rex Harrison at the Haymarket in 1983; and in an even more lavish Cameron Mackintosh production of James Goldman and Stephen Sondheim's *Follies* at the Shaftesbury in 1987.

Although she was a 'Bond girl' in one of the lesser James Bond movies, *On Her Majesty's Secret Service* (1969), with George Lazenby, and Vincent Price's avenging daughter, Edwina Lionheart, in the comedy horror movie *Theatre of Blood* (1973) – a role her daughter, Rachael Stirling, wittily reprised in the National Theatre stage version in 2005 – her career on celluloid stuttered. She appeared as a murdered actress in Guy Hamilton's all-star Poirot mystery *Evil Under the Sun* (1982) and a mother superior in the remake of Somerset Maugham's *The Painted Veil* (2006).

Otherwise, she made sporadic yet powerful incursions on television: as Regan to Laurence Olivier's valedictory King Lear (1984), Lady Dedlock in *Bleak House* (1985), an obsessive mother in the BBC mini-series *Mother Love* (1989) for which she won the Bafta best actress award, and as Mrs Danvers in *Rebecca* (1997), co-starring Emilia Fox and Charles Dance, for which she won an Emmy when it was broadcast in the US.

However, it was in the theatre that Rigg crowned a remarkable career, with a string of scintillating performances at the Almeida, Islington, during the 1990s: first, in John Dryden's *All for Love*, then as a rampaging Medea (both 1991), with the latter transferring to the West End and Broadway, where she won a Tony award; as a ferocious Martha in Albee's *Who's Afraid of Virginia Woolf?*, with a ginger hairstyle and leopardskin print slacks, fighting to the near-death with David Suchet in 1996; and then as both Racine's Phaedra and his bigamous Messalina in *Britannicus* in 1998.

These performances attracted critical acclaim and a clutch of awards from the *Evening Standard*, the Variety Club and the South Bank Show and, for good measure, she slotted in a slightly less successful Mother Courage at the National Theatre in 1995.

Rigg returned to the National in 2001 to play Simon Russell Beale's exotic mother in Charlotte Jones's *Humble Boy* and continued in extravagant vein as Mrs Venable in Michael Grandage's 2004 West End revival of Tennessee Williams's *Suddenly Last Summer*, followed three years later by the less-than-urgent stage version of Pedro Almodóvar's *All About My Mother* at the Old Vic in 2007.

She had lived for some years in a château in a village south of Bordeaux in France, and one of her neighbours there, the producer Duncan Weldon, was instrumental in arranging her casting at the Chichester Festival Theatre in 2008 and 2009, in roles that should have been ideal: Ranevskaya in Chekhov's *The Cherry Orchard* and Judith Bliss in Noël Coward's *Hay Fever*, but neither production was a success and both failed to arrive in the West End.

But she was superb when she stepped into another Chichester revival, Shaw's *Pygmalion*, at the Garrick in 2011, returning to the play she first graced in 1974, as Mrs Higgins, alongside Rupert Everett and Kara Tointon in Philip Prowse's beautiful production. Her Mrs Higgins in a 2018 production of *My Fair Lady* at Lincoln Center in New York, the first Broadway revival of the musical in 20 years, earned her a Tony nomination.

In 2014, on the Edinburgh Festival fringe, she gave an anecdotal solo show based on her irresistible 1982 book of rotten reviews, *No Turn Unstoned*. Later screen appearances were in an episode of *Doctor Who*, *The Crimson Horror*, in 2013, with her daughter (whom, in character, she blinded); as onscreen mother to Rachael in the second and third series of the TV comedy *Detectorists* (2015 and 2017); the outspoken Duchess of Buccleuch in Daisy Goodwin's second series of *Victoria* for ITV in 2017; and, briefly, as an imperious aristocrat in Andy Serkis's movie *Breathe* (2017) starring Andrew Garfield and Claire Foy.

Rigg was chancellor of Stirling University for ten years from 1997, and Cameron Mackintosh visiting professor of contemporary theatre at Oxford University in 1999. She published a second book, *So to the Land*, an anthology of countryside poetry, in 1994.

After a long relationship with the television director Philip Saville, in 1973, Rigg married the Israeli artist Menachem Gueffen. They divorced in 1976. In 1982, she married the Scottish laird Archie Stirling, a former army officer who became a theatre producer. When it emerged that Stirling was having an affair – with Joely Richardson, Natasha's younger sister – Rigg sued for divorce and took his suits to the nearest Oxfam shop.

She was appointed CBE in 1988 and made a dame in 1994. She is survived by Rachael and a grandson, Jack.

---

*Enid Diana Elizabeth Rigg was born in Doncaster on 20 July 1938 and died aged 82 of cancer in London on 10 September 2020.*

# Barbara Jefford

*Vocally resplendent, Jefford exuded intensity and
stillness on stage in a vast range of Shakespearean roles,
ranging from fresh-faced juveniles to hoary old queens.*

THE GLORY DAYS OF BARBARA JEFFORD as the leading classical actor
of her generation at the Old Vic came in the 1950s. In that distant
decade, she played every Shakespearean female role going, from Imogen
and Portia to Beatrice, Rosalind and Desdemona. It was reckoned that
she appeared in all but four of Shakespeare's three dozen plays.

She made her name as Isabella in Peter Brook's 1950 staging of
*Measure for Measure* – rarely done in those days – at Stratford-upon-
Avon. Brook wanted an unknown to play the virginal novice opposite
John Gielgud's Angelo. And he asked her, as she knelt before the Duke
to plead pardon for Angelo, whom she had 'bed-tricked' in order to
save her condemned brother, to hold a pause for as long as the audience
would allow. Two minutes is an eternity of silence, and that's what she
invariably commanded.

Few actors exude such intensity and stillness on a stage as was Jefford's
stock-in-trade. She was thought to be a definitive Viola in *Twelfth Night*
in 1958 – bursting with joyful exuberance – but in that same Old
Vic season she played Regan in *King Lear*, and a 'fire-breathing' (said
Kenneth Tynan) Queen Margaret in *Henry VI*.

As she matured, she acquired a majesty and a grandeur that most
critical writing about her performances noted, as she blazingly
personified Tamora, Queen of the Goths, in *Titus Andronicus* and was
the most possessed Saint Joan since Sybil Thorndike's introduction of
the role in 1924, throughout the UK and on tour in Russia at the start
of the 1960s.

She was not involved in the early days of the Royal Shakespeare
Company and the National Theatre, partly because she had played all

the great roles open to her before they were launched, but a new London audience discovered her matchless power and dignity when she took over as Gertrude from Angela Lansbury to Albert Finney's Hamlet at the National in 1975 and partnered him, too, as Zabina in Peter Hall's magnificent 1976 revival of Marlowe's *Tamburlaine*.

Jefford was born in Plymstock, near Plymouth, in Devon, the daughter of Percival Jefford, a bank manager, and his wife, Elizabeth (née Laity). She was educated at Weirfield School, Taunton, where she excelled in verse-speaking competitions before being taught elocution by Eileen Hartley at her studio in Bristol. 'Whenever I do poems in recitals,' said Jefford, 'I can still hear her advice, her instructions, her orders.' She then trained at RADA in London, where she won the Bancroft gold medal.

Her London debut came at the Q theatre in a stage version of Ingmar Bergman's *Frenzy* in which she played the Mai Zetterling role ('I wore a plastic mac to show I was a prostitute'). She played three more seasons at Stratford: she was the Queen of France to Richard Burton's break-out Henry V in 1951 and toured with Anthony Quayle's company to Australia and New Zealand in 1953-54 as Desdemona, Rosalind and Lady Percy in *Henry IV*.

After Andromache opposite Michael Redgrave in Jean Giraudoux's *Tiger at the Gates* (translated by Christopher Fry) at the Apollo in 1955, she began a five-year stint at the Old Vic, ending with Lavinia ('superbly suggesting rats at work beneath a smooth white surface', said one critic) in Eugene O'Neill's *Mourning Becomes Electra* in 1961 and a US tour as Lady Macbeth, as well as St Joan.

When Hall launched several autonomous companies at the National in 1986, she joined the group led by the director Michael Rudman to play the mother in *Six Characters* (she had been the stepdaughter at the May Fair), stoically bereaved and eloquently granite-faced, and made a rare sortie into contemporary drama as a mine owner in male attire in Nick Darke's *Ting Tang Mine*.

Rudman's company included two unforgettable new faces – Ralph Fiennes and Lesley Sharp – as well as Richard Pasco, Alec McCowen and Robin Bailey, and they all shone in Brian Friel's *Fathers and Sons*, adapted from Turgenev. She then obligingly repeated her Duchess of York and Queen Margaret for a 1988-89 season at the Phoenix starring Derek Jacobi as both Richard II and Richard III, directed by Clifford Williams, but this was old-style Old Vic, dated and dusty.

Ten years later, in 1998, she joined a far more exciting West End season at the Albery (now the Noël Coward) for Jonathan Kent's double-header of Racine, playing Oenone, a confidante of steel and ice, to Diana Rigg's Phèdre (translated by Ted Hughes), and Albina in *Britannicus*, with Toby Stephens as a livid, unpredictable young Nero on the rise.

There was a final rerun of Queen Margaret for Kenneth Branagh's *Richard III* at the Sheffield Crucible in 2002, a Simon Gray play, *The Old Masters*, with Edward Fox and Peter Bowles, at the Comedy in 2004 and a magisterial valedictory as Mrs Higgins at the Theatre Royal, Bath, and the Old Vic, in Hall's superb 2007 revival of Shaw's *Pygmalion*, with Tim Pigott-Smith and Michelle Dockery.

Her most memorable film performance was her erotically supercharged Molly Bloom in Joseph Strick's *Ulysses* (1967), and she 'dubbed' no fewer than three female James Bond actors, Daniela Bianchi in *From Russia With Love* (1963), Molly Peters in *Thunderball* (1965) and Caroline Munro in *The Spy Who Loved Me* (1977). She adorned Roman Polanski's *The Ninth Gate* (1999), Terence Davies's *The Deep Blue Sea* (2011) and Stephen Frears's *Philomena* (2013).

On television, she was a charity worker in Ted Kotcheff's *Edna, the Inebriate Woman* (1971) starring Patricia Hayes, Ian McKellen's mother in *Walter* (1982), the first drama on Channel 4, directed by Frears, and Ian Richardson's wife, first lady of the college, in the TV adaptation of Tom Sharpe's *Porterhouse Blue* (1987).

When Jefford was appointed OBE in 1965, she was at that time the youngest ever civilian recipient of the honour. Her first marriage, to the actor Terence Longdon, ended in divorce. She married actor John Turner, who survives her, in 1967.

---

*Barbara Mary Jefford was born on 26 July 1930 near Plymouth, Devon, and died at home aged 90 on 12 September 2020, having completed a career stretching over 70 years.*

# Nicola Pagett

*Stage and screen actor of sensual charm and inner
mystery best known for playing Elizabeth Bellamy in
the 1970s TV series* Upstairs, Downstairs, *ideal when
cast in period costume or Pinter.*

NICOLA PAGETT WILL NOT EASILY be forgotten by anyone who saw
her on stage or screen over a career of 30 years. She was a glacial,
beautiful presence in plays from Shaw to Pinter and she illuminated
*Upstairs, Downstairs* on television in the early 1970s.

She played Elizabeth Bellamy, the spoilt and self-absorbed daughter
of the upscale Belgravia household in Eaton Square, who makes the
mistake of marrying a poet with no interest in the physical side of
love. She has an affair with his publisher and conceives a child. Other
amorous adventures follow before she leaves for New York.

Other starring roles soon followed: Elizabeth Fanshawe in *Frankenstein:
The True Story* (1973) on television, widely considered to be one of the
best Frankenstein films; the title role in ten 50-minute episodes of
*Anna Karenina*, a 1977 BBC television epic co-starring Eric Porter as
Karenin and Stuart Wilson as Vronsky; and Liz Rodenhurst in *A Bit of
a Do* (1989) adapted from the Yorkshire novels of David Nobbs, with
David Jason and Gwen Taylor. Liz was the promiscuous, middle-class
mother of the bride who starts an affair with Jason's working-class Ted
Simcock, father of the groom.

However, her career was overshadowed by a long period of mental
illness, which she wrote about in a book, *Diamonds Behind My Eyes*,
published in 1997. Her behaviour became increasingly erratic and
she developed an obsession with Alastair Campbell, Tony Blair's
spokesperson, whom she bombarded with love letters, some of them
containing underwear.

Her final stage appearance was at the National Theatre in 1995 in
a revival of Joe Orton's madhouse black comedy *What the Butler Saw*

with Richard Wilson and a young newcomer called David Tennant. Her book suggested a recovery of sorts. But it was only partial. Some days were better than others. She was nothing if not resilient.

Nicola was born in Cairo, where her father, Herbert Scott, was a peripatetic Shell Oil executive who had met her mother, Barbara (née Black), in Egypt, where she had been stationed with the Women's Royal Naval Service during the war.

The family travelled around – Nicola had a younger sister, Angela – and it was in what is now known as Saint Maur International School, a Catholic establishment in Yokohama, Japan, that a seven-year-old Nicola stood on a desktop and declared she was going to be an actor. After another business posting of her father to Hong Kong, she was sent, aged 12, to the Beehive boarding school in Bexhill-on-Sea, where her godmother, Anne Maxwell, served in loco parentis.

She was just 17 when she went to RADA in 1962. On graduating she changed her surname to Pagett, then spent several years in repertory theatres, including the Glasgow Citizens and the Connaught, Worthing, before making a London debut in *A Boston Story* (1968) at the Duchess theatre, adapted by Ronald Gow from Henry James, starring Tony Britton and Dinah Sheridan.

She immediately became a West End regular, employed by the producer Michael Codron in no less than three important roles opposite Alec Guinness: in John Mortimer's *A Voyage Round My Father* (1971) at the Haymarket; in Julian Mitchell's adaptation of Ivy Compton-Burnett's *A Family and a Fortune* (1975) at the Apollo – in which she met the actor/writer Graham Swannell, whom she married in 1975 – and as Jonathan Swift's muse, Stella, in Alan Strachan's 'entertainment' *Yahoo*, based on the life and work of the mordant Irish satirist. In all three roles her beauty was tempered with a fascinating mixture of steeliness and reserve.

This quality of mystery and an inner, secret life is a rare one in an actor, and it really counted in the plays of Harold Pinter, most notably in a 1985 revival of *Old Times*, in which she played the fawn-like wife of Michael Gambon's filmmaker visited by their mutual friend of 20 years ago, played by Liv Ullmann. The play's territory of power games in a sexually ambiguous, dream-like atmosphere was one she inhabited as of right. She stood out, too, in Pinter's *Party Time* on a double bill with *Mountain Language* at the Almeida in 1991.

Pinter directed her at the National in 1983 as Helen, a stunning and slyly provocative enchantress, in *The Trojan War Will Not Take Place*, translated from Jean Giraudoux by Christopher Fry (his text is better known as *Tiger at the Gates*), so it was no surprise that she occupied the Vivien Leigh role of a not-so-kittenish Lady Teazle in John Barton's production of *The School for Scandal* at the Duke of York's later that year.

She was wonderful, too, as a seductive Countess in Jean Anouilh's *The Rehearsal*, translated by Jeremy Sams, at the Almeida and then the Garrick in 1990. And she offered what Michael Billington described as 'a highly intelligent study in devouring sensual rage' in David Hare's *The Rules of the Game*, adapted from Pirandello and directed by Jonathan Kent, also at the Almeida, in 1992.

Her television work had not dried up, exactly, but was more sporadic outside of the series with David Jason. In *Scoop* (1987), a two-hour film scripted by William Boyd, based on Evelyn Waugh's great 1938 novel, she was Julia Stitch alongside Michael Maloney as the hapless war reporter William Boot and Denholm Elliott as the chaotic newspaper editor.

A film career that began with the small role of Princess Mary in *Anne of a Thousand Days* (1969), starring Richard Burton and Geneviève Bujold, included Roy Boulting's *There's a Girl in My Soup* (1970) with Peter Sellers and Goldie Hawn, Michael Blakemore's *Privates on Parade* (1983) with John Cleese and Denis Quilley, and Mike Newell's *An Awfully Big Adventure* (1995), adapted by Charles Wood from Beryl Bainbridge's novel and starring Hugh Grant and Alan Rickman as unequivocal theatrical types.

After divorcing Graham in 1997, she lived alone in East Sheen, southwest London – with a couple of Persian cats keeping her suitably feline company – stoically dealing with her illness, making a domestic agenda of cooking and gardening, and going for power walks whenever she could. She is survived by her daughter, Eve, from her marriage, and by her sister, Angela.

---

*Nicola Mary Pagett (Scott) was born 15 June 1945 and died suddenly of a brain tumour aged 75 on 3 March 2021.*

# Paul Ritter

*Unheralded character actors are the lifeblood of*
*British theatre and film, and Paul Ritter was one of*
*the very best, notable for his roles in the TV comedy*
Friday Night Dinner *and the miniseries* Chernobyl.

THE BRILLIANT CHARACTER ACTOR Paul Ritter, who has died, too young, of a brain tumour, came to the notice of wide audiences only later in his career – as the long-haired wizard and would-be biographer Eldred Worple in the sixth of the Harry Potter film series, *Harry Potter and the Half-Blood Prince* (2009); as the villainous power plant worker Anatoly Dyatlov in the chilling HBO/Sky miniseries *Chernobyl* (2019); and, from 2011 onwards, as the combustible, inexplicably shirtless Martin Goodman in Channel 4's *Friday Night Dinner* ('lovely bit of squirrel,' moving fork to mouth) with Tamsin Greig.

In all three roles he was never recognisable as whoever he really was. For Ritter was an actor who really did 'disappear' inside his character. He seemed to be patiently volcanic and, on the other hand, anonymously scrofulous. When he was on stage – and he appeared often with the RSC and the National Theatre, especially – I tried, and failed, to pin down his identity.

I settled for what he might really look like as the bespectacled wreck of an unsuccessful pianist in a 2005 revival of Harold Pinter's *The Birthday Party*: the lone inmate of a boarding house in a resort where his father had once 'nearly' come down to see him play in a concert. But that was probably just another ruse.

He took the role of Shakespeare's great orator Ulysses in *Troilus and Cressida* in his underpants (Old Vic, 2000); a mysterious postman in *Christmas* (Bush Theatre, 2003) by Simon Stephens with, said Michael Billington, 'wheedling aggression …[and a] cawing, nasal voice that mixes Manchester with Mile End'; and John Major in Peter Morgan's *The Audience* (Gielgud Theatre, 2013), attending his weekly meeting with Helen Mirren's Queen, as a bendy-limbed fidgeter with a sly flirtatiousness and a guilty secret of only three O-levels.

The more he showed himself, the more he remained hidden, one definition, possibly, of all great acting. Ritter was not exactly secretive, but he let the acting do the talking.

He was born Simon Paul Adams in Kent, though both his parents hailed from Oldham, Lancashire (now Greater Manchester). His father, Kenneth Adams, who had relocated the family to Gravesend, was a fitter and turner in power stations for the Central Electricity Generating Board – he had attended the same Ward Street Central school in Oldham as Eric Sykes, whom Paul played with uncanny accuracy in a 2014 TV film about Tommy Cooper. His mother, Joan (née Mooney), was a school secretary who had been a classmate of Bernard Cribbins. Paul had four older sisters.

He was educated at Gravesend Grammar School for boys and St John's College, Cambridge, where he took a degree in German and French. In a year abroad as part of his studies in Cambridge – where his friends and contemporaries included the actors Stephen Mangan and Paul Chahidi, the television writer Sarah Phelps, the journalist James Harding and the playwright Jez Butterworth – he walked on at the Deutsches Schauspielhaus in Hamburg.

After graduating, he went back there for a year and, on returning to Britain, changed his name to Paul Ritter as there was already a Simon Adams on Equity's books; he admired a German actor of that surname. He then went straight into regional rep and fringe theatre in London, appearing in plays at the Gate Theatre, Notting Hill, and the Bush, including Snoo Wilson's extraordinary *Darwin's Flood* (1994), alongside James Nesbitt as an Ulster Jesus.

He was soon on the radar of the RSC and the Royal Court, appearing with the former in their 1996 Stratford-upon-Avon season of *Troilus and Cressida* and Webster's *The White Devil*; and the latter in a 1998 Young Writers' season and, in 2002, in Butterworth's second play, *The Night Heron*, in which he played an intimidated policeman caught up in a farrago of sacked Cambridge college gardeners trying to take revenge on their former employers by fixing a poetry competition.

The National Theatre first came calling in 2000, when he appeared in Howard Davies's revival of Arthur Miller's *All My Sons* and Di Trevis's beautiful staging of Pinter's un-filmed 1978 screenplay of Proust's

*Remembrance of Things Past.* Subsequent NT productions included Patrick Marber's *Howard Katz* and Tom Stoppard's *The Coast of Utopia*, in which Ritter played Karl Marx.

Later in that decade at the National in 2007 he was a brilliantly funny Robin Day (cruel wit, cruel glasses) in Nicholas Wright's *The Reporter*, directed by Richard Eyre; a hilarious, floppy-haired employee in a revival of *The Hothouse*, Pinter's second play, an institutional black satire; and, in 2010, a creepy government policy wonk in Tamsin Oglesby's *Really Old, Like Forty Five*, devising two-speed pavement strategies and euthanasia directives for the elderly.

His notable television appearances included an effete, sinister intelligence officer in *The Game* (2014), the wrong 'Dave Stewart' in *Bob Dylan: Knockin' on Dave's Door* (2017, with his friend Eddie Marsan as Dylan) and a plausibly smooth Jeremy Hutchinson QC in *The Trial of Christine Keeler* (2019).

He loved working at the Old Vic with Matthew Warchus on that theatre's community work in homeless shelters. He re-appeared there as a safari-suited Reg – trapped in adolescent, hobby-filled dreams – in a brilliant 2008 revival of Alan Ayckbourn's *The Norman Conquests* (with Mangan as the libertine librarian), which won him a Tony award nomination in New York.

Apart from the Harry Potter film, he clocked in on the Bond movie *Quantum of Solace* (2008); as a brutally discouraging teacher in Sam Taylor-Wood's John Lennon biopic, *Nowhere Boy* (2009); and in Juan Carlos Medina's British horror story of Victorian murders, *The Limehouse Golem* (2016). He last appeared on stage in a 2016 Warchus revival of his great hit, *Art*, by Yasmina Reza.

Ritter is survived his wife, Polly Radcliffe, a senior research fellow at the National Addiction Centre in King's College London, whom he married in 1996, their sons, Frank and Noah, and his sisters.

---

*Paul Ritter (Simon Paul Adams) was born on 20 December 1966 in Gravesend, Kent, and died of a brain tumour aged 54 at home in Faversham, Kent, on 5 April 2021.*

# Helen McCrory

*One of the leading stage actors of her generation, stunning in Ibsen, Rattigan and as Medea, who found wider fame in the Harry Potter films and TV's Peaky Blinders.*

HELEN MCCRORY, WHO HAS DIED, far too young, was already established among the leading stage actors of her generation when she became known as a smartly observed Cherie Blair in Stephen Frears's movie *The Queen* (2006), starring Helen Mirren, and with Michael Sheen as Tony; and as the witch Narcissa Malfoy, mother of Draco, in the last three Harry Potter films.

Her brisk and slinky Cherie Blair was one in a line of suited authority figures and lawyers played by McCrory, culminating in an acidulous, brutally frank but deluded Tory prime minister in David Hare's television drama *Roadkill* (2020), refusing to give a 'big job' to Hugh Laurie's shameless MP. In comparison, Narcissa was a 'turn', a Gothic hoot, for all her verve and suffocating evil.

It was, however, her imperious matriarch Aunt Polly in *Peaky Blinders* (five series, 2013-19), ruling the roost in the inter-war criminal Shelby family in Birmingham, and keeping tabs on the ill-gotten gains, that suggested her roots in complex dramatic performance on the stage.

In her last two roles at the National Theatre, she was truly outstanding: as Euripides' murderous Medea in Carrie Cracknell's 2014 revival on the Olivier stage, playing the full range of the character as a barbarian refugee descended from the sun god; and as the emotionally ravaged Hester Collyer in Terence Rattigan's *The Deep Blue Sea*, revived in 2016 in the Lyttelton, also directed by Cracknell, fully embodying the illogicality of passion, her features ablaze, said Michael Billington, 'like a city in illumination'.

McCrory was small of stature but huge of spirit, ferocious, even feral, on the stage, and consistently played great roles. Twenty years ago, I had her down as 'the next Judi Dench'. Now, as Richard Eyre has said, we are deprived of all the great performances she might have delivered in the coming years, in new plays as well as in the classics.

Born in London, she was the eldest of three children of Iain McCrory, a Glaswegian diplomat from a Catholic background, and his wife, Ann (née Morgans), a Cardiff-born physiotherapist from a Welsh Protestant family. The family was peripatetic due to her father's postings abroad – in Cameroon, Tanzania, Norway and France.

Helen returned to Britain to attend Queenswood school, in Hatfield, Hertfordshire, where her instinctive acting talent was encouraged by the drama teacher Thane Bettany (father of actor Paul Bettany). She auditioned for the Drama Centre school in London and told the director who turned her down, Christopher Fettes, that she would apply every year until they admitted her. One year later, after she had worked in Paris and travelled in Italy, they did.

She made a professional debut at the Harrogate theatre in 1990, as Gwendolen Fairfax in *The Importance of Being Earnest*. Critics started sitting up when she played the flighty Lydia Bennet in *Pride and Prejudice* at the Royal Exchange in 1991 – 'excellent' said the *Independent*, while *The Times* noted 'a streak of gleeful recklessness'.

Eyre brought her almost immediately into the National, where she joined the 1992 revival of Declan Donnellan's fine 1989 production of Lope de Vega's *Fuente Ovejuna*, translated by Adrian Mitchell. She put down a serious marker first as Rose Trelawny in John Caird's wonderful 1993 revival of Pinero's hymn to a changing theatre, *Trelawny of the Wells*, then as an exuberant and radiant Nina in Caird's staging of Chekhov's *The Seagull*, particularly impressive as the crushed leftovers of her own dream in the last act.

On the night of the 9/11 attacks in 2001, it was eerily silent along the Euston Road, but the incongruity of a Chekhov play – Hare's version of *Platonov* – opening in a vast hangar-like shed at King's Cross, a temporary outpost of the Almeida, was mitigated by her performance as the seductive general's widow Anna Petrovna in Jonathan Kent's epic production: 'Smoke me like a cigarette,' she challenged Aidan Gillen's chaotic, womanising antihero, before steam-rollering him.

Sam Mendes signed off at the Donmar Warehouse in 2002 with a brilliant double of *Uncle Vanya* and *Twelfth Night*. A crack company included Simon Russell Beale, Emily Watson, David Bradley and Mark

Strong. McCrory was Chekhov's languorous Yelena and Shakespeare's Olivia, again charting a revelatory journey from mourning her father to coming alive, blazing sexily. The shows were a knockout success in London and New York.

Another fire was lit in 2003 when she met Damian Lewis in rehearsals for Joanna Laurens's eccentric verse play *Five Gold Rings* (a Christmas family reunion of rattling skeletons in cupboards and an adulterous pact) again at the Almeida, directed by Michael Attenborough. Off stage, they became a glamorous power couple; the one film credit they shared was in Richard Bracewell's *Bill* (2015), Lewis a shadowy naval bigwig, Sir Richard Hawkins, McCrory a scabrous Queen Elizabeth I.

She chipped in with another Tory MP in Mendes' second Bond film, *Skyfall* (2012), and featured in Tom Hooper's wartime horror film involving a bunch of evacuated children in a haunted house, *The Woman in Black: Angel of Death* (2014). Her last movie was the extraordinary *Loving Vincent* (2017), 'the first fully painted feature film' about the artist Van Gogh and the circumstances of his death. One of her last television roles was a stern defending counsel, Sonia Woodley QC, in James Graham's *Quiz* (2020), about the 'coughing major' on *Who Wants to be a Millionaire?* and she voiced Stelmaria in the BBC's *His Dark Materials* adaptation (2019-20).

McCrory married Lewis in 2007. Both were active patrons of the charity Scene & Heard, which puts volunteer professional actors to work on scripts written by children in north London schools. They also raised more than £1m for a charity arranging food for NHS staff during the Coronavirus pandemic. McCrory was appointed OBE in 2017. She is survived by Lewis and their children, Manon and Gulliver; by her parents; and by her siblings, Catherine and Jon.

---

*Helen Elizabeth McCrory was born in Paddington, London, on 17 August 1968 and died aged 52 of breast cancer at home in Tufnell Park, north London, on 16 April 2021.*

# Tony Armatrading

*Stage and screen actor who enjoyed success with the
RSC and in many TV and film roles, including
Empire Road and Notting Hill.*

TONY ARMATRADING, WHO HAS DIED aged 59 of cancer, was a big, warm-hearted actor in the second wave of black British performers who began to make an impact in theatre and television in the mid-1970s. Before relocating to Los Angeles in 1999, he had three busy seasons with the Royal Shakespeare Company and featured impressively in contemporary black theatre classics at the Theatre Royal, Stratford East, and the Tricycle (now the Kiln) in Kilburn.

His debut role came in the BBC's ground-breaking black drama series *Empire Road* in 1979. His elder sister, Joan Armatrading, had been invited to record a title song, but the BBC at Pebble Mill in Birmingham could not afford her fee (the reggae band Matumbi took the gig and had a big hit). Over lunch with the show's producer, Peter Ansorge, who was having trouble finding a teenager for the *Blues in the Night* episode, she suggested he take a look at her little brother.

Anthony, as he was known early on, was just 17 and working backstage at the Birmingham Rep, where he had quickly become head flyman. Having played his *Empire Road* role, for the rest of the series he spent time with the cast – which included Norman Beaton, Corinne Skinner-Carter, Thomas Baptiste and Joseph Marcell – and worked with the crew; he became one of the gang.

He was interested in all aspects of production, as a fine jazz musician – he played keyboards and bass guitar, and Jelly Roll Morton on a national tour of a dramatic biography, *Jelly Roll Soul*, in the 1980s – and a technical geek, too, as he proved later in LA.

In 1981 he made his National Theatre debut in Michael Rudman's exuberant Caribbean production of *Measure for Measure* (the authority figures Escalus and the Provost were played by white actors) and then signed up for a year in 1982 on the TV series *Angels*, created by Paula Milne, about student nurses, followed by a 1985 stint as the music teacher Mr McCartney in *Grange Hill*.

Born in Birmingham, he was the second youngest of six children of Amos Armatrading, a carpenter, who had emigrated in the 1950s from St Kitts with his wife, Beryl (née Benjamin), from Antigua, a cousin of the Lib Dem peer and entertainer Floella Benjamin, first going to Cornwall, before settling in Birmingham.

Tony was educated at the Central Grammar for boys, whose alumni include Tony Garnett, the BBC Play for Today producer, and the actors Nicol Williamson and, contemporary with Tony, Kevin McNally. He was popularly known as 'Ant' until he grew much bigger and became 'Fly' (a larger insect than an ant). He excelled at rugby and, outside school, ice-skating and drama classes, and was a lifelong supporter of Birmingham City FC.

The central passage of his career were the three seasons (1986-89) he spent with the RSC. He was a noble, steadfast Banquo to Miles Anderson's feverish Macbeth, directed by Adrian Noble, and played Tybalt in *Romeo and Juliet*, directed by Terry Hands, and Orsino in *Twelfth Night*, on regional tours.

For the opening 1986 season in the Swan Theatre in Stratford-upon-Avon he was a stalwart: Trevor Nunn directed Thomas Heywood's *The Fair Maid of the West* (with Imelda Staunton as a barmaid turned pirate, Simon Russell Beale and Sean Bean) as a joyous Elizabethan romp; he experienced the more sober-sided John Barton's scrupulous textual excavation of Aphra Behn's *The Rover*, alongside Jeremy Irons, Imogen Stubbs and Sinéad Cusack.

Either side of these seasons came a tense and brooding performance – he had the most beautifully modulated, rolling vocal delivery – as the emigrating trolley-bus driver Ephraim in Errol John's 1958 play *Moon on a Rainbow Shawl* at Stratford East in 1986; and, in one of August Wilson's century cycle works, *Joe Turner's Come and Gone*, at the Tricycle in 1990, a truly devastating performance as Herald Loomis, a migrant mystery man in a Pittsburgh boarding house of 1911.

On film, he made small, but telling, contributions to Philip Noyce's *The Saint* (1997), starring Val Kilmer, as a customs officer; and to Roger Michell's *Notting Hill* (1999), as a security guard keeping tabs on Hugh

Grant trying to access the set of a period drama starring Julia Roberts.

Propelled by these screen credits, and newly married in 1997 to the actor and producer Suzan Crowley (his best man was his best friend, the *Archers* actor Tim Bentinck, 12th Earl of Portland), he decided to try his luck in Los Angeles.

This worked up to a point. He guest-starred in many big, networked TV series – *The Philanthropist* (with James Purefoy), *NCIS* (with Chris O'Donnell and Linda Hunt), *Sheena* ('queen of the jungle') and *Providence*, about a plastic surgeon and his dysfunctional family on Rhode Island. But only for the occasional episode.

He loved the life, and the sunshine, and he had British friends, Ralph Brown and Jenny Jules, nearby in the hillside neighbourhood of Los Feliz. He and Suzan acquired US citizenship. Putting his RSC experience to good use, he taught Shakespeare at CalArts (California Institute of the Arts) and created a small multimedia company in London with corporate clients.

However, we saw what we had been missing for several years when he returned to London, and the Almeida Theatre in Islington, in 2007. The play was a forgotten classic, Theodore Ward's *Big White Fog* (1937), a precursor to Wilson's Pittsburgh chronicles in charting a southside Chicago family's fortunes (and lack of them) across the 1920s through the Depression.

Armatrading gave a radiant, sharp-witted performance as a salesman who becomes a slum landlord, advocating beating the system by joining it. He was locked in ideological conflict with Danny Sapani's heavily politicised labourer, his brother-in-law. On a tiny stage pulsating with two dozen actors, he was back where he belonged.

He is survived by Suzan and his siblings, Everett, Carl, Joan and Andrew. Another sister, Jackie, predeceased him.

---

*Tony (Anthony) Armatrading was born in Birmingham on 24 August 1961 and died of cancer aged 59 in the Ronald Reagan UCLA Medical Centre, Los Angeles, on 10 May 2021.*

# Una Stubbs

*Sparkling revue and pantomime star whose range*
*extended from Cliff Richard's movie co-star to*
*Shakespeare on stage and* Sherlock *on TV.*

BRIGHT AND BUBBLY, TART AND TWINKLY, Una Stubbs was a revue regular and a Palladium pantomime principal boy who parlayed her natural song-and-dance talent into a later, diverse career on the classical stage.

In earlier years she was best known for her roles alongside Cliff Richard in two high-spirited pop musical movies – *Summer Holiday* (1963) and *Wonderful Life* (1964) – and as Alf Garnett's daughter, Rita Rawlins, married to a socialist layabout (played by Anthony Booth, Cherie Blair's father and Tony's father-in-law), in Johnny Speight's classic TV series *Till Death Us Do Part* (1965-75) and in episodes of its 1980s sequel, *In Sickness and in Health*.

Both incarnations are unimaginable today: a docile, amenable dolly bird hanging around Cliff and the Shadows, and a tolerant but incipiently trendy daughter of a loud-mouthed racist bigot – in Warren Mitchell's brilliant and relentless performance – in the post-war Wapping sitcom that became a whopping hit.

Stubbs transcended, or at least sidestepped, these cultural contrasts by the simple expedient of always being herself, honest and translucent in all she did. She had the ability to shine in revues (at the Mermaid theatre) based on the works of Noël Coward and Cole Porter, as well as in Shakespeare and Schiller directed by Michael Grandage – her latter-day mentor – in Sheffield and the West End, or even Ibsen at the National Theatre.

Wherever she went, she sparkled, and the longevity of her career was remarkable. She started out as a 16-year-old dancer in a Folies Bergère-style musical revue, *Pardon My French*, with the great hangdog comic

Frankie Howerd and the pianist Winifred Atwell at the Prince of Wales in 1953, and finished as a touchingly concerned Mrs Hudson in the BBC's Sherlock, starring Benedict Cumberbatch and Martin Freeman (2010-17).

She was geared to be fast and funny. There were no barriers. She was 'the Dairy Box girl' in an early TV ad in 1955, her breathy, adenoidal voice instantly memorable, and she was soon starring in the West End revue *On the Brighter Side* (1959-60) at the Phoenix – with the incomparable Stanley Baxter, Betty Marsden and Ronnie Barker.

Una was born in Welwyn Garden City, Hertfordshire, where her mother, Angela (née Rawlinson), worked in the cutting room of Denham film studios nearby, and her father, Clarence Stubbs, was a factory worker with Shredded Wheat. Her great-grandfather was Ebenezer Howard, an urban planner who founded Welwyn Garden City.

The middle of three children – a sister, Claire, was two years older, a brother, Paul, two years younger – Una struggled to assert herself as they all grew up in Hinckley, Leicestershire. She trained at the La Roche School of Dancing in Slough ('There's posh,' she said) and made a debut at the Theatre Royal, Windsor, as the fairy Peaseblossom in *A Midsummer Night's Dream*.

In 1955 she was dancing at the London Palladium, and in 1956 appeared in both ITV's *Cool for Cats*, the first-ever teen pop music show, with the Dougie Squires dancers, and as 'a starlet' at the Venice film festival in *Grab Me a Gondola*, an unjustly forgotten British musical in which Joan Heal gave a celebrated performance as a wannabe film star. Stubbs met her first husband, the actor Peter Gilmore (the lead mariner in BBC TV's *The Onedin Line* in the 1970s), whom she married in 1958, on these gigs. The marriage ended in divorce in 1969.

After the Cliff Richard films and during *Till Death Us Do Part*, there was a step-change when she met Nicky Henson, whom she married in 1969, and joined the Young Vic. She appeared there as the Princess in *The Soldier's Tale* (Henson was the Soldier), and in *Little Malcolm and His Struggle Against the Eunuchs*. In 1975 Stubbs played the lead role in *Irma la Douce*, directed by Dougie Squires, at the Watford Palace, in which she exploded like a firecracker in the big set-piece number 'Dis Donc'.

Her place in popular television culture was sealed in the next few years as she appeared in *Fawlty Towers* with John Cleese (in *The Anniversary* episode, oddly hitched with Ken Campbell); as the ferocious Aunt

Sally in *Worzel Gummidge* (1979-81) with Jon Pertwee; and as team captain, opposite her great friend Lionel Blair, in the television show that brought parlour game charades into the 1980s, *Give Us a Clue*.

Her second great phase as a stage actor began at the Royal Exchange in Manchester in the 1990s – Mrs Hardcastle in *She Stoops to Conquer*, Lady Markby in *An Ideal Husband* – culminating in a devastating and wholly unexpected performance as Terence Rattigan's confused and desperate heroine Hester Collyer in *The Deep Blue Sea*, in a 1977 production directed by Grandage at the Mercury Theatre in Colchester.

She began the new millennium as a hilarious sidekick to Penelope Keith in a touring (and West End) stage adaptation of the Noël Coward short story *Star Quality* (2001-02) and got serious as the Nurse in *Romeo and Juliet* at Chichester in 2002 (Emily Blunt was Juliet). In 2005 she joined the National Theatre, playing Mrs Holt in Ibsen's *Pillars of the Community*, with Damian Lewis and Lesley Manville; two years later, her 'legit' status increasing, she joined Peter Hall's summer season at the Theatre Royal, Bath, to play a delightful Mrs Pearce in *Pygmalion*, a revival that, with Tim Pigott-Smith as Higgins and Michelle Dockery as Eliza, transferred to the Old Vic.

When Grandage took over at the Sheffield Crucible, then succeeded Sam Mendes at the Donmar Warehouse, Stubbs was a regular part of his team, and a revelation, as a pert and fiery Maria in *Twelfth Night*, a starchy lady-in-waiting in Schiller's *Don Carlos*, with Derek Jacobi, and a choric mainstay of a wonderful revival of TS Eliot's *The Family Reunion*, with Samuel West and Penelope Wilton, in 2008.

She enjoyed embroidery and painting, writing two books on the former – *Una Stubbs in Stitches* (1984) and *A Stitch in Time* (1985), which expanded into a self-help volume on single motherhood – and indulging her well-trained eye for the latter in co-hosting (with Richard Bacon) the first series, in 2015, of BBC TV's amateur artist show *The Big Painting Challenge*.

Her marriage to Henson ended in divorce in 1975. She is survived by their sons, Christian and Joe, and by Jason, the son of her first marriage.

---

*Una Stubbs was born in Welwyn Garden City on 1 May 1937 and died, after a few months of illness, aged 84 at home in Edinburgh on 12 August 2021.*

# Lionel Blair

*Superb dancer and choreographer, host of 1980s TV gameshows such as* Give Us a Clue *and* Blankety Blank.

ALTHOUGH HIS STAR STATUS was rooted in talent and solid achievement, on the musical stage, in revue and in television light entertainment, Lionel Blair was one of the first media celebrities famous for being sort of famous. He played up roguishly to his image of a bouffant-haired, perma-tanned dancer, impossible to send up in any meaningful way because he was already sending himself up, on gameshows in the 1980s (*Give Us a Clue, Blankety Blank*) and reality shows in the new century (*Celebrity Big Brother*).

Blair was a genuine hoofer and a superb choreographer, who performed a scintillating dance routine with his friend and idol Sammy Davis Jr at the 1961 Royal Variety show and directed one of Danny La Rue's most lavish spectaculars at the Palace Theatre in 1970. He was quick on his feet and witty in speech, and audiences loved his unique brand of extravagant ingratiation, even if the critics squirmed.

Endearingly, he owned up to having lied about his age in his autobiography (he shaved off four years), on the daytime chat show *Loose Women* in 2016. But in 2010, as one of six oldie celebs on the BBC reality show *The Young Ones* – along with Sylvia Syms (with whom he had appeared as a dancing sailor in the 1960 movie *The World of Suzie Wong*), the newsreader Kenneth Kendall, cricket umpire Dickie Bird, actor Liz Smith and Fleet Street editor Derek Jameson – he was easily the most agile and youthful.

He was born Henry Lionel Blair Ogus, in Montreal, Canada, where his parents – of Russian and Polish extraction – had emigrated from the East End of London in 1926. In 1930, the family returned to Hackney before settling in Stamford Hill, north London. Lionel's father, Myer

Ogus, was a barber; his mother, Deborah ('Della', née Greenbaum), was a tailor. Lionel very much cared about his hair and his clothes all his life (and his legs were once insured for half a million pounds, a sum then comparable to the $1m quoted – admittedly two decades earlier – to cover Betty Grable's pins).

He was educated at Craven Park School – where he first met his lifelong friends Mike and Bernie Winters, the comedians – and Egerton Road School, connected to a synagogue. During the war years, he and his younger sister, Joyce – a budding Fred and Adele Astaire sibling song-and-dance act who were soon billed as 'England's youngest swingsters' – entertained Londoners in the air raid shelters at Manor House station on the Piccadilly line.

Lionel made a professional debut as a munchkin in *The Wizard of Oz* at the Grand, Croydon, in 1942, shortly after that theatre reopened following the heavy bombing of Croydon earlier in the war. In 1943, he was one of the children in the post-West End tour of Lillian Hellman's *Watch on the Rhine*, a powerful anti-Nazi play, and made a West End debut in 1944 in *Flying Colours*, a revue starring Binnie Hale and Douglas Byng.

In the same year, he joined the Memorial Theatre at Stratford-upon-Avon to play five roles in the summer season directed by Robert Atkins, including Macduff's son in *Macbeth*; Gregory in *The Taming of the Shrew*; and third player in *Hamlet*. After a season in rep in Belfast there was a short run in R.F. Delderfield's cosy comedy *Peace Comes to Peckham*. When his father died in 1947, Lionel became the family breadwinner – Joyce was just starting at a dance school – and decided to change his surname and concentrate on dancing as a more likely way of maintaining a regular income of sorts.

This he did, as a waiter, in *Bob's Your Uncle* (1948) at the Saville, a musical comedy vehicle for Leslie Henson with a score by Noel Gay, then on the touring production of *Annie Get Your Gun* and in *Kiss Me, Kate* at the Coliseum in 1951.

By the mid-1950s he was choreographing the celebrated *Five Past Eight* shows, swishly staged by Dick Hurran at the Alhambra, Glasgow, with headline stars such as Jimmy Logan, Eve Boswell and Stanley Baxter, and this led to his pre-eminence on BBC television in the 1960s, choreographing and dancing with his own show girls.

In that same period, he choreographed several movies and appeared in Michael Winner's *The Cool Mikado* (1963) with Frankie Howerd and Stubby Kaye, and in Richard Lester's *A Hard Day's Night* (1964) with the Beatles. He was a regular in the biggest London pantomimes, commanding a fee of £15,000 a week as Buttons, Dick Whittington, Jack on his beanstalk and Aladdin.

He was now subsumed in his television work, and his last 'legit' West End stage appearances included a cheerful 1968 revival of the Gershwins' *Lady Be Good* at the Saville, partnering the self-parodying squeaky 'blond bombshell' Aimi MacDonald (who had won television prominence in *At Last the 1948 Show* with John Cleese and Marty Feldman); and critically acclaimed 'turns' as the Player King in a touring production of *Rosencrantz and Guildenstern Are Dead* at the Piccadilly in 1987, and as the oleaginous compere of *Pageant* ('like Liberace on speed', said Sheridan Morley) at the Vaudeville in 2000.

On *Give Us a Clue* (1979-92), he and Una Stubbs captained teams competing in charades. On *Name That Tune*, which had been running in some shape or form since being imported from the US in 1956, he took over as presenter from Tom O'Connor from 1983 until 1988. And he filled in missing words on *Blankety Blank* during the best years of that show, with Les Dawson chaotically in charge.

On a Christmas special of *Extras* by and with Ricky Gervais in 2007, Blair paid the ultimate humiliating price for self-preservation with a needy plea to extend his career on *Celebrity Big Brother*; and this eventually came to pass in 2014 (he was the third house guest to be evicted).

In the same year, on the BBC drama *Doctors*, he played an old actor stricken with Alzheimer's disease. Latterly, he occasionally dusted down a one-man show, *Tap and Chat*, for the delectation of his loyal fans.

For many years he lived in Surrey with his wife, Susan Davis, whom he married in 1967. He is survived by Susan, their daughter, Lucy, two sons, David and Matthew, and three grandchildren. His sister, Joyce, a well-known performer in her own right, died in 2006.

---

*Lionel Blair (Henry Lionel Blair Ogus) was born in Montreal on 12 December 1928 and died aged 92 on 4 November 2021. With the comedian Alan Carr he once saved a would-be suicide on Blackpool pier, who was hanging on by his fingertips.*

# Antony Sher

*His celebrated and extraordinary performances in a
long career with the Royal Shakespeare Company used
his identity struggles to some advantage. He was also a
gifted writer and artist.*

AS BREAKTHROUGH PERFORMANCES GO, Antony Sher's as Richard III at Stratford-upon-Avon in June 1984 was beyond astounding. He gate-crashed this play's performance history and threw down an audacious gauntlet to the hallowed shades of Edmund Kean, Henry Irving, Laurence Olivier and, on that same Stratford stage, Ian Holm.

Just as Irving's bells stopped ringing on 'the lascivious pleasing of a lute' in the opening soliloquy, so did Sher's background music, and he instantly produced, with an obscene flourish, a pair of black medical crutches, resuming the speech with two swinging, ape-like hops to the front of the stage, an unforgettable creepy arachnoid.

That, in a lesser actor, might have been that. But Sher developed this spitefully animated cartoon into a complicated study of pathology, unctuousness and glistening malevolence way beyond anything revealed in the role, arguably, before or since.

In *Year of the King*, the first of his many books, Sher told the story of Bill Alexander's RSC production, accompanied by a plethora of remarkable drawings – he was a fine artist, an accomplished writer and an indisputably great actor.

And, as with all great actors, there were areas of critical dispute, of 'going too far' or of 'hogging the stage'. You could equally argue that there is far too little of that sort of thing in the theatre these days, and more's the pity. Sher was a great admirer of Steven Berkoff, in whose expressionist, balletic adaptation of Kafka's *The Trial* he appeared as a bespectacled Joseph K at the National Theatre in 1991; in the same season, he referenced his RSC crutches by surging manically down stage on a pair of upended tommy guns as Brecht's Arturo Ui, for which Shakespeare's hunchbacked toad was a prototype.

Most of his career was at the RSC after he joined in 1982 to play a capering, clownish Fool to Michael Gambon's mighty King Lear. He stole a few notices there, too, and allegedly had to be reminded by Gambon that Shakespeare's play was called *King Lear*, not 'King Lear plus a crass clown in a red nose'. He was the first Fool ever killed on stage by his master – not without feeling, one imagined, this act of smother-love.

Richard was followed by a flurry of extraordinary performances rooted in Sher's innate sense of not-quite-belonging as a gay, Jewish South African. In some ways you could see that his long struggle with his own identity paid off more than handsomely in a savagely embittered Shylock, a Greek Orthodox-style Malvolio, a murderous, full-throttle Vindice in *The Revenger's Tragedy* and a grubby, unpleasantly perverse Iago to the refined South African Othello of Sello Maake ka-Ncube in 2004. Recrimination and vengeance were his forte.

He was less successful as Falstaff, and perhaps saw with hindsight the wisdom of Olivier in never having played the role. But he strode magnificently through *The Winter's Tale* as Leontes; as Macbeth (opposite Harriet Walter, the best RSC pairing since Ian McKellen and Judi Dench in 1976), both of these in 1998-99; as a wizened old Prospero (2009) in another pertinent South African reimagining; and finally as King Lear (2016), appearing first enthroned in a glass cage, swathed in furs, prone to violent mood swings and, said Michael Billington, 'unbearably moving' with David Troughton's blinded Gloucester on the Dover cliff. He was a marvellous Willy Loman, too (Walter, again, as his stoically forbearing wife), in Arthur Miller's modern tragedy *Death of a Salesman* (2015).

Sher's grandparents were Jews who experienced persecution in Lithuania in the 1890s and fled to Cape Town, where he grew up insulated against the injustices of apartheid. His father, Emmanuel Sher, was an exporter dealing in animal skins and hides, and he remained particularly close to his mother, Margery, who encouraged and enjoyed his success.

Along with his two brothers and sister, he was well educated – at Sea Point boys' junior and high schools in Cape Town – and the household had black servants. From the beach at Sea Point he could see Robben Island, where Nelson Mandela was incarcerated.

After his compulsory year in the South African army, he came to the UK – it was reading the monthly magazine *Plays and Players* that ignited his theatrical ambitions – and he took a BA acting course at Manchester Polytechnic (now Manchester Metropolitan University), where he was briefly married to an American fellow student. He trained at Webber Douglas – other London drama schools rejected him – from 1969 to 1971, and plunged into repertory theatres in Liverpool, Nottingham and Edinburgh.

At the Liverpool Everyman, where I first saw him, he played Ringo Starr in Willy Russell's *John, Paul, George, Ringo ... and Bert* (1974). Then he donned a leopardskin as Enoch Powell in *Tarzan's Last Stand*, a withering and unnerving impersonation. This now legendary Everyman company – the theatre had been co-founded in 1964 by the director Terry Hands, who would become Sher's key mentor at the RSC – included Julie Walters, Alison Steadman, Bill Nighy and Jonathan Pryce.

He blossomed further in the London new plays explosion of the 1970s, notably with the pioneering company Gay Sweatshop alongside his friend and rival Simon Callow, and in significant early pieces by David Hare (*Teeth 'n' Smiles*, 1975, with Helen Mirren and a rock band) and Caryl Churchill (*Cloud Nine*, 1979, with Julie Covington, Miriam Margolyes and Jim Hooper) at the Royal Court. He was in a partnership of 17 years with Hooper, who featured in *Characters*, his 1989 sketchbook of favourite performers and performances.

Sher achieved an early prominence on television as the leering, lecherous academic Howard Kirk in Malcolm Bradbury's *The History Man* in 1981 (in line with the 1970s setting, Sher sported kipper ties, flares and an afro haircut) and followed through on stage in Mike Leigh's hilarious *Goose-Pimples* (1981) at the Hampstead Theatre and the Garrick; his character was a small-time entrepreneur who mistakenly thinks he has arrived in a brothel in Dollis Hill, north London, when he fetches up with a nightclub croupier (Marion Bailey) whose landlord is a house-proud car salesman (Jim Broadbent).

When he collected several theatre awards in 1985, Sher said he was proud to be nominated as both king and queen in the same year: Richard III and Arnold Beckoff, the drag queen hero of Harvey Fierstein's *Torch Song Trilogy* at the Albery (now the Noël Coward), to whom he lent a restrained, almost melancholic, suburban glamour.

He was now increasingly interjecting his classical triumphs – a barbaric and overweening *Titus Andronicus* co-presented by the Market Theatre in Johannesburg and the National (1995), a tremendous, moving *Cyrano de Bergerac* at the RSC (1997), using the Anthony Burgess translation – with some telling adventures in the contemporary repertoire.

For the RSC, he played leads in David Edgar's *Maydays* (charting the classic journey of left-wing agitators moving rightwards), Peter Barnes's farcical medieval pandemic epic *Red Noses* and, the first contemporary play in the new Swan at Stratford in 1989, Peter Flannery's *Singer*, a furious caricature of the 60s London landlord Peter Rachman. Later, in 1997, he delivered one of his sweetest, most obsessional performances as the painter Stanley Spencer, the priapic mystic of Cookham, in a play by Pam Gems at the National.

By then he had kicked a self-confessedly serious cocaine habit. He went into a rehab clinic in 1996, supported by his partner, the RSC director Gregory Doran, whom he had met when they first worked together in Stratford in 1987.

The first, and most acclaimed, of Sher's several novels, *Middlepost* (1988), was a fictional saga of his grandfather's journey from the Russian shtetl to South Africa. Part critical love affair, part exorcism, his relationship with his home country seeped further into his work with every passing year. His first play, *I.D.*, at the Almeida in London in 2003, was about the assassination of Dr Hendrik Verwoerd, the South African prime minister and architect of apartheid, by a Greek Mozambican immigrant in 1966.

Two other plays reflected his passion and commitment to politics and aesthetics: *Primo* (2004), a one-man show for himself set in Auschwitz and based on the writings of Primo Levi; and *The Giant* (2008), which fascinatingly fictionalised a struggle between Michelangelo (John Light) and Leonardo da Vinci (Roger Allam) over the commission for the David statue in Florence, with their mutual apprentice a catalytic agent in Renaissance gay culture.

His film career was virtually non-existent, though he was an excellent Benjamin Disraeli in Dench's belated breakthrough movie, John Madden's *Mrs Brown* (1997), and popped up as Dr Moth in *Shakespeare in Love* (1998) and as Adolf Hitler in Peter Richardson's ribald spoof *Churchill: The Hollywood Years* (2004).

Sher worked with Doran as his director at every opportunity, before and after the latter succeeded Michael Boyd as the RSC's artistic director in 2012. They formed a civil partnership in 2005 and were married in 2015, sharing homes in Islington, north London, and outside Stratford-upon-Avon.

Sher's last stage appearance in Stratford in April 2019 was as a bibulous old thespian with terminal liver cancer cared for by a black South African nurse – played by John Kani, the play's author. *Kunene and the King*, a co-production by the RSC and the Fugard theatre in Cape Town, was directed by Janice Honeyman. Its transfer to the West End in January 2020 was closed by the pandemic two months later.

Sher was knighted in 2000, and held honorary doctorates from the universities of Liverpool, Warwick and Cape Town. He is survived by Doran who was given compassionate leave by the RSC to care for Sher in the last three months of his life.

---

*Antony Sher was born in Cape Town on 14 June 1949 and died of cancer, aged 72, at home in Stratford-upon-Avon on 2 December 2021.*

# Dennis Waterman

*A notable early years career with the RSC in*
*Shakespeare and the Royal Court in controversial plays*
*prefaced fame and fortune in much-loved television*
*series* The Sweeney, Minder *and* New Tricks.

DENNIS WATERMAN WAS SUCH A FAMILIAR FACE on television for more than 40 years, playing similar sorts of streetwise characters, that it is hard to imagine that he was once a child actor in Hollywood and appeared in the opening season of the Royal Shakespeare Company in Stratford-upon-Avon in 1960. He also featured on the West End stage – in 1961, he led the first act closing number in Meredith Willson's *The Music Man* at the Adelphi theatre.

He is indelibly associated with two of the most successful television series of all time, both shown on ITV: *The Sweeney* (four series, 1975-78), co-starring with John Thaw as members of the flying squad branch of the Metropolitan police tackling violent crime and armed robbery; and *Minder* (1979-94), with two extended breaks in the overall ten series, playing the hapless gofer and bodyguard Terry McCann to George Cole's dodgy, throwback petty crook and wheeler-dealer, Arthur Daley.

Unmistakably and always a south Londoner, Waterman was a tough nut, detective sergeant George Carter, in *The Sweeney*, a series that coincided with an extensive inquiry into corruption inside the Met itself. Carter himself was highly corruptible, as well as sexist, usually meeting violence head-on with violence.

In *Minder*, more of a sitcom than a serious crime drama, he revealed a more winning streak of vulnerability and ineptitude in a wonderfully evoked milieu of the criminal underside in west London. He was now on the other side of the law as Terry McCann.

Waterman's rough-edged charm and gravelly tones were effective when playing either criminals or crime-fighters, both parties walking a fine line between humour and danger and liable to cross that line unexpectedly from one side to the other.

Several other sitcom and crime drama series employed him throughout the 1990s before his third major long-running success in the BBC's *New Tricks* (2002-14). Alongside James Bolam and Alun Armstrong, he played a retired police officer, Gerry Standing, part of a 'cold case' squad specially formed to reinvestigate unsolved murders and other crimes.

As in *The Sweeney*, where he and Thaw had to contend with an officiously demanding detective chief inspector (Garfield Morgan), he often crossed swords with his *New Tricks* detective boss (Amanda Redman). These hierarchical tensions allowed him to display quite a subtle range of hard-headedness, seething resentment and bitterness.

All three of these three hit series shared qualities of gritty realism, truth, humour and not just in the scripts – in the acting, too. Waterman also acknowledged that the public seemed to like watching characters old enough to retire but still doing the job properly. Made them look on the bright side of getting on, perhaps.

Also, he said, 'the police, the old bill, like it. They feel it's exactly like they are in their office, taking the piss out of each other. You're doing a serious job but there's always got to be a laugh.'

The happy-go-lucky, rackety 'Jack the Lad' image was not one Waterman had any problem in developing. He cheerfully admitted that acting came easily to him as an extension of his own personality and outlook in life. Drink, women and football were his cornerstone activities. Some of that spilled into darker areas, with drink-driving convictions and accusations of domestic violence from his third wife, the actor Rula Lenska, claims he discussed openly in a television interview with Piers Morgan ten years ago.

Waterman, born in Clapham, south-west London, was the youngest (by six years) of nine children brought up on a council estate in nearby Putney. His father, Harry Waterman, was a ticket collector at Clapham Junction station, his mother, Rose (née Saunders), made curtains and soft furnishings. Dennis attended Granard Primary School in Putney and, after being inducted into the theatre by an elder sister who was busy in amateur dramatics, trained at the Corona Stage School in Hammersmith.

One of his brothers became a professional welterweight boxing champion, another joined the RAF, and three of Dennis's sisters ended up working in the film industry in Los Angeles. Even before he joined the RSC, Dennis had appeared as Moth in *Love's Labour's Lost* in Brixton Town Hall and had made his first movie, *Night Train for Inverness* (1960), playing the kidnapped diabetic son of a newly released prisoner.

At Stratford-upon-Avon, in Peter Hall's first RSC season, he was a boy player in *The Taming of the Shrew*, starring Peggy Ashcroft and Peter O'Toole, and young Mamillius, son of Eric Porter's ragingly jealous Leontes, in *The Winter's Tale*.

After completing that Hollywood gig, recording a sitcom, *Fair Exchange*, starring Judy Carne, for Lucille Ball's production company, he was cast by Peter Wood, who had directed *The Winter's Tale*, in Graham Greene's strangely religious *Carving a Statue* (1964) at the Haymarket; he played the recalcitrant son of an eccentric sculptor played by Ralph Richardson. This led to the most significant period of Waterman's theatre career, at the Royal Court in Sloane Square, a place he described as his drama school.

Over three years, 1965-68, he appeared in two controversial plays by Edward Bond – *Saved* (1965) and *Early Morning* (1968) – which, as a result of being banned by the Lord Chamberlain, and performed in less than watertight club conditions, led to the abolition of censorship in the Theatres Act of 1968.

In *Saved*, Waterman's disaffected teenager, Colin, was the first of the gang to throw a stone at the baby in the pram in the park. In *Early Morning*, which presented a lesbian relationship between Queen Victoria (Moira Redmond) and Florence Nightingale (Marianne Faithfull), he played another miscreant teenager who cannibalises a character standing in front of him in a queue.

Both plays, directed by William Gaskill, met with a hostile reception from most critics and audiences, but are now rated modern classics. Also at the Court, Waterman played Fabian in *Twelfth Night* and Nick, the bastard son of Sir Walter Whorehound, in Thomas Middleton's tumultuous Jacobean city comedy *A Chaste Maid in Cheapside*.

There followed a series of movies before he hit the small screen big-time: the 1968 inferior re-tread of Ken Loach's television drama *Up the Junction*; *My Lover, My Son* (1970), a modern version of the Oedipus myth, in which Romy Schneider offered the wrong sort of mother love to Waterman as her murderous son; and Roy Ward

Baker's *Scars of Dracula* (1970) in which Christopher Lee, on the point of impaling Waterman on the castle turrets, was struck by lightning and engulfed in flames.

He returned to the RSC in 1978 for a revival of a famous old 19th-century American comedy, *Saratoga* by Bronson Howard, and returned to musicals in 1982 playing the manipulative journalist Hildy Johnson in another American stage landmark, a musical version by Dick Vosburgh and Tony Macaulay of the great newsroom comedy *The Front Page* by Ben Hecht and Charles MacArthur, *Windy City*. This was highly enjoyable, though Michael Billington opined that *The Front Page* needed music like the Sahara needed sand.

Music, though, was a serious string to Waterman's bow. He had enjoyed a pop chart success with his recording of the theme tune of *Minder* (co-written by his second wife, the actor Patricia Maynard), 'I Could Be So Good for You', and did likewise on several other of his TV shows, a habit that led to a satirical spoof – which he loved – on the *Little Britain* comedy show.

Many fine actors succeeded O'Toole in the title role of Keith Waterhouse's *Jeffrey Bernard Is Unwell* (1989) and it was Waterman's turn in 1993, when he played the role in Australia, then on tour in Britain, opening at the Theatre Royal, Bath.

His most notable later stage appearance, though, was in the National Theatre's revival of *My Fair Lady* in 2001, with Martine McCutcheon as Eliza Doolittle and Jonathan Pryce as Professor Higgins. Waterman's dustman Doolittle rescued the role from Stanley Holloway knees-up cosiness in a spectacular stag night scene ('Get Me to the Church on Time') on a manic pub crawl complete with dancing girls in black bodices and fishnet tights.

Unlike his colleagues in *New Tricks*, Waterman embraced retirement enthusiastically, ceasing to actively pursue employment in 2014. He swapped his house in Berkshire for a smaller house in Spain, going from a four up, four down, to a two up, two down.

'I've found out a remarkable thing about myself,' he said. 'I'm really, really good at doing bugger all. I've always sneered at people who've retired early, but I've taken to it like a duck to water.'

Nonetheless, he took the odd job that appealed. His last movie, *Never Too Late* (2020), was filmed in Australia, a comedy drama with four Vietnam war veterans planning a second escape from depressing circumstances in their residential retirement home.

Waterman was married four times. Three marriages ended in divorce. He is survived by his fourth wife, Pam Flint, whom he married in 2011, and by two daughters from his second marriage, Hannah – an actor who appeared in *EastEnders* as Laura Beale – and Julia.

---

*Dennis Waterman was born on 24 February 1948 in Clapham, south London, was a fanatical supporter of Chelsea FC, and kept a home in Spain, where he died suddenly aged 74 on 8 May 2022.*

# David Warner

*The mystery of Warner was how he inhabited a force
field of magnetic, vibrantly unsentimental goodliness
while remaining the most modest and self-deprecating
of great actors. My first, and greatest, Hamlet.*

WHEN DAVID WARNER WAS MAKING a film some years ago with his
old friend and RSC associate Ian Holm, he asked him what he was
doing next. 'Kafka with Jeremy Irons,' said Holm. 'And you, David?'
'*Teenage Mutant Ninja Turtles II: Secret of the Ooze.*'

Warner told this sort of story against himself all the time. Tall and
gangly, diffident and slightly injured, the actor who was the greatest
Hamlet of my lifetime (he was also my first, in 1965) had a busy but
decidedly chequered career after he moved to Hollywood in 1987.

There was even a downside to the big films. As the malicious bursar
in *Titanic* (1997) he should have been fêted at the London premiere.
But as he stepped on the red carpet, a photographer shouted, 'Hey,
David, is anyone famous coming?'

At least he got into the cinema on that occasion. At a lesser film
opening, he was bundled off his own red carpet altogether. 'Well, I
hadn't turned up in a limo, you see,' he guffaws. 'I was in Hollywood
for fifteen years and I was never in the same room as Tom Hanks or
Tom Cruise. I never went to any A-List parties and I was never at the
Oscars.'

This adopted loser status continued a trend dating from his first
movie, Tony Richardson's *Tom Jones* (1963). 'Tony cast Albert Finney,
who gets all the women. As Blifil, they wanted someone with bad skin
who looks as though he couldn't get any. When I looked on the make-
up schedule, I saw: "No make-up!" '

Sixties movie stardom followed anyway with Karel Reisz's *Morgan,
a Suitable Case for Treatment*, Jack Gold's *The Bofors Gun* and the Sam
Pekinpah collaborations on *The Ballad of Cable Hogue* (with Jason

Robards) and *Straw Dogs*. His character in *Straw Dogs* moves with the most horrendous limp.

That limp was real. For reasons never revealed, he jumped out of a window in Rome and broke both his heels. He was only given a 50/50 chance of ever walking again. Warner never discusses what happened. 'I once told a journalist that I was in bed with Claudia Cardinale and my wife came in, so I jumped out the window. If only it were true!'

He talks a lot about 'physical problems' then smashes his right fist into his left palm as he declares that he hit a wall. Let's put this another way: he has not touched drugs or alcohol for 22 years.

Back in England, separated from his second wife, the Californian production assistant Sheilah (sic) Kent, he made a statement of sorts by opening as King Lear at the Chichester Minerva Theatre in the 2005 summer season. In a modest way, he was reclaiming the kingdom he lost when debilitated by stage fright in 1973, just after a disastrous West End production by Tony Richardson of *I, Claudius*.

What form, exactly, did the stage fright take? 'It was different from Ian Holm's. He simply couldn't go on one night, and that was a public thing. Mine gradually took me over. I looked at the stage and it became tiny. I perspired and said to myself: how can they learn all the lines; how can they stand in front of all those people? I don't know where the obsession came from. Every single year Peter Hall would ask me to do something and every single year I turned him down with some excuse or other. I never told him what I was going through.'

Then, suddenly, in 2001, he sidled back on to the stage in New York as Bernard Shaw's arms dealer Andrew Undershaft in *Major Barbara* and was acclaimed by the critics. Michael Billington saw the performance and reported how this bluff panjandrum, played in the movie by Robert Morley, was totally re-thought by Warner as a power-broker perpetuating his position through a quiet, intense love for his daughter.

There was, said Billington, an almost Lear-like affection (for Cordelia) at play here. The fact that Warner's then 23 year-old daughter Melissa, who studied politics, had never seen him on stage, must have been a factor in this evidence of impassioned paternal role-playing. Some years later, Melissa transitioned smoothly into a son called Luke, and Warner's affection was no whit diluted.

Michael Billington grew up in Leamington Spa, Warwickshire, where, as chance would have it, he was a short-trousered customer of the strikingly blond, acne-ridden Warner in the local newsagents, Burgess and Colbourne. The picture is delightful: the tall, whey-faced future Hamlet dishing out papers and gob-stoppers (well, they didn't work, did they?!) to his unawares future critic and chronicler.

Warner had spent a peripatetic childhood, moving around with his parents from Manchester (where he was born) to Newcastle and the Midlands. He failed every school exam going and in Leamington drifted around coffee bars and into the amateur theatre, thanks to the encouragement of a teacher who had cast him as the tallest Lady Macbeth in the history of school productions.

Then his dad – he doesn't speak about either parent and does not deny that his childhood was unhappy – said he might as well apply to the RADA, and he was away. While a student, he made his stage debut at the Royal Opera House, Covent Garden, as a body-painted Nubian slave in a lavish *Aida*.

'I can't tell you who was singing in it,' he says, 'and I've never been back to see an opera since.' During his RSC phase he married a Swedish girl and started on some strange journey of withdrawal from his own fame, living in Stratford-upon-Avon, hiding in country pubs, with the occasional sortie to his favourite hostelry, the Dirty Duck, near the theatre.

My favourite photo on the walls of the Duck in those years, and for many years afterwards, was of Warner and fellow RSC actor Roy Dotrice perched on the pub terrace in broad daylight, nursing pints. Warner's bubble caption reads, 'Where is everyone?' Dotrice: 'They've all gone home for breakfast.'

Even in *I, Claudius*, Warner was mesmerising. But it is impossible for anyone who saw that Hamlet, or indeed the beautiful RSC studies in wracked saintliness that preceded it, Henry VI and Richard II in the *Wars of the Roses* sequence, to think of Warner as anything less than a great original. His Hamlet, in a long red scarf, leather boots and unruly mop of blond hair, whined and scowled with dyspeptic candour.

We didn't know it at the time, nor did they, but he was a student radical three years before student radicals existed. Every Hamlet since Warner has had something of his roughness, or awkwardness, or insolence. Every Hamlet before him was romantic, or glamorous, or struck with high intellect. 'He seemed,' said Billington, 'to be one of us, and he shaped how the role has been done ever since.'

Warner hated talking about those early performances, waving away nostalgia with a wild flurry of disclaiming gestures, and refusing to accept that he was all that influential. 'If I see someone like Jonathan Pryce do it – and I did, he was great – I think, God, I wish I'd thought of doing that. Not the whole thing, necessarily, but moments in it.'

Warner's Hamlet was the first to speak the verse as if it wasn't Shakespeare. Which is not to say he didn't speak it well. This Hamlet's first comic cousin in the West End that year (1965) was the loutish art student hero of David Halliwell's *Little Malcolm and his Struggle against the Eunuchs*, which lasted two weeks only at the Garrick Theatre. Malcolm Scrawdyke was, like Hamlet, socially disjointed and sexually confused, but his rebelliousness was also ridiculous.

Warner's Hamlet was accused at the time of being 'un-prince-like' by which critics meant he was nothing like Gielgud and his disaffection was palpably modern. He became a prophetic emblem of the student revolt in the Paris *événements* of 1968. And when his friend and RADA contemporary John Hurt, who had played Malcolm on stage, made the movie in 1974, Warner joined in as one of his ludicrous fanatical acolytes, Dennis Charles Nipple.

A more immediately direct consequence of the Hamlet, was Warner's casting as David Mercer's Morgan Delt – the suitable case for treatment – in the 1966 Karel Reisz movie. This disarming, delightful, eccentric performance as a failed Communist artist seeking revenge on his upper-class wife (Vanessa Redgrave) and her gallery-owning lover (Robert Stephens) by disguising himself as a gorilla, cemented his newfound status as an authentic cultural pin-up of the 1960s.

Warner was always at pains to point out that he went on to make many more excellent films, three of them with Sam Pekinpah, his favourite director. Others not to be sneezed at include *The Omen*, in which he was decapitated by a flying plate of glass; Alan Resnais' *Providence*, beautifully scripted by *Morgan* writer Mercer, Warner's best friend for many years, co-starring Dirk Bogarde, John Gielgud and Ellen Burstyn; and Carl Reiner's *The Man With Two Brains*, a joyously daft Frankenstein spoof with Steve Martin and Kathleen Turner.

Adding in three *Star Trek* movies, the television work and mini-series, the jobs Warner admitted were done to pay the rent, it all amounted to a career of astounding diversity but little coherence. His Lear was acclaimed but his return to the London stage in 2002 was a flop.

*The Feast of Snails* at the Lyric was a meal of dross, in which Warner struggled valiantly as an Icelandic tycoon with Parisian ideas above his gustation. The play crept along until you screamed inside for your dinner, and not necessarily at L'Escargot round the corner.

Latterly domiciled in a flat in Pimlico, and partnered since 2006 with the actor Lisa Bowerman, he has characteristically accepted any work coming his way, from the G.K. Chesterton serial, *The Club of Queer Trades*, on radio ('I love radio: you don't have to learn the lines and you don't have to shave'), to a nice cameo as the village doctor in *Ladies in Lavender* followed by the role of a former CID officer afflicted with Alzheimer's disease in a BBC television drama, *Conviction*; and 'a stupid sort of villainous character, no subtlety involved' in the League of Gentlemen movie, *Apocalypse*.

Before that *Lear* opened in Chichester, I met Warner over dinner in Covent Garden. He had been running through the final entrance carrying his dead daughter, with all that howling. His hips felt a bit sore. 'You just get on with it and follow Donald Wolfit's advice: "Get yourself a light Cordelia and keep your eye on the Fool." I've worked out where the performances fit in with the cricket. I'm living very near the theatre, so my summer will be *King Lear* on the stage and the Ashes on the telly. Who could wish for anything more?'

---

*David Hattersley Warner was born in Manchester on 29 July 1941 and died of a cancer-related illness aged 80 in Denville Hall, the actors' residential home, in Northwood, London, on 24 July 2022.*

# Angela Lansbury

*Descended from East London left wing political stock,*
*Lansbury had a long career on stage and screen, best known*
*as the TV sleuth Jessica Fletcher in* Murder, She Wrote,
*but also famed for her svelte, smart, slightly sinister turn as*
*Mama Rose in the London premiere of* Gypsy.

ALTHOUGH SHE WAS BORN IN LONDON, and retained a classic English poise all her life, Angela Lansbury was a Hollywood and Broadway star for more than seven decades, and one who was completely unclassifiable.

On her film debut, she played Ingrid Bergman's cockney maid in George Cukor's *Gaslight* (1944) and was promptly nominated for an Oscar, though she was never to win one. She graduated to play Laurence Harvey's evil, possibly incestuous, mother – although she was only three years older than Harvey – in John Frankenheimer's *The Manchurian Candidate* (1962), and then a dotty amateur witch in Disney's follow-up to *Mary Poppins*, *Bedknobs and Broomsticks* (1971).

This versatility, allied to her natural grace, vitality and chastely appealing features – her eyes were full, blue and unblinking, her face almost perfectly round, her mouth a cupid's bow from the studio era – propelled her to stage stardom in Jerry Herman's *Mame* (1966) and, in London at the Piccadilly Theatre in 1973, as the show-stopping Mama Rose in *Gypsy*, by Jule Styne, Stephen Sondheim and Arthur Laurents.

Lansbury had been initially reluctant to assume Ethel Merman's mantle in *Gypsy* but, like Merman, she gave the performance of her life, full of steel and tenderness in equal measure. Her performance was more nuanced and needy than Merman's; the critic Robert Cushman described 'a slow steady build towards magnificence'.

She became best known worldwide for *Murder, She Wrote*, an American television series running from 1984 to 1996, with four subsequent TV films. She played the incisive and level-headed Jessica Fletcher, a retired English teacher, mystery writer and amateur sleuth in the coastal town of Cabot Cove, Maine, a sleepy location with a criminal body count as delightfully high and unlikely as in our own *Midsomer Murders*.

'It really was a fluke success,' Lansbury said, 'and came at a time when that kind of family entertainment seemed needed.' She added that, of all the characters she played, Fletcher was the one most like herself: intuitive and sensitive, a voice of calm and reason in a troubled time. She gradually assumed ownership of the CBS series. Peter Shaw, whom she had married in 1949, was joint director of the production company. Her son, Anthony, and stepson, David, were executive producers, her brother Bruce was supervising producer.

Family was always of paramount importance to Lansbury. She came from strong, muscular stock. Her father, Edgar Lansbury, was a lumber merchant and one-time member of the Communist party and Mayor of Poplar (his father was George Lansbury, a reforming leader of the Labour party). Her mother, Moyna MacGill, was an Irish actor who took Angela to the Old Vic theatre in London from an early age. One of her cousins was Oliver Postgate, the British animator best known for the children's television animated puppet show *Bagpuss*.

She was educated at South Hampstead High School for girls and trained at the Webber Douglas Academy of Dramatic Art. Her father died in 1934, and her mother merged her family – Angela and her younger twin brothers, Edgar and Bruce – with that of a former British Army colonel in India, Lecki Forbes, under one roof in Hampstead.

It was not a happy arrangement. At the outbreak of war, Moyna decamped with her children to New York, and Angela continued her training for two more years at the Feagin School of Dramatic Art. While her mother toured Canada in a variety show for the troops, Angela did cabaret turns in Montreal. When Moyna's agent sent her to Hollywood for an audition, she decided to move the children out there with her.

Nothing much happened at first, so mother and daughter took jobs as sales clerks at Bullocks Wilshire, the art deco department store in Los Angeles, while continuing to audition. Angela was still only 17 when she landed the role in *Gaslight*, and this set a pattern of playing older than her age.

A notable exception was *The Picture of Dorian Gray* (1945), in which she played Sibyl Vane, the chirpy music-hall singer, a role that brought her second Oscar nomination; through her co-star, Hurd Hatfield, she met her future husband, Shaw. She had been married previously, for just nine months, to the actor Richard Cromwell, who was almost twice her age.

By this point a Hollywood fixture, Lansbury played Elizabeth Taylor's older sister in *National Velvet* (1944), sang Jerome Kern's 'How'd You Like to Spoon With Me?' in *Till the Clouds Roll By* (1946), fooled with Danny Kaye in *The Court Jester* (1955), peaked in glory in *The Manchurian Candidate*, with her third and final Oscar nomination, and joined another great cast list in *The Greatest Story Ever Told* (1965), on which David Lean took over as director from George Stevens.

Lansbury took American citizenship in 1951 and made her Broadway debut opposite Bert Lahr in Feydeau's *Hotel Paradiso* in 1957, following with Helen in Shelagh Delaney's *A Taste of Honey* in 1960 and, most significantly, as Cora Hooper Hoover, the corrupt mayor in Sondheim and Laurents's 1964 flop *Anyone Can Whistle*. The show, which has since become a concert favourite, closed in a week, but Lansbury came out of it with flying colours, commended by critics for her agility and engaging personality. She was even likened to a young Bette Davis.

This led to her *Mame* acclaim, and her first Tony award. Lansbury played Auntie Mame, a free-spirited woman who picks herself off the floor of the stock market crash to sing 'Bosom Buddies' (Lansbury duetted with Bea Arthur) and who ultimately recoups her fortunes by marrying a southern aristocrat. She won a second Tony in Herman's next show, *Dear World* (1969), a musical based on Jean Giraudoux's *The Madwoman of Chaillot*, in which she appeared to be dressed in 'a wedding cake made of cobwebs,' according to the critic Walter Kerr.

A belated London debut followed in 1972, when she joined the Royal Shakespeare Company at the Aldwych in Edward Albee's *All Over*, playing the mistress of a dying man, locked in battle with Peggy Ashcroft as his wife. She took *Gypsy* back to Broadway in 1974 for a few months, winning her third Tony, then joined the National Theatre at the Old Vic in 1975 to play a fairly youthful, glamorous Gertrude to Albert Finney's thickset, plainspoken and powerful Hamlet, directed by Peter Hall; the production was part of the opening season in the National's new home on the South Bank in 1976.

Back on Broadway, she hit another great milestone in Sondheim and Hugh Wheeler's *Sweeney Todd* (1979), playing the gleefully cannibalistic, pie-making Nellie Lovett (and winning a fourth Tony) opposite Len Cariou's demon barber in a dark and scintillating production by Hal Prince that played on Broadway for a year before touring the US for another 11 months.

Before *Murder, She Wrote*, a series of starry film roles included John Guillermin's *Death on the Nile* (1978) with Peter Ustinov, David Niven, Bette Davis, Mia Farrow and Maggie Smith; Guy Hamilton's *The Mirror Crack'd* (1980), in which she did some sleuthing stretches by playing Agatha Christie's Miss Marple, with Elizabeth Taylor, Kim Novak, Tony Curtis and, in his penultimate movie, Rock Hudson; Wilford Leach's rocked-up *The Pirates of Penzance* (1983), opposite Kevin Kline as the Pirate King; and Neil Jordan's wonderfully weird *The Company of Wolves* (1984), in which she played yet another eccentric old granny figure.

She did voices for two animated movies – *Beauty and the Beast* (1991, for Disney) and *Anastasia* (1997, for 20th Century Fox) – but was not in a feature movie again until she played Great Aunt Adelaide in Kirk Jones's *Nanny McPhee* (2005), starring and written by Emma Thompson. Subsequently, she was with Jim Carrey in *Mr Popper's Penguins* (2011).

For many years, Lansbury kept a home in County Cork, Ireland, where she and Shaw would spend two months each year while maintaining their base in Brentwood, Los Angeles. She rented an apartment in New York in 2007 to return to Broadway in Terrence McNally's *Deuce*, a specially crafted two-hander for her and Marian Seldes about former tennis partners reliving past glories while watching a match at Flushing Meadow, and switching their heads from side to side during the rallies.

The play was not a huge hit, but Lansbury was electrifying and was greatly moved by the affection with which audiences greeted her. She had not been on Broadway since a possibly ill-advised 1983 revival of *Mame*.

Regarded by now as a national treasure, in 2009 she won her fifth Tony as Madame Arcati in Noël Coward's *Blithe Spirit*, wearing a bright red wig and 'with a superfluity of bad jewellery, the gait of a gazelle and a repertory of poses that bring to mind Egyptian hieroglyphs', wrote Ben Brantley in the *New York Times*.

At the end of the same year in New York, she appeared for six months as Madame Armfeldt in Trevor Nunn's Menier Chocolate Factory revival of Sondheim and Wheeler's *A Little Night Music*, winning plaudits for her nostalgic litany of fading qualities in 'Liaisons': 'Where is style? Where is skill? Where is forethought? Where's discretion of the heart? Where's passion in the art? Where's craft?'

The Academy of Motion Picture Arts and Sciences compensated for her lack of an Oscar with an award for 'some of cinema's most memorable characters' in 2013, and the following year she was made a dame, and took Madame Arcati to the Gielgud Theatre in London. She was Aunt March in the BBC's adaptation of *Little Women* (2017), and in 2018 she both appeared as a balloon-seller in *Mary Poppins Returns*, and joined up with another member of that cast, Dick Van Dyke, as guardian angels in the Christmas tale *Buttons*.

Shaw predeceased her in 2003, and she is survived by Anthony, David, her daughter, Deirdre, three grandchildren, five great-grandchildren and her brother Edgar.

---

*Angela Brigid Lansbury was born in London on 16 October 1925 and died in her sleep in her Los Angeles home aged 96 on 11 October 2022.*

# Leslie Phillips

*Veteran of the* Carry On *films, Phillips, another
survivor of the London school of hard knocks, was a
stylish smoothie with impeccable credentials and a
pedigree crossing West End farce with RSC classics.*

LESLIE PHILLIPS WAS A LIGHT COMEDIAN of the old school, closely
associated with a roster of smooth-talking cads and lady-killers in the
series of *Carry On* and *Doctor* films he graced from the late 1950s
onwards.

He first coined his trademark phrase 'I say, ding dong!' as the
lubricious Jack Bell in *Carry On Nurse* (1958) and made the simple
greeting 'hello' sound like a frolicsome, impure invitation, earning him
the nickname 'King Leer' and lending itself to the one-word title of his
immensely entertaining autobiography (2006).

He became a national Sunday lunchtime institution on BBC Radio's
*The Navy Lark*, in which he appeared as a hopeless lieutenant on HMS
*Troutbridge* – alongside Stephen Murray, Jon Pertwee, Tenniel Evans,
Heather Chasen and Ronnie Barker – between 1959 and 1977. It was
never clear – deliberately so – whether he was a simpleton or a crook
in this company of Royal Navy undesirables on the recommissioned
frigate stationed off Portsmouth.

Despite his louche and carefree acting persona, Phillips was an
ambitious and hard-working artist who in the late 1960s toured the
world in his own West End hit, *The Man Most Likely To...* – he rewrote
Joyce Rayburn's play, took the lead, produced and directed it.

He joined the Royal Shakespeare Company in his mid-70s and
featured in several major films, including George Cukor's *Les Girls*
(1957), with Gene Kelly and Kay Kendall, Sydney Pollack's *Out of
Africa* (1985), Steven Spielberg's *Empire of the Sun* (1987) and Roger
Michell's *Venus* (2007), playing an old thespian alongside Peter O'Toole
and Richard Griffiths.

He was surprised to receive a gong at an awards ceremony for the latter film and went to the stage without an acceptance speech. When he arrived at the microphone, he told the *Oldie* magazine, all he could think of was his mother. Starting with his trademark leery 'Hello', he said, 'In 1993, at the age of 92, my mother was mugged in the street and killed. She would have been very proud of me tonight.' He brandished the trophy and walked off to a stunned silence.

Phillips's prodigious work-rate derived from his impoverished background in Tottenham, north London, where from an early age he was the family breadwinner. His suave and polished persona was as much a creation as that of Terry-Thomas or Rex Harrison, and it gave his acting an edge of seditious malice, an air of unofficial naughtiness.

With the confidence that came from being told frequently he was a good-looking lad he developed a taste for fast cars, high living and beautiful women when the money rolled in. For a time, he was the highest earning actor on the West End stage, and joined the Ibiza crowd in the 1970s, keeping a house there in a colony of artists and writers that included his great friend Denholm Elliott.

He was married three times and had a long relationship (between the first and second marriages) with Caroline Mortimer, the daughter of Penelope Mortimer and stepdaughter of John Mortimer, both writers.

This was all a far cry from his humble London beginnings as the third child of Cecelia (née Newlove) and Frederick Phillips, a maker of cookers at Glover & Main in Edmonton. The family moved from Tottenham to Chingford, by the river Lea on the fringes of Epping Forest, in an attempt to improve Frederick's health, but he died of a chest illness in 1935, and Cecelia, spotting an advert in a newspaper, packed her son off to the Italia Conti school to train as an actor.

Phillips had shown talent in plays at Chingford School and soon supplemented his income from delivering papers and singing at weddings and funerals in All Saints Church, Chingford, by playing a wolf – his stage debut, in 1937, aged 13 – in *Peter Pan*, starring Anna Neagle, at the London Palladium.

After a spell as a cherub in a stained-glass window in Dorothy L. Sayers's *The Zeal of Thy House* at the Garrick, he returned to the Palladium for the 1938 production of *Peter Pan*, now playing John Darling in a cast led by Seymour Hicks ('vile', according to Phillips) as Captain Hook and Jean Forbes-Robertson ('lovely') as Peter.

By the time he was called up in 1942, he had sung in the children's chorus at the Royal Opera House, Covent Garden, and acted with John Gielgud and Marie Tempest in Dodie Smith's *Dear Octopus* at the Queen's – the start of a long association with the producers Binkie Beaumont and H.M. Tennent – and Vivien Leigh and Cyril Cusack in Shaw's *The Doctor's Dilemma* at the Haymarket.

Everyone in the business liked him, and this would stand him in good stead after the Second World War. He sounded posh enough to gain a commission as second lieutenant in the Royal Artillery, transferring to the Durham Light Infantry, where he was put in charge of the Suffolk transit camp at Chadacre Hall, before being invalided out in 1944.

His first post-demob job was in the box office at the Lyric, Hammersmith. He played Guildenstern in *Hamlet* at Dundee rep, and discovered his talent for light comedy in a stint at the York rep. His first major West End role was in a sentimental comedy, *Daddy Long Legs* (1946), at the Comedy (now the Harold Pinter).

The first of more than 100 film appearances came in *Lassie for Lancashire* (1938). The Hollywood adventure of *Les Girls* could have led to a latter-day C. Aubrey Smith-style career in California, but he preferred London and Pinewood Studios – he was the last living actor to have worked there when they opened.

He was also in the cast of the first live BBC broadcast from Alexandra Palace in 1948 – *Morning Departure*, set on a wartime submarine with Michael Hordern – and played his first BBC television lead in 1952 in *My Wife Jacqueline* (opposite Joy Shelton), a pioneering but mediocre (he said) sitcom about married life, broadcast live from Lime Grove in six 30-minute episodes.

Over the next ten years he established himself in the *Doctor* films as the philandering consultant, Dr Tony Burke, and in the *Carry Ons*, usually stuck on Joan Sims. He followed the huge stage success of the superb farce *Boeing-Boeing* (taking over from David Tomlinson in 1963) with the first series of *Our Man at St Mark's* on television, in which he played an eccentric new village vicar. When his affair, while still married, with Caroline Mortimer became public, he was no longer deemed suitable as a clergyman, and was succeeded in later series by Donald Sinden.

Opening at the Vaudeville in 1968, he played 655 performances as the upper-class lounge lizard Victor Cadwallader in *The Man Most*

*Likely To…* and later toured to Australia (where one audience member in Adelaide was reported to have literally died laughing), New Zealand and South Africa, defying the cultural boycott and working in the townships as well as the commercial theatres.

He played in another 'saucy' comedy, *Sextet*, at the Criterion in 1977 (Julian Fellowes, author of *Downton Abbey*, was also in the cast), and then led a hugely successful revival of Ray Cooney and John Chapman's *Not Now, Darling* at the Savoy in 1979, followed by another world tour.

Phillips said that he broke his own mould when cast by Lindsay Anderson as a dithering, weak-willed Gayev in *The Cherry Orchard* at the Haymarket in 1983 (Joan Plowright played his sister), and he went even further in a brilliant revival by Mike Ockrent of Peter Nichols's lacerating comedy *Passion Play* at the Leicester Haymarket, and then Wyndham's in the West End, in 1984. In 1990, he popped up unexpectedly in *Chancer*, the television series which launched Clive Owen, playing Owen's scheming boss.

There was now no pattern or predictability as he entered the last phase of an astonishing career. He played the professor in another Chekhov, Julian Mitchell's rewrite of *Uncle Vanya*, *August*, with Anthony Hopkins at Theatr Clwyd, Mold (1994), and then joined the RSC to play a fruity saloon bar roué of a Falstaff in Ian Judge's *The Merry Wives of Windsor* (1996) on the main Stratford-upon-Avon stage and, in the Swan, a cynical hotelier in Steven Pimlott's discovery of Tennessee Williams's 'lost' fantasia, *Camino Real*. Also in 1996, he played a frisky old Sir Sampson Legend in *Love for Love* by William Congreve at the Chichester Festival Theatre.

*On the Whole, It's Been Jolly Good* was the appropriate title of a Peter Tinniswood one-man play he took to the Edinburgh Fringe in 1999, reverting to more raffish type as Sir Plympton Makepeace, a bitterly 'dumped' Tory MP from the Shires with no good to say of anyone: 'That woman with the loud voice … I think she was the PM but to me she looked like a power-mad swimming baths attendant.'

His last stage appearance came as Uncle Fred, an ageing judge with a back problem in John Mortimer's *Naked Justice* at the West Yorkshire Playhouse in 2001, a courtroom drama occasionally reminiscent of Mortimer's *Rumpole of the Bailey* TV series. With sly ingratiation and a stream of hoary old anecdotes, Uncle Fred was an instant audience favourite and, after stuttering over few lines, Phillips was soon operating with his accustomed effortless, silken aplomb.

In the new millennium he had good TV roles in *Monarch of the Glen* and *Miss Marple*. An excellent television version of Evelyn Waugh's *Sword of Honour* trilogy, adapted by William Boyd (2002), had him in the role of Gervase Crouchback, father of Daniel Craig's anti-heroic Guy, and he regained his dog collar in Nigel Cole's charming movie *Saving Grace* (2000), starring Blenda Blethyn. For the Harry Potter films he voiced the Sorting Hat at Hogwarts.

In 1997 he received a lifetime achievement award from the *Evening Standard* and, ten years later, another from the Critics' Circle. In 1998 he was appointed OBE and, in 2008, CBE.

Phillips married the actor Penelope Bartley in 1948, and they had two sons and two daughters. They divorced in 1965, and Penelope died in a fire when he was on tour in Australia in 1981. He chose not to return to England for the funeral, a decision, he admitted, for which he had not been forgiven by the family.

In 1982 he married the actor Angela Scoular. She had a medical history of alcoholism and depression and died in 2011 after ingesting acid drain cleaner and pouring it on her body 'while the balance of her mind was disturbed', said the coroner. Two years later, Phillips married Zara Carr, and she survives him, along with his children.

---

*Leslie Samuel Phillips was born in Tottenham, north London, on 20 April 1924, was a schoolboy breadwinner as a chorister and singer, and died in his sleep aged 98, after suffering two strokes several years earlier, at home in London on 7 November 2022.*

# Glenda Jackson

*As fierce and uncompromising in real life as she was on
stage and screen, Jackson gave her two Oscar statuettes to
her mother who used them as bookends – after she had
polished off all the gold plate.*

MANY LEADING BRITISH ACTORS have mixed art and politics, but
no great actor ever made such a decisive break from one to the other
as Glenda Jackson, who was elected Labour MP for Hampstead and
Highgate in 1992.

For the previous 30 years, she had been an outstanding, ferocious
presence in theatre, cinema and television, a leading light of the Royal
Shakespeare Company in its most radical phase, and as memorable in
screen comedies with George Segal and Walter Matthau as she was in
more tempestuous movies by Ken Russell.

She never had to prove a point about her politics: she was known
for having concerns rather than ideas, and these were rooted in her
background of working-class poverty, and her belief that the arts had
both a higher purpose and a responsibility to educate and inform.

It is extraordinary that, at the height of her fame in the 1980s, she
appeared in London stage productions of ambitious, difficult plays
by Botho Strauss, Eugene O'Neill, Racine, Brecht, García Lorca and
Howard Barker. She evinced an uncompromised intelligence, and a
scrubbed beauty that had nothing to do with makeup or vanity.

She was always strong, never sentimental, with a great aptitude for
sarcasm and sourness. She was impatient with frivolity; except, of
course, when it came to working with Morecambe and Wise. She
first appeared on the great comedy duo's television show in 1971 as
Cleopatra in a cod classical sketch – 'All men are fools and what makes
them fools is having beauty like what I have got' – and returned on
four of their subsequent Christmas shows.

Jackson was as fearless in sending herself up as she was in going for the jugular on stage; she was totally without affectation. She didn't think much of her looks, having been, she said, 'an archetypal spotty teenager who suffered the tortures of the damned because I wasn't like those girls in the magazines', and she never tampered with her imperfectly aligned teeth; for her legion of admirers, such honesty redoubled her sensuality.

There was a profound unhappiness about her, too, which she could always turn to dramatic advantage. 'When I have to cry,' she once said, 'I think about my love life. And when I have to laugh, I think about my love life.' The American director Charles Marowitz said that 'It was always the sense of being close to elemental forces that accounted for Glenda's fascination; the knowledge that she is capable of manifesting those potent inner states, that in most of us remain contained or suppressed.'

She was born in Birkenhead, Merseyside, the eldest of four daughters of Harry Jackson, a bricklayer, and his wife Joan, a cleaner, moving soon afterwards to the coastal village of Hoylake on the Wirral in Cheshire. Her family was distinctly matriarchal, a fact compounded by the absence of Harry for six years during the war, serving on the minesweepers.

Glenda was educated at Holy Trinity Church of England Primary School in Hoylake and West Kirby Grammar School for Girls, where she became, by all accounts, sullen and introverted. She did badly in her exams and, at the age of 16, took a job selling laxatives in the local Boots pharmacy, a stultifying experience.

A developing interest in the cinema, a school visit to see Donald Wolfit as Shylock in *The Merchant of Venice* at the Liverpool Empire, and a brush with amateur dramatics led her to audition for RADA in 1954. She began studying there in January 1955, financed by a discretionary award from Cheshire Education Committee. She was one of the first wave of students going against the grain of the old-style 'finishing school' RADA in the wake of the arrival of Albert Finney, Peter O'Toole and Alan Bates.

On graduating, she acquired an agent, the redoubtable Peter Crouch, and worked in repertory theatres in Worthing and Hornchurch, making her London debut in *All Kinds of Men* at the Arts Theatre in September 1957, followed by a six-month season at Crewe, where she met and married the stage manager, Roy Hodges. Further seasons at the Dundee Rep and the Lyric, Hammersmith led to a West End debut in Bill Naughton's *Alfie* (transferring from the Mermaid) as one of John Neville's girlfriends.

Peter Brook bowed to the insistence of his colleague Marowitz in hiring Jackson for the RSC's notorious Theatre of Cruelty season at the London Academy of Music and Dramatic Art (LAMDA) in 1964, an experimental project using improvisation based on theories of the mad genius Antonin Artaud, leading to 'club' performances (to bypass the Lord Chamberlain): in one of them, Jackson was stripped naked and dressed in prison clothes while a report on Christine Keeler (of the Profumo affair notoriety) was read out; she was later transformed into Jackie Kennedy.

In an intense period with the RSC between 1964 and 1966, she secured her reputation for danger and pent-up savagery in Brecht's schizophrenic masterpiece *Puntila*, Peter Weiss's *The Investigation* (playing witnesses at Auschwitz), and the David Warner *Hamlet*; her electrifying Ophelia had all the qualities needed, said Penelope Gilliatt in the *Observer*, to play the title role.

Most controversially, she appeared in two landmark Brook productions (both later filmed by him), the *Marat/Sade*, in which she played a psychotic Charlotte Corday, whipping the bath-bound Marat with her long hair; and *US*, a quietly enraged, inquisitive response to the Vietnam war, and how we might deal with it on our own doorstep.

She was one of Chekhov's *Three Sisters* (alongside Avril Elgar and Marianne Faithfull) in William Gaskill's fine production of Edward Bond's translation at the Royal Court in 1967, and then her film career (which had started in Lindsay Anderson's *This Sporting Life*, with Richard Harris, in 1963) really took off: she won two Oscars, before she even set foot in Hollywood, for her brilliant performances in Ken Russell's D.H. Lawrence fantasia, *Women in Love* (1969), and Melvin Frank's delightful romcom, *A Touch of Class* (1973), revealing an unsuspected talent for bitchy high comedy as a divorced fashion designer in a hectic affair with George Segal.

These years can now be seen as the pinnacle of her career: an amazing performance over six different episodes of *Elizabeth R* (1971) on BBC television, ageing from 16 to 69, ending with a parched, cracked face, and two Emmy awards in America; another Ken Russell histrionic special, *The Music Lovers* (1970), in which she writhed naked on the floor of a train compartment to the sounds of Tchaikovsky; and another take on the Virgin Queen in a recreation of Schiller's fictional encounter between Elizabeth and her cousin Mary Stuart in *Mary, Queen of Scots* (1971), opposite Vanessa Redgrave; and a finely poised Lady Hamilton in Terence Rattigan's *Bequest to the Nation* (1973).

That film reunited her with Peter Finch, with whom she had starred in John Schlesinger's grown-up look at bisexuality in *Sunday Bloody Sunday* (1971), written by Gilliatt. Jackson, in fine fettle as a divorced businesswoman, shared her beefcake lover (Murray Head) with Finch's conflicted gay doctor.

Two stage performances in Jean Genet's *The Maids* at Greenwich in 1974, with Susannah York, and Ibsen's *Hedda Gabler*, directed by Trevor Nunn at the RSC in 1975, were also filmed. Jackson's Hedda was so withering and scornful, you wondered how she'd lasted one night of the honeymoon, let alone six months; she certainly played up the crypto-lesbian side of her relationship with Jennie Linden's Mrs Elvsted.

Hedda's volatility and confusion carried through to Jackson's private life as she embarked on a tempestuous affair − it would last six-and-half-years, on and off − with the show's hard-drinking lighting designer, Andy Phillips (who had been a humble, but always, she found, entertainingly 'mouthy' electrician on the *Marat/Sade* at the RSC).

This ended her marriage to Hodges and propelled her through a couple of indifferent Hollywood romcoms (*House Calls* with Walter Matthau in 1978, *Lost and Found* with Segal again in 1979) and a mixed bunch of stage shows, one of which, Edward Bond's version of the Jacobean masterpiece *The White Devil* at the Old Vic in 1976, signalled both the launch and instant demise of a Jackson/Phillips production company.

She returned briefly to the RSC in 1978 to play Cleopatra, directed by Brook, another disaster, misconceived on the main stage as a close-up studio production. The announced Antony, Stacy Keach, was replaced at the last minute by Alan Howard, and the chemistry simply wasn't right. Jackson's crop-haired Queen of old Nile was a mercurial majesty in orange kaftans, but the tragedy never did justice to its own poetry.

At this point, with her Hollywood status in decline, she unexpectedly surfaced in 1982 in the West End as Eva Braun, Hitler's mistress, in Robert David MacDonald's witty conversation piece *Summit Conference*, first seen at the Glasgow Citizens.

Her involvement with the Citizens under Giles Havergal and Philip Prowse led to her final decade of outstanding theatre work, which included a brilliant Phedra (Racine's) in Glasgow and at the Old Vic, and a wonderful revival of Lorca's *The House of Bernarda Alba*, alongside Joan Plowright, at the Globe (now the Gielgud) in 1986.

Her last hurrah was a typically ebullient and uncompromising performance as the Renaissance painter Galactica in Howard Barker's *Scenes from an Execution* at the Almeida in 1990, followed by Prowse's revival of Brecht's *Mother Courage* at the Citizens; she was loud, brassy, wolfish, pugnacious, resilient and scornful – 'God help her opponents in the House of Commons, should she get there,' I wrote at the time.

Although her friend Neil Kinnock tried to dissuade her from standing in 1992, on the grounds that she was a great actor first and a Labour party member second, he acknowledged her determination and swung his electioneering machine behind her. Despite the overall Labour débâcle in losing to John Major, she achieved a swing of twice the national average, proving as popular a new 'celebrity' MP as were Sebastian Coe and Gyles Brandreth on the Tory side.

In 1997, re-elected in the Tony Blair landslide, she served briefly as a junior transport minister, but she became an increasingly critical voice on her own side, especially over the Iraq war. Constituency boundaries were re-drawn for the 2010 general election, and she was left to fight a tough battle for Hampstead and Kilburn; doughty to the last, she held on, after a re-count, with a vulnerable majority of just 42 votes.

Still, she eventually resigned her seat and made a surprise return to acting in 2016. What would she do? Only an 80-year-old King Lear at the Old Vic, scowling and raging her way through the pitiless storm, a truly great gender-neutral performance, impressive in its range, stamina and bravery. She returned to Broadway in Edward Albee's *Three Tall Women* in 2018, winning a Tony award, and reprised her Lear in New York in 2019.

Jackson was appointed CBE in 1978, and is survived by her son with Roy Hodges, Daniel, who worked for her in the Commons, and is a noted political commentator of a different hue, and by two grandchildren.

---

*Glenda May Jackson was born on 9 May 1936 in Birkenhead, Merseyside, and died at home, after a brief illness, in the basement flat of her son's house in Blackheath, south London, on 15 June 2023.*

Published in 2023 by Unicorn
an imprint of Unicorn Publishing Group
Charleston Studio
Meadow Business Centre
Lewes BN8 5RW
www.unicornpublishing.org

ISBN 978-1-911397-62-5
10 9 8 7 6 5 4 3 2 1

Designed by Felicity Price-Smith
Printed by Gutenberg Press Ltd